deadly vows

deadly vows

*The True Story of a Zealous
Preacher, a Polygamous Union
and a Savage Murder*

Leif M. Wright

New Horizon Press
Far Hills, New Jersey

Requests for permission should be addressed to:
New Horizon Press
P. O. Box 669
Far Hills, NJ 07931

Leif M. Wright
    Deadly Vows: The True Story of a Zealous Preacher,
    a Polygamous Union and a Savage Murder

Cover design: Charley Nasta
Interior design: Scribe Inc.

Library of Congress Control Number: 2013935928

ISBN 13: 978-0-88282-454-3

New Horizon Press

Manufactured in the U. S. A.

18   17   16   15   14   1   2   3   4   5

AUTHOR'S NOTE

This book is based on the author's experiences and reflects his perception of the past, present and future. The personalities, events, actions and conversations portrayed within this story have been taken from interviews, research, court documents, letters, personal papers, press accounts and the memories of some participants.

In an effort to safeguard the privacy of certain individuals, some names and identifying characteristics have been altered. Some characters may be composites. Events involving the characters happened as described. Only minor details may have been changed.

TABLE OF CONTENTS

PROLOGUE

On January 9, 2004, a lone camper hiking around the desert near his campsite stumbled upon a strange rock structure resting on the baked earth.

In his many travels through the area, he'd never seen a rock formation quite like the one underneath the palo verde tree about three hundred feet north of the nearest unnamed dirt road. The area was just north of the Barry Goldwater Air Force Base, and that was just north of the Mexican border. There's nothing in the vicinity except scrubby desert but the hiker loved the area and spent lots of time exploring it. Buried under the palo verde tree lay a mystery. A mystery that looked very much like a tomb.

And he also had never smelled that scent before. He had smelled plenty of dead animals in his day, but this?

"You could smell...a different smell from an animal," he said. Anyway, the tomb, he said, was "too big to have an animal like a dog buried there."

The next day, the hiker's son, a federal ranger with the Bureau of Land Management, went out to the area his father described and began gently moving the stones to see what lay underneath.

"I found a partial portion of a head and a torso," the ranger said. "It just became apparent it wasn't an animal."

Investigators were horrified when they found the decayed remains. Was it a man or woman, old or young? The story the bones told was violent, graphic and desperately depraved. The body, which was almost completely decomposed except for the bones, a little flesh on the legs and ten-inch dreadlocks still clinging to the skull, was laying on its left side in a loosely fetal position beneath the rocks that had entombed it. The badly decayed body was brought back to the medical examiner's office for autopsy.

Dr. Laura Fulginiti is the forensic anthropologist in Phoenix, Arizona, who examined the body. The first thing she did with the remains is the same thing she does anytime someone brings in skeletal remains: she laid the body out carefully, putting each piece as close to its anatomical position as she could. Some answers came quickly. Fulginiti determined the victim was young, female and African-American; it became apparent rather quickly that some pieces were missing and her skull and ribs were practically screaming that something terrible had happened to the poor woman. It was clear from her bones, especially her hip bones, that she had given birth at least once.

But Fulginiti's discoveries soon became more alarming. The bone where the chest connected to the clavicle and to which the first rib attached had been completely severed just a centimeter above the sternum. The aorta, the largest artery in the body ascending from the heart, lies directly beneath that bone. The end result of such a wound would be massive and fatal bleeding. The left side of that same bone, which is where most people assume the heart sits, had deep cuts, as if someone had jammed a knife between the woman's first and second ribs, beneath which her vital organs sat vulnerable to the blade.

Her sternum, which was just below that bone and the bone to which the rest of the ribs attached, wasn't completely there, but what was there bore signs of trauma, with scratches and cuts all over it. Several of the multiple stab wounds alone were enough to be fatal, Fulginiti said.

Many of the ribs recovered from the woman's left side were rife with signs of being stabbed through, including two that were completely severed by the knife. Whoever had killed this woman had wanted to make damn sure she was dead. In fact, her hyoid bone, which sits in the neck just below the chin, directly above the "adam's apple," and helps control the tongue and larynx, had been damaged by what appeared to be a saw blade as if someone had tried to cut the young woman's head off.

Whoever had stabbed this poor woman to death had been aiming to kill. The injuries were all to the left side and center of the chest, where the heart is located. And whoever had done it was trying very hard to make sure the woman was good and dead.

But that kind of trauma wasn't really unusual in homicides. It certainly wasn't something the forensics investigators hadn't seen before. Killing was a brutal, nasty business, and the damage it left behind was almost always stark and compelling.

"The most stunning thing is the back of the sternum is sliced off," Fulginiti said. "That's the most startling thing. The sternum is thick, but not so heavy. When the knife went in, it must have caught, and (the killer) pulled down on it so hard that (the killer) literally sliced the back half of the sternum off of the front half."

That wound, Fulginiti said, is the most striking aspect of what happened.

"I have never seen that before," she said. "And I never expect to see it again."

But this poor woman had been through more than just a brutal, vicious stabbing death, unusually violent as it may have been. The skull to which the long dreadlocks had been attached, even after an extended period of decomposition, was missing something important: a face. The familiar smiling skull with which anyone who has been spooked on Halloween is familiar wasn't all there. Between the orbs that once housed eyes, there should be a bone called the maxilla, which forms the nasal cavity and at its bottom houses the top row of teeth. That bone was mostly missing, though the part that should have contained teeth was still there. The woman's cheekbones had been smashed, and lay in pieces near the skull to which they had once been joined.

But the bone that should have held her top row of teeth? It had been sawn clean on the bottom where the teeth would have been attached. The teeth hadn't just been sawn out; the bone that held the teeth had been sawn away, and the sawing had been done so violently that the blade had ended up cutting into a wisdom tooth at the back of the bone that the killer probably hadn't known was there.

"It had to be a pretty bloody, gory business," Fulginiti had said. "[The killer] would have had to cut the skin away on her face several inches, sort of like the Joker. I bet [the killer] couldn't see the wisdom teeth because of all the blood and gore."

That lone wisdom tooth had a twin on the jaw, where the killer had also sawn away the bone so violently that the blade had become buried in the actual bone that attaches the jaw to the skull. On the other side, part of the wisdom tooth that was hiding there had also been sawn into. On both the top and the bottom, the roots of this woman's teeth were visible, where they had been exposed by the killer's saw.

The front of the woman's jaw showed cuts that indicated what might have been false starts with the saw blade that had cut her teeth out. But finally, the killer had gotten an angle he or she liked and had made one clean cut all the way across her entire jaw, hacking and hacking away at it until there were no more teeth—and no more gums—left in her mouth.

Her killer hadn't been satisfied with just stabbing the woman brutally and trying to cut her head off. When that had failed, the killer had instead violently and repeatedly bashed her face in with what looked to be a hammer, from the marks it left, and then had sawn her mouth completely off.

But that wasn't all the killer had done.

As she examined the bones that were laid out in front of her, some were missing, but that was to be expected with the condition the body was in. What wasn't expected was that each hand was too short. By one bone on each finger.

Human fingers are composed of three bones each, with the smallest bone lying between the fingernail and the fingerprint. On this woman's hands, that bone had been cut off of each finger, likely by the same blade that had so violated her mouth.

"Goddamn CSI," Fulginiti said. Her anger was triggered by the condition in which they found the body, as if someone had planned to prevent investigators from identifying her. "Somebody had watched too much TV and they knew exactly what to get rid of to try to thwart us."

Chapter 1

HOLY FIRE

S ean Goff was outgoing, charitable and the kind of guy people often describe as a person who would "give you the shirt off his back."

I even saw him literally do that once.

He was raised on a fundamentalist Pentecostal doctrine that is opaque to outsiders. Fundamentalist Pentecostal women almost always wear dresses and almost never use makeup. Jewelry, if it is allowed at all, is generally restricted to a wedding ring, but certainly not necklaces or earrings, which are considered flashy and prideful. Generally, their hair is kept long, because the Bible tells them that God has invested the glory of a woman in the length of her hair. Such a notion is completely sensible to those who interpret the Bible as literally breathed out of the mouth of God and onto the page from which they read it.

"Did you know that the word of God spoken by a Christian is the only way the supernatural world is bridged into the natural world?" Sean preached in 1995. "You see the words on the pages of the Bible? Do they do you any good laying on the page like that? No, they don't. When you read the story of the upper room, you know what is there but nothing has been spoken; it only goes into your mind. It is still just a spiritual thing until you speak it, which is when it becomes natural. That's when God's word comes into the natural world from the supernatural world."

Preaching, fundamentalist Pentecostals believe, is the way God's will is communicated to the faithful. Even those who read the Bible every day can't understand the fullness of God's will for their lives unless a preacher who is inspired (they say "anointed") by God reveals it to them. As Sean said, the Bible is just words on a page until someone puts those words into action, either by speaking them or acting them out. That's why they don't see it as odd that women, following the commandments found in the New Testament, grow their hair long, refuse to wear pants and eschew most jewelry and makeup. It's not just because those things are on the page but because preachers for generations have hammered "holiness" into them as the primary virtue to be aspired to.

Holiness is the ultimate goal of every fundamentalist Christian and that means even if you look foolish to non-fundamentalists (who fundamentalists call "the world"), following God's will as revealed through his "anointed" servants takes precedence above all other considerations.

The men, even in homes where the wife also has a job or a career, are served literally hand-and-foot by the women, who are considered "help mates," which is a term from the book of Genesis generally interpreted by literalists to mean that women were put on the earth to assist men.

The man's role is clearly defined: bread-winner, family defender, spiritual leader, lawmaker. The woman's is just as clear: mother, nurturer, housekeeper, caregiver.

Sean loved recounting the story of how his uncle once sat at the dinner table, served by his wife, Sean's mother's sister. After his wife had cooked the meal, she served it up on plates for Sean's uncle and their children. By the time she had served up everyone's plates (the uncle's was first), Sean's uncle was getting low on tea, so he simply rattled the ice in the glass and his wife silently and automatically got up from her just-started meal, fetched the tea pitcher and filled the glass. When he was done eating, he sat back, pushed his plate away and grunted "Sumpin' sweet!" His wife got up from a meal she had taken only a few bites of and fetched a piece of pie for him.

In Sean's opinion, that was a good view—if a bit cartoonish—of what family life should be. The woman was designed by God to be a helper for the man, whose role was to support the family and protect them. And the woman's role was to be absolutely submissive to the man, whom God had appointed as the "priest" of the household—the family's intermediary with God.

In actual practice, the roles are often more fluid, but in Sean's mind that was one great failing of the church, which he thought had bowed to the will of Jezebels who had demanded to be treated as equals to men—in clear defiance of God's will. It was a recurrent theme with Sean that didn't become obvious as carrying such importance until someone had known him for a long time. But the structure of the family was near the very top of his priority list, and he had no respect for anyone who strayed from that God-inspired structure.

He once told me he resented his mother—and in some ways his father for allowing it to happen—because his mother "ruled the roost" in their home as he grew up. She, he told me, was an expert at manipulating his father and the children to get her way, and in the Pentecostal tradition manipulation is an evil on par with witchcraft, which is an abomination in the eyes of God.

Such statements make outsiders wince, and some question whether anyone could actually believe such things in modern times, but fundamentalist Pentecostals believe in a very real devil whose only purpose for existing is to deceive good folks into stepping off the straight and narrow path that leads to heaven. That spiritual danger is always lurking behind the scenes, manipulating circumstances to push believers into a place of vulnerability where they become susceptible to the devil's primary weapon: the subtle whisper of temptation, which becomes ever more reasonable as circumstances guide the believer down the devil's winding trail of deception.

In some fundamentalist churches, Satan is preached about far more often than God is, with "spiritual warfare" strategies doled out by the dozens to help believers fend off the never-ending attacks from a devil still furious at being kicked out of heaven by a God who refused to let anyone else receive worship.

"We have to come to the place where we feel good about the warfare we're fighting," Sean preached. "We did not enlist in this army to stay in one place and let other people fight for us. We need to come to the place where as far as our integrity and our anointing are concerned, we have our eyes set on the war that is before us. I believe it is God's will for me to come into this service this morning and impart into you a spirit of warfare."

Such preaching is not considered fringe inside fundamentalist belief, which propounds a very real and ongoing war between God and Satan in which humans are both pawns and prizes. And in that war, the devil is willing to stoop to any depth to ensure that we turn away from the truth and anointing of God so he can steal our souls from heaven.

"We are continually in warfare," Sean preached. "We have to be vigilant against the attacks of the enemy; the word of God declares that we should not fear and we can go into battle and, even though the enemy may come in like a flood, the Spirit of the Lord will raise up a standard against him."

Pentecostals, like other fundamentalists, believe the Holy Bible to be literally "breathed" by God, word-for-word, as a letter to mankind spelling out the path to redemption from a sinful nature passed down to everyone from Adam and Eve. That belief provides its subscribers with a solid foundation from which to reject the encroachments of moral relativists and those who adulterate old-time religion with modern compromise.

"You got some new Bible?" I had once heard Sean's cousin preach while defending the King James Bible against new translations. "Why? Are you serving some new *God*?"

That belief in the literal inspiration of scripture is comforting to fundamentalist Pentecostals, who find it reassuring to have an unchanging standard by which to compare every situation—even if that standard may be somewhat subject to the interpretation of the denomination reading it.

Sean's uncle Jake pastors a truly miraculous and stunningly raw fundamentalist Pentecostal church off the main highway that runs through Locust Grove, Oklahoma, in the lush, green foothills of the Ozark Mountains. The area is a flyover state paradise, surrounded by lakes and rivers, green well into December and January, protected from outsiders by Oklahoma's "dust bowl" image, which eastern Oklahomans use to their advantage.

Jake fit in perfectly with the close-knit community of northeastern Oklahoma. He's one of them; a white Native American married to a full-blood Native American with mostly-Native American kids. He has a gentle southern drawl just deep enough to identify him as an insider while not pigeonholing him as a hillbilly.

And Jake's way of ministering had a clear and profound influence on Sean, who even looked like Jake when he preached.

Jake's church, inside an old gas station turned sanctuary, was loud, raucous, emotional—and packed just about every service as believers crammed into the tiny building to hear the dynamic preaching that thundered from the pulpit with a conviction and moral authority few others could muster and none could challenge.

But if visitors expected to hear "The Old Rugged Cross" played on a venerable pipe organ, they had another "think" coming. Jake, an aging former hippie who sang and played guitar for the church's music service as well as preaching just about every sermon, sounded more like an amalgamation of Mick Jagger, Keith Richards and Bob Dylan than something you'd expect at a fundamentalist church. Amps cranked all the way up, Jake would fire up his Stratocaster and launch into the first, droning chords of Dylan's "Saved," and you'd swear you were at a concert, not a church service. The drummer, Jake's daughter—who for all intents never hit the snare drum unless it was a booming rim shot—pounded along in time. Jake's son thumped along on the bass guitar as Sean's mother rounded out the sound on piano and harmony vocals with Jake of the perfect kind only siblings can ever hope to fully achieve. As the music built and roiled, congregation members sang, wailed loudly, praised God, lifted their hands and jumped up and down in time to the music, eyes slammed shut, tears streaming down their faces. Song after song built on the raw emotion until it reached a climax, another Dylan song, "Pressin' On," in which Dylan proclaims *People try to stop me/shake me up in my mind/saying 'Prove to me he is Lord/show me a sign.'*

If it was signs they wanted, Jake's church was the place to be. Divine healings were so common that the congregation was more surprised if they *didn't* happen than if they did. Every service opened with a "testimony" period, where parishioners could stand and tell the rest of the congregation what wonders God had worked for them recently, the stories frequently ending in tears and shouts of "Amen!" and "Hallelujah!" from everyone as the service built in tenor and power, arcing toward the sermon, which was when the real fireworks began.

The miracles they reported weren't of the pedestrian kind, either. God was very real, very present in the lives of the members of Jake's church. When God worked a miracle, it was something you *knew* was a miracle, not something that could be *interpreted* as a miracle. Doctors were frequently flummoxed in the stories as God's impossible healings blew their over-educated minds.

But if the song service and the testimony period were a spectacle, the real show didn't start until Jake stood up, set his guitar down and began to preach, the rhythm in his voice carrying over from the just-finished songs that were still ringing in the congregants' ears. As the sermon began to build in cadence and power, Jake's voice changed from preaching to a combination of shouting and singing, both lyrical and staccato at the same time, mesmerizing, captivating as he bounded from one side of the stage to the other. His piercing blue eyes—a defining symbol of the clan that Sean inherited—rested on each and every person as he delivered a sermon tightly woven with passion and emotion, calling the congregation to mortify the sins of the body, reject the lust of the eyes and press themselves into God's "anointing" so he could invest them with the power to live holier lives.

Sin, always waiting at the door for just the tiniest crack to slip in through, was an ever-present danger lurking behind every believer, just biding its time until it could rob them of that "anointing," a term that stood for the active power and presence of God in their lives.

A signature of the family's preaching style—including Sean's—was an unwavering and unassailable moral conviction based on the unshakeable belief that God is real, alive and active in determining the most minute details of the lives of those who serve him. God wasn't far off, letting events on earth unfold as they would; the same God who could count the hairs on every one of six billion heads could certainly get his hands dirty cleaning up the gritty details of your life.

Sickness wasn't just a cause for aspirin, it was an affront to a life dedicated to a God who heals. In Jake's church, long before big-time TV preachers such as Benny Hinn began aping the phenomenon for effect, people would drop to the ground, stunned, as the power of God overwhelmed them. The event, called being "slain in the Spirit," happened so often that people began to stand behind those being prayed for in order to catch them as they fell onto the hard concrete floor. Jake, however, wasn't having it.

"If someone falls and hurts themselves, it wasn't God who knocked them down," he thundered from the pulpit one day in 1989. "If they're faking and get hurt, they get what they deserve. Don't catch them."

No one caught any falling parishioners after that, though to preserve the women's modesty, they did throw pieces of cloth over their exposed legs as they lay on the ground, enraptured with the "anointing," some shaking, some chattering in tongues, some just laying there, soaking up the glory, eyes jammed shut, hands reaching into the air as if to physically grab hold of the God who had knocked them to the ground.

Words ring hollow in describing the feeling in Jake's church in the late 1980s and early 1990s. There was a raw power there, hanging in the atmosphere, like a cat waiting to pounce—even before the services began, it felt like a place where people just *knew* the darkest secrets of your life, because in that place God revealed everything. Over the years, Sean took many friends from college on the three-hour trip from the University of Oklahoma in Norman to Jake's church in Locust Grove. It was a significant number of people and none of them left unimpressed. The most skeptical ones might not leave Jake's church as believers, but they also wouldn't walk away unchanged. It was an amazing place that, for that time at least, seemed to have captured an intangible *something* that embedded itself in the minds of everyone who experienced it.

In Jake's church, when you came up to the altar for prayer, you had better be serious about it, because Jake could tell. As dozens of people shouting in tongues filled the air with the cacophony of their prayers, Jake would slather his hands in olive oil, straight out of the bottle, and then lay them on the heads of those seeking prayer, praying in loud, rapid-fire staccato tones that commanded the sickness to "leave! Right now! In *JESUS's* name!"

There was no gentle asking God to heal. There was no "if it is your will." In Jake's preaching, it *was* God's will to heal; he was simply waiting on people to speak that will into the air so that he could get about the business of healing.

One man came to the altar, Sean once recounted, asking God for healing for his hands, both of which were bloodied and broken. When Jake asked the man what had happened, the man said he had hurt his hands beating up his son-in-law, who had been smacking the man's daughter around.

"I believe God isn't mad at me," the man told Jake, "and I'd like him to heal my hands."

According to Sean, after Jake prayed, that's exactly what happened. Whether or not it was true, Sean believed it enough that he told the story frequently.

Stomping his feet in time with the music, swaying with the beat, eyes closed, mouth pursed between smile and wince, Jake would lay his hands on each member of the congregation who came up for prayer, each one leaving with the impression that they had been forever changed by the power of God. And if Jake was in the mood, he would "prophesy," which is church lingo for proclaiming to someone their deepest thoughts, fears and prayers, and then purportedly God's answer to those prayers.

"Sister," Jake would say to one woman, "God says you've been praying late at night, begging Him to draw your husband in. He said you weep and cry and pray, and I want you to know God has heard your prayers, hallelujah. You stay faithful, sister, and know that God is going to do what you've asked when his time has come!"

The woman would jump up and down, hands raised to God, eyes slammed shut in thankfulness, tears rolling down her cheeks as she spoke in tongues and cried, thanking Jesus for hearing her prayers. But unlike some who were fakes and would "prophesy" in sweeping generalities that could apply to anyone, Jake seemed to be the real deal. He called people out for things that it seemed no one could know without supernatural intervention.

"Brother," he said. "I know you're feeling those lustful thoughts for the woman you work with who wears the jean skirts, but I want to tell you that God is here to strengthen you, to tell you to resist, because the temptation of the devil can't overcome you while Jesus is in you."

Jake's church was exciting, powerful and unforgettable, but Sean's nature would not let him avoid looking for ways he could improve it.

"That church should have 5,000 members by now," he said to me on one of our trips back to Norman in his white Daihatsu Charade, which tore down the road on a tiny three-cylinder engine ("It has a Trinity of cylinders," he used to joke.). "If Jake knew how to manage, that church would be huge!"

The idea that Jake might not *want* a huge church never occurred to Sean. It wasn't in him to think small. No matter what someone had going on, Sean saw a way to improve it, to make it bigger, and not in a disrespectful way. Sean openly admired people like Jake while still thinking of ways to make him better. It's a mean balancing act, but Sean pulled it off.

That virtue—seeing the bigger and better in everyone, no matter how good they already were—served Sean well through the years. It made him a valuable person to know, for everyone from college students struggling to figure out what to do with their lives to multimillionaire TV preachers who needed someone to infuse them with fresh ideas for expanding and improving their ministries. Sean could not stop himself from helping them, from brainstorming ways that they could accomplish their goals.

It was one of his strengths, and ultimately, it would be part of what led him down the dark and terrible path to a ghastly decision.

But Sean wasn't always a powerful preacher and he also wasn't always a confident guy who just seemed to know the answers to everyone else's problems. When he was a child growing up in the small northeastern Oklahoma city of Wagoner, Sean wasn't even Sean.

He was "Bear."

Until his senior year in high school, that's how everyone knew him. His high school yearbooks even list him in pictures and indexes as "Bear Goff." The Goffs raised their children in a lower middle-class neighborhood in Wagoner.

Both parents worked for the phone company, scrimping and saving money when they could to help their children when they became adults.

When he was a child, someone asked Sean what he wanted to be when he grew up. His reply was simple: "A bear."

And the nickname was born—and stuck. The entire time I knew him, Sean's brothers still called him "Bear," as did his cousins and extended family. It was a nickname that, at least as an adult, bothered him to no end. He accepted that people from his past were going to use it, but he didn't like it and he didn't want anyone new to use it. In school, however, he was anything but a bear. Sean quietly made the honor society each year. He quietly assumed a position on the student council. He quietly became the president of the foreign language club (his language was French). Everything he did, "Bear" did as a leader, but one who didn't really stick out in people's minds.

"Bear would make an interesting story, for sure," said Adam Miller, who served with him on the student council. "He was affable, aloof, smart and cheerful for the most part."

The oldest Goff brother was out of school by the time Bear was getting around. Sean's next oldest sibling was ahead of him by a year, and his youngest brother was two years behind him, so he always had family around him, and when it wasn't family, it was a group of Oklahoma teenagers who had grown up with the slight, silent yet incredibly smart boy.

The eldest brother was "the toughest man I ever met," Sean later told me.

Sean's next oldest brother is an imposing man, with a voice as commanding as his stature. When they were younger, he became the brunt of a family joke when he said, out of the blue, "When I sing, I can sound like anybody. *Anybody*. I don't know. I just can. It's a gift."

Sean's mother, without missing a beat, dead-panned: "OK, let's hear some Ethel Merman."

Sean's older brother didn't brag about his singing after that, but occasionally, one of his other brothers, out of the blue, would quip, "When I sing, I can sound like anybody. I don't know, it's a gift," and the older brother would jab at them, smiling.

Sean's younger brother, three years his junior, was also much bigger than Sean, who was always delicate. The younger brother was a star quarterback at Wagoner High School, and he had received "plenty" of scholarship offers, Sean told me proudly, but he had decided to not play college football because he believed God didn't want him to.

Sean was no football star, no homecoming king, a member of the student council but not the president. Academically, he was ahead of just about everybody else, but socially, he fit nicely into the background. He was not a nerd, but he also wasn't the life of the party.

His freshman yearbook features a quarter-page photo of Sean solving a Rubik's Cube, then the nation's biggest craze, lauding the fact that the "whiz kid" had the ability to solve the deceptively simple puzzle "in a flash."

"His mannerisms were unusual," Adam said. "I remember sitting over and behind him; he had these long, delicate fingers, and he would move them like he was playing piano while he was sitting in class. Maybe he just did that when he was bored."

Though he seemed cheerful enough, "Bear" kind of kept to himself, appearing at school and extracurricular functions but never really being the center of attention.

"He knew he was smarter than just about everybody else," Adam said. "But he didn't try to rub your face in it. If he was asked, he would answer a question in class, but he was more introverted. He wasn't like goth or anything but he also wasn't a joiner. He didn't sit with his head on the desk wearing all black or broody or anything. He was just more mature than the rest of the kids in the class."

He also wasn't the chick magnet he eventually became, classmates agreed. No one seems to be able to remember "Bear" having a girlfriend at all, though he did go on one date with a girl, taking her to church with him.

"It was real strange," a friend of hers said. "He took her to this weird church up in Locust Grove, and they were all speaking in tongues and acting crazy. She was petrified during the service and she started crying and screaming at him to 'take me home!' She cried all the way back.

"I don't think they ever had another date."

If "Bear" had any girlfriends in high school, he was discreet about it, because no one seems to be able to recall him having one.

"If he had a girlfriend, it would have been a real wallflower type," Adam said. "He wasn't a cocky guy strutting down the hall with a gal on his arm. He didn't go out on Fridays or Saturdays to hang with the guys. He didn't really socialize a lot."

"Bear" was already showing signs of his future behavior in high school.

"He liked to control his immediate environment," Adam said. "He was meticulous. His handwriting was like everything else about him: delicate. He was probably the most docile and effeminate guy I knew there who wasn't gay."

Sean's mannerisms weren't limited to playing air piano, either. Unlike most guys his age, Sean crossed his legs at the knees like a woman, instead of putting one ankle on the other knee—a habit he carried into adulthood. But his introverted childhood was already preparing "Bear" to become Sean, the powerful preacher, the chick magnet, the advisor to people in power.

"There's a lack of Bible study in the church today, isn't there?" he preached in 1992, when he was twenty-four. "We have conditioned ourselves to whatever buzzwords and scriptures are going on our television sets, and through whatever movement we're in, we'll study those things and those things alone. You find very few people in any church have read the whole Bible. Listen, by the time I was twelve years old, you couldn't preach on a scripture that I hadn't heard. Either I heard it at church or read it at home or something. And it sure helps when someone is preaching something that's not true if you've heard the story before. Otherwise, they can give you all kinds of heresy and it'll just soak right in."

His time not hanging out with the other kids—reading books, studying the Bible, taking friends and girls to his uncle's innovative church—was about to pay off, making him a respected minister. But that period was also laying the foundation of a systemic misogyny that would ultimately lead him to rage against a woman who wanted to usurp his control and leave him.

Chapter 2

OU

"Darryl? Is that you?"

As the summer of 1987 waned, Sean and I had known each other less than two hours and we were already fast friends, hanging out in my dormitory room at the University of Oklahoma, beckoning to every student who was lugging his belongings up the stairs to the second floor, trying to find Darryl Hoyt, the lanky country boy who was to be my roommate.

Earlier in the day it had been just me, my amplifier cranked, jamming as hard as I could on my Flying V guitar, hoping to make my mark early and let everyone know I was there. I was scared, just as everyone else probably was. It was my first real time away from home, and it felt like I was responsible for my own life—a terrifying proposition.

The guitar blast had worked, too. I had already met my next-door neighbor that way, an incredibly nice guy named Kevin Thornton, who would later go on to fame in '90s pop group Color Me Badd.

I had also met Kevin's roommate, Luc Phan, and Sean's roommate, a guy named DB who freaked out because Sean had a snake in an aquarium, and "black folk don't do snakes," he said. Kevin had introduced himself and informed me that he also was in a band that sang a capella Christian music.

"Maybe we can jam sometime," he offered.

"No, man," I said. "I don't do Christian music."

The irony wasn't lost on me a few years later, when all I played was Christian music and Kevin's group had a hit with a song titled "I Wanna Sex You Up."

Later that day, I had grown tired of marking my territory with the guitar and had instead plugged my stereo into the amp, blasting the new album by Ace Frehley, my guitar hero, to everyone within earshot. And that's when Sean walked in, strolling with an easy gait, long, confident strides and a cocky grin on his face, wearing skinny-leg Levi's with penny loafers at the ends.

"Whatcha listening to?" he asked, as if we had known each other all our lives.

"Ace Frehley," I replied. The guitarist had quit his band, Kiss, five years earlier, and in the summer of 1987 he had finally released his long-awaited first solo album, "Frehley's Comet," which I soaked up like a sponge, ignoring the horrible lyrics because I loved the guitar playing.

"It's wild," he said, not wanting to offend. "I'm Sean, and I only listen to Christian rock, but this is really good."

What *was* it with this place and Christian music? I had never heard the words "Christian" and "rock" used together. It was the 1980s, and Tipper Gore and the Moral Majority had been spending tons of time and wads of cash convincing everyone who would listen that rock and roll music was the tip of a slippery slope sucking poor, innocent kids into drugs, sex and ultimately murdering their parents in the name of Satan.

"Christian rock" seemed like an oxymoron to me.

Still, I was intrigued.

"Ace Frehley *is* a Christian," I said, for lack of a better response. I had absolutely no social graces, so I didn't even think to introduce myself; instead, I immediately flew into defending my guitar hero against the implication that he was playing the devil's music. I pointed to the lyrics for his song, "Rock Soldiers," which tell how Frehley survived a horrific drunk driving incident: *When I think of how my life was spared/ From that near fatal wreck/If the Devil wants to play his card game now/He's gonna have to play without an Ace in his deck.*

Sean, to his credit, simply said, "Wow. That's cool."

Years later, he laughed as he told the story, recounting how I had thought Ace Frehley's music was Christian rock. But at the time he wasn't laughing. Instead, he formed a friendship with me that transcended our differing views on religion: he was a staunch believer, while I enjoyed thumbing my nose at religion, once telling my religious step-father that I was "fornicating" when he called and asked whether he had interrupted anything important. It was a stark contrast that somehow worked. We connected on a more cerebral level, possibly, or maybe it was just Sean's nature that he continued to reach out even when the cause seemed hopeless.

By the time our first day in the dorms was nearly over, Darryl still hadn't arrived, so Sean and I passed the time throwing water balloons at arriving students and taunting them from behind the safety of the cinderblock walls beneath the roll-out windows.

"Bye, Mommy, I'll miss youuuu," I teased one kid as he hugged his mother in the parking lot opposite Sean's room on the north side of the dorm. The kid flipped me off and Sean launched a balloon at him as we scurried across the hall, laughing hysterically, and slammed the door to my room on the south side in case the kid figured out that the taunts—and the balloon—had come from our hallway. We did that all day long, laughing giddily, speculating about each person who moved his stuff in on the floor, whether it was Darryl or not.

"That guy's a stoner for sure," Sean said as one dude moved in at the end of the hall. Then a lanky guy nicknamed Skip arrived on the other side of my room. Sean leaned over and giggled: "Did you notice he shaved his legs?"

Turned out, Skip was a bicycle racer and his penchant for shaving his legs was part of a push to make his body as aerodynamic as possible, but that didn't stop us from giving him a hard time about it all year long. Later in the year, we were all riding in a Jeep, and we saw Skip on his bike, so I squirted him with a water gun as we passed him. Much to our surprise, Skip was a lot faster on his bike than we had assumed, and he actually caught up to the Jeep, grabbing the water bottle from his bike's frame and squirting us all with water.

One guy who called himself "Moose" moved in next to Sean, and he immediately supplied us with hours and hours of discussion material, because he had somehow found a mannequin and had dressed it up like Freddy Krueger, the creepy killer from the *Nightmare on Elm Street* movies, and then perched the mannequin at the window of his dorm room, peering down on every person who walked past the building. Moose had also hung a banner across his room the first day he was there that read, "Dyslexics of the world UNTIE!" Sean and I both thought that was really clever, so we liked Moose, weird as he was, from the beginning.

Sean was the first person I really connected with at college, and the only one with whom I formed a lasting friendship. Though our friendship later would coalesce around two pillars—religion and writing—in the beginning, we were just a couple of guys who liked poking mostly good-natured fun at other people for a few laughs. From the day we met, we were nearly inseparable, the odd couple through and through.

For me, college was my first real taste of freedom and I found myself going wild, gravitating toward anyone who had drugs or alcohol. I paid my own way, unlike many students, so I had literally no extra money to spend on things like that, but I wasn't above hovering at parties and borrowing others' libations. Almost immediately, I got a job at a fast food restaurant about a mile down the road, and I would walk back and forth to the restaurant, working until closing time, which was when the employees could select whatever leftover food they wanted and take it home. The chain has since discontinued that practice, but at the time, it meant the difference between eating and starving for me. Every night, when I came home and stocked my dorm fridge with leftover food, people would gravitate by to pick through the haul. Sean was no exception, and every night, we would sit and watch my tiny TV while chowing down on old burgers and fries.

That week, unbeknownst to me, he made a list of everyone in the dorm —all four floors—in order of the likelihood that they could be converted to evangelical Christianity.

I was at the bottom of the list, on the "forget about it" portion of the page.

Sean made lots of friends in the dorm, and I was friendly with lots of people, but didn't really make any close friends. Kevin and I hung out a bit (and Sean and I penny-locked him into his room, blowing talcum powder into the room with a hair dryer, the cloud from which forced him to climb out a window), and Luc and I spent some time hanging out and comparing our martial arts skills (his were better) and him trying in vain to teach me to fence, but other than the guys at the end of the hall with whom I got high, Sean was the only person with whom I spent significant time. Because he was smarter than just about everyone, Sean never really seemed to need to study, so he had time to hang out.

He was disarmingly normal for my view of what a Christian was supposed to be. When I bought a cable splitter and stole the cable signal from the dorm's lounge, running it up to my room through a cracked window, Sean didn't get morally superior on me; instead, he'd come into my room, ask what was playing and we'd watch whatever it was. He made fun of me, of course, when a couple of months later the dorm's resident advisor caught me and forced me to give up my larceny, but it was a good-natured ribbing; there was nothing malicious about his humor at all.

Even though I was literally at the bottom of his "salvation" list, Sean went out of his way to share his faith with me. He never came right out and said anything like "you need to get saved." Instead, he occasionally would mention something about church, and then he would wait to see if I asked questions. If I didn't, we transitioned to something else. If I did, he didn't jump in and start trying to seal the deal; instead, he simply answered the question and if it led to other questions, he'd answer them. If it didn't, we'd move on. The strategy wasn't immediately successful for him, but he trudged onward. I wasn't the only one, either. Shortly after the university term began, he started spending a lot of time with a girl on the third floor who eventually became his girlfriend.

Sean's weekly Bible studies moved up to his girlfriend's room and I started attending, because it seemed plenty of girls were going, too. There were two girls on the third floor whom I was interested in, one an ice skater and the other an aspiring singer. Both were regulars at Sean's Bible studies, which sort of meant I had to be a regular, too. The Bible study part bored me; I had no idea what they were talking about, nor did I care. But Sean seemed to know what *he* was talking about. Sometimes he flipped to some random Bible passage, read it and then related it to modern life, no matter how tenuous the connection or obscure the scripture.

I guess I looked interested enough, however, because at some point Sean and his girlfriend invited me to church with them at Crossroads Cathedral, a 6,000-seat behemoth literally at the crossroads of Interstates 35 and 40 in Oklahoma City. I agreed to go and it was shocking to a guy who had never been in a church service more upbeat than old-school Southern Baptist. In the church my parents attended, everything was pretty straightforward: we found a seat in the balcony and sat quietly until the service was over, listening dutifully to the sermon and getting pinched by my mother if we squirmed too much.

When I left for college, my dad had given me only one piece of advice: Stay away from Pentecostals.

But Crossroads Cathedral was another thing entirely. The first shock I had was a drum set on stage. These days, they seem pretty common in church, but in the fall of 1987, drums were nearly unheard of in a church. The next shock was how the congregation (I remember calling them the "audience") reacted to the music. They stood, swayed, danced, sang along and lifted their hands above their heads like the surrendering antagonist in an old Western movie. And one lady halfway across the church, eyes slammed shut, hands thrust into the air, silently chattered throughout the service, tears pouring down her face the whole time. I was transfixed. I watched her the entire service.

After church, back at his girlfriend's dorm room, I asked about Chattering Lady.

"Don't worry," Sean said, smiling, "we think she's weird, too."

With that offhand comment, he effortlessly defused a confusing and awkward experience and made the Pentecostal religion seem perfectly reasonable to a non-believer. I didn't find out until much later that the Crossroads Cathedral was exactly the thing that my dad had warned me about: it was Pentecostal; it was actually Oklahoma City's First Assembly of God, disguised under a different name.

"Why do people put their hands in the air?" I asked Sean, still oblivious to the fact that I had been to a Pentecostal church service. All I knew was it was different. "Is it like antennae, to get better reception?"

Sean laughed.

"Actually, that's an excellent analogy," he said. "They're reaching out to God, literally."

I wasn't a convert, but I didn't mind going to church with him and his girlfriend and they became good friends of mine. By the time I learned that Crossroads Cathedral was Pentecostal, I no longer minded; the people there were friendly, the services weren't that crazy once you got used to them and I enjoyed hearing the pastor, Dan Sheaffer, preach. He was funny. When the congregation wasn't shouting "amen" loudly enough, Sheaffer jumped down from the platform and sat down on the front row and shouted into the microphone, "Amen, Brother Sheaffer, preach it!" and then hopped back up and continued his sermon.

Crossroads was one of the first of what is now called "mega-churches," and it showed. Each service, even those on Wednesday nights, easily was attended by more than 1,000 people, and the Sunday morning services were packed with nearly 6,000.

Sean could not stop talking about how successful Sheaffer had been in building the church and he often spoke about how other churches could learn from him. Early on, when Sheaffer was building the tiny First Assembly of God into a mega-church, he noticed that less than half of the congregation had shown up to a Wednesday night service. The following Sunday, he said, "Folks, I don't know where you were Wednesday night, but we are here to build a church. If you are not going to be here on Wednesday night, then I don't want you here on Sunday mornings. I will need your seat pretty soon for a person who wants to serve God and build here what God has asked us to build. You either have to get in, get committed and pray through, or you will have to find somewhere else to go."

Not one person left, and Sean *loved* stories like that, where people who made their living from preaching nonetheless stood up to those they were preaching to and offered them an ultimatum: serve God or get out. To Sean, that signified the height of faith. Sheaffer was also renowned for being a pioneer in racial integration of the church, another position that appealed to Sean, who believed white churches had a lot to learn from black churches. Sean and I settled in at Crossroads and, although I still wasn't a believer, I came to enjoy the experience.

But Sean and his girlfriend had a secret plan to "win" me that I didn't know about. Over the course of the semester, I had drawn a picture of Eddie, the Iron Maiden mascot, on my dormroom door. Eddie was essentially a reanimated corpse, and looked the part. His eye was the peephole for my door, so when I looked through the peephole, I was looking through the eye of a corpse. It was positively creepy to people like Sean and his girlfriend, who believed such images were inspired by Satan.

When I came back from Thanksgiving break, Eddie was gone. Later, Sean told me he and his girlfriend had spent hours erasing the drawing.

"We cast the demon out of your door," he said, smiling.

Eventually, I stopped going to church with them, because other things were demanding my time, but Sean and I remained close. He visited me periodically and never commented about the beer can pyramid, the smell of marijuana or the liquor bottles littering the floor. As religious as he was and I wasn't, Sean never openly judged me, which may be why we remained friends while we were so at odds over religion.

It was a key to Sean's personality—until he considered you "under his authority," Sean never corrected you. Even after I converted, Sean never said a cross word to me, because I was a man and, as such, in his mind an equal. We disagreed many times, but Sean's way of correcting men he saw as out of line was much gentler, much more collaborative than his method of correcting women, who even then he viewed as less spiritually solid than men. He never voiced such a thing in public, but in private, he confided that women needed men to lead them.

With men, he presented his case in such a way that it provided an opening for you to agree with him and thus avoid the appearance of having lost an argument. It was an intuitive method of arguing that Sean probably picked up from growing up with three brothers who were larger and stronger than he was. But with women, his approach was much more direct, because he believed women needed to be led, not collaborated with.

The way Sean presented that point of view, much as the way he presented just about everything, made it less offensive—and even plausible. It wasn't misogyny, he said, to fulfill the roles God intended for us when he created humans. Was it anti-dog to teach your four-legged friend to sit, not to beg and not to urinate on the carpet? In Sean's way of thinking, the two ideas were parallel; though he didn't view women as dogs, he certainly viewed them as being under the authority of men, and thus it wasn't anti-woman to simply fulfill the roles God created for humankind. Men were second only to God in the hierarchy of authority; women and children were third and fourth, respectively.

And dogs, he added with a wry grin, were probably fifth on that list.

I never could accept Sean's way of thinking about women, but he believed it wholeheartedly. In fact, it was a foundational aspect of his entire theological worldview. God, he believed, ran an explicitly ordered universe, and when humans slipped outside that order, they were placing themselves in positions to reap the negative consequences of being apart from God's will. God was all about order in his kingdom, where Satan was all about chaos. Being out of order was akin to being in league with Satan, at least in practice, and that meant you were vulnerable to his influence the farther you slipped outside the plan of God.

For Sean, that understanding was a foundation that must be laid first, before any other information could be adequately added or comprehended, and once that was understood, the true theology of God's kingdom—and the spiritual warfare that accompanied it—could be built on top.

Spiritual warfare, however, wasn't the only kind of violence the whisper-thin kid preacher was into. One day I was shocked when Sean was on the third floor with his girlfriend. The third floor was where all the girls lived, so of course most guys spent a lot of time there. There was a goofy kid from the fourth floor named Stan who was also on the third floor, being goofy as usual, and he happened to drop the F-bomb in Sean's girlfriend's hearing.

Sean flipped out.

Before Stan knew what had hit him, Sean ran over, grabbed him by the shirt and began yelling at him. The dorm had no air conditioning, so the windows were open and at the end of each hall there was a full-size window. Sean pushed Stan up against that wall and then he pushed Stan's torso outside the window, holding him up by his shirt.

"Apologize," Sean said in a weirdly calm voice, a smile/smirk plastered on his face. There was no yelling, only a calm forcefulness to his voice. "Apologize to her for talking like that or I'm going to drop you out of this window."

Stan, eyes wide, held up both hands in surrender and said, "Okay, okay!"

When he was safely back in the hall, Stan apologized to Sean's girlfriend and slunk back to his own room. Word spread quickly through the dorm of how the preacher man had lost his cool and beat up Stan.

Of course, Sean hadn't beaten up anyone, but it was easy to see how he might have.

Other events intervened and the incident at the window faded in most people's memory, but Sean's boiling undercurrent of violence would come back later on to haunt him in the starkest way possible.

Chapter 3

FOUR CORNERS

S ean's future wife was fifteen when Sean met her during my sophomore year at Oklahoma University. I almost never ran into Sean that year; I was living off-campus, working at the fast food restaurant to help pay the bills and playing guitar whenever I could in local bars, getting high with my cousin and trying to find new ways to kill brain cells as I experimented with drug after drug.

Sean said he had stopped by my apartment one time that year to invite me to a church function, and it had taken me several minutes to answer the door, shirtless, eyes glazed and hair down to the middle of my back.

"You were terrifying," he said to me years later, smiling. "I decided you probably weren't going to be going to church with me, so I left."

I don't remember the incident, but his description of me was accurate, so I'm sure it happened. I didn't see much of Sean until much later, but he was busy anyway, courting his future wife.

When she met him, Sean's future wife was swept off her feet by him.

She had always wanted to marry a man with jet black hair and blue eyes, she confessed to friends. In fact, she had been praying that God would send along just such a man for her. Fifteen may seem like an early age to start praying for a husband, but she thought she knew what she wanted and she decided she would ask God to give it to her.

And, by all appearances, he did.

Sean cut a dashing figure: well-dressed, well-groomed, thin, deceptively good-looking, and when he spoke, there was a simmering intelligence and passion behind every word, even those dropped idly, that seemed ready to boil above the surface at any time. Just as many other women at the time, Sean's future wife was captivated.

And then when he preached, the deal was sealed.

Sean had landed a gig as youth leader at a church called Harbor of Praise, where he was in charge of mentoring and leading teenagers through the difficult times of puberty in God's direction—and though he was just barely past puberty himself, Sean always seemed older than his years and he was the perfect pick, the church's pastor had decided. With Sean preaching to his youth group, the pastor was assured that the kids would learn about holiness and living for God.

"He was anointed," said one of the congregation members at Harbor of Praise who later left with Sean when he formed a new church. "He was a man of God."

The woman's husband remembers that Sean was an amazing preacher at age twenty-one, a time when most other people—like me—were partying their heads off, being as irresponsible as possible.

The husband believes that Sean was just ahead of everyone else. When Sean was scheduled to preach, the amount of people in attendance was substantially more than those who showed up when the pastor preached. The husband believes that the pastor was worried that Sean would take over.

But Sean wasn't interested in taking over—the church, anyway. There was that cute girl in the youth group who always seemed to be making eyes at him, and Sean was definitely thinking about taking *her* over. Attractive, with long dark hair, big, sparkling eyes and a ready smile, she was just the kind of girl Sean was looking for: young (and thus, as he later told me, "teachable"), pretty and submissive to whatever her spiritual leader said. For Sean, it was the trifecta: attractive, malleable and youthful. He started immediately working his way into her family's confidence and quickly developed a romantic relationship with the completely smitten teenager, who had never encountered anyone as good-looking, worldly and blazingly intelligent.

Sean's girlfriend from OU could only handle so much of the man being the boss all the time, so she and Sean hadn't lasted very long after their initial fire in the dorms at OU.

"He took over everything," his girlfriend told me years later, as she and her husband spoke with me just before he and I left to accompany Sean on an evangelistic trip to Kentucky. "It was too much; he had to have his way, and he always had to be right. It just wasn't for me."

After her, Sean wouldn't repeat the mistake of dating a woman his equal in age or independence again. In his future wife he found a girl, not a woman, who naturally submitted to his authority as her youth leader, and that appealed to him religiously, while her looks appealed to him physically—though not as much as those of her younger sister.

"If her sister had been older, I would have chosen her," he told me in 2003. "She was prettier, but way too young."

In reality, both of the girls were pretty and Sean, twenty at the time, latched onto the one closest to his age: fifteen, almost sixteen. It shouldn't have been a surprise to anyone who knew him closely that Sean would put rational considerations above emotional ones in choosing the older sister over the younger one. He was contemptuous of people who allowed emotions to influence important decisions (or even small ones) and he would never allow his decisions to be influenced by emotion, even one as powerful as love.

In his mind, he wasn't falling in love so much as making a logical decision for his future. Here was a future wife he could live with, maybe not as attractive as her younger sister, but old enough—almost—to marry. That's not to say that his future wife was hard on the eyes and that made it better for Sean, because he needed his wife to be pretty as well as spiritual and submissive. Was it her personality that drew Sean to her? No. Was it her scintillating conversation skills? No. For Sean, "love" wasn't about not being able to live without her. It was about choosing to make a life with someone he deemed compatible and suitable. It was, ultimately, the logical choice.

That determination turned almost pathological for Sean. He sneered at those he considered easily manipulated by emotions and he took great pride in using that "weakness" to get them to do what he wanted them to do. And he saw nothing wrong with it; it was in a perverse way his own take on the survival of the fittest. If people were weak-minded and easily led, it was up to strong-minded leaders to lead them. And he was up to the task.

"We were all really young," a congregation member said later about Sean's ability to get people to do what he wanted. "He knew how to manipulate that. He had been in it his whole life and, being so intelligent, he was really good at it."

For Sean, however, it wasn't manipulation to be able to control people through their emotions. It was simply God's way of culling the herd, letting the dominant bulls make sure everything went the way it should, including reserving the best females for themselves, which would lead to a better future not filled with so many lemmings. If that sounds harsh, in Sean's mind it wasn't. It was simply the way things were.

Later he claimed to me that he was never sexually inappropriate with the underage girl, though he did tell me once that he "accidentally" saw her naked by walking in on her taking a bath at her parents' house, where he was accepted as a nearly-every-night guest. He winked and smiled as he said "accidentally." Why he felt the need to tell that story was always a mystery, except that, in fundamentalist Christianity, sexual immorality is in the top tier of sins, and seeing a woman naked when you're not married to her can only lead to lust, which is second only to fornication in the pantheon of sexual immorality. It's "naughty," and Sean loved to walk the line between holy and naughty. He wanted to stay on the "holy" side of the line, but he didn't mind flirting with the edges, especially when those edges involved his secret favorite subject: women.

Most people in their early twenties have already seen a few people of the opposite sex naked and it seems to begin losing its novelty by the time they're in their mid-twenties, but for Sean, it wasn't the sexual arousal at all that did the trick; it was the conquest. Women were prizes to be won, and seeing them at their most vulnerable—naked—was the white flag that signified that the prize had been secured. Nudity is a taboo to fundamentalist Pentecostals, so seeing someone he wasn't married to without her clothes on was a big deal, one that made a lasting impression on Sean.

After the "accidental" bath incident, one thing led to another, and in May of 1990, when his wife-to-be was seventeen, Sean called me up to invite me to his wedding.

I had only recently converted to Christianity, so I was anxious to reconnect with Sean, who seemed so well versed in my new religion. It was a chance to spend a few days in Peggs, Oklahoma, deep in the woods outside Locust Grove in Oklahoma's hilly and green northeastern corner, with his grandmother, who had been pastor of the Four Corners Church there since her husband had died.

Though Pentecostals are generally strict fundamentalists, they largely differ from other fundamentalists in the area of women in the clergy. Sean, who had big problems with women exercising authority over men, made exceptions for female pastors in certain circumstances, most especially that of his grandmother, for whom he seemed to have an almost worshipful respect.

His grandmother commanded that respect by her very presence, and Sean gave it. There was a sternness about her presence that seemed obvious until she started to speak, when an almost unplumbed depth of warmth and compassion radiated from her. Her long salt-and-pepper hair (mostly salt) was always impeccably tied into a bun, her eyes piercingly perceptive, nuggets of wisdom easily falling from her lips, seemingly without effort or thought. Jake seemed to have inherited his mother's aura of perception; it just seemed that she knew your deepest secrets, and though she might not approve of everything she saw, she wouldn't push you away because of it. In her, you could see the active presence of a very real God, and you could feel both the disappointment and the unmitigated love and forgiveness you expected from such a being.

I found myself trying to not even think bad thoughts when I was around Sean's grandmother, because I was pretty sure she would find out, and there was nothing I wanted to avoid more than a disapproving, yet knowing, look from her. It was in her house and her church that I first understood the idea that so many fundamentalist Pentecostals cling to: holiness. Holiness, as embodied by Sean's grandmother, was a clean place, a tidy, pristine room where sin could not bear to even peek through the windows at a place so sanctified and revered. Holiness was a refusal to sin, not for fear of hell, but because the very thought of sin offended a holy God, whose presence could not tolerate even the slightest evil.

When she preached, it was immediately obvious where the boys had gotten their passion and preaching style. Her delivery was powerful and persuasive, though not as explosive as Sean's or Jake's. Her power was more gentle, more feminine and matronly.

Sean invited me up onto the platform to play guitar during the service before his wedding, and I was completely at a loss. I had been a believer less than a month; I knew no Christian songs, and the chord progressions in the old Pentecostal spirituals were foreign to a guy raised on three-chord riff rock. If they had wanted me to play Led Zeppelin, I could have happily accommodated them, but "Power in the Blood" was another thing altogether, and I just didn't understand it. Worse, I was playing an acoustic twelve-string guitar after playing nothing but electric six-strings for fourteen years. I was terrified that my newness in the faith would become obvious as I stumbled all over the songs these people held so sacred, so mostly I pretended to play and instead observed everything going on around me—and there was a *lot* to observe.

Sean's grandmother's Four Corners Church, a member of a loose affiliation of churches called the Church of God of the Apostolic Faith, was orders of degrees wilder than the Crossroads Cathedral I had attended with Sean in Oklahoma City. My first trip to Jake's church was still in the future and my church was a basic Baptist-ish pod of normalcy, so I had never been in a church quite like Four Corners.

The closest city to Peggs is Tahlequah, most famous for being the headquarters of the Cherokee Nation. Tahlequah has about fifteen thousand residents. Peggs has one hundred. To citizens of Peggs, Tahlequah is a big city.

But Four Corners is actually down a few dirt roads deep in the woods outside Peggs, in an even more remote part of the countryside, too small to actually have a name. Sean's uncle, typical of the men in the area, went "shelling" and "frogging" for a living, Sean told me. I'm still not sure if he was pulling my leg or not, but the fact that it was believable should in some way indicate just how out of the mainstream the area is.

Sean's aunt, his mother's baby sister, played piano at Four Corners and the music was fast, loud and powerful. Her daughter played the drums, banging out rim shot after rim shot. In the congregation, people sang along as loud as they could, bobbing, swaying and dancing to the music, faces heavenward, hands in the air, tears streaming down their faces. It seemed to my eyes almost as if a fog descended into the room as the congregation worshiped and cried. It was a thin haze that seemed to permeate the building.

Between the songs, cries of "Hallelujah," "Praise God" and "Thank you, Jesus" refused to be suppressed by people who appeared absolutely sincere and worshipful. Throughout the congregation, smatterings of people speaking in tongues would periodically waft through the air, and strange as it sounded to me, it wasn't jarring like it had been at Crossroads Cathedral, where it had felt assumed and less genuine. Here, among the poor hill folks, it seemed like even outbursts of tongues just *belonged*. There was a raw honesty that permeated the place. These people, I thought, weren't putting on airs. They weren't trying to do anything other than humble themselves before God. And in that place, in that time, it seemed like they might be onto something.

It felt like it was okay to just let all your dirty secrets hang out in a place like that, because everyone was there to repent, to get back into alignment with God. It wasn't a place where sin was judged, it was a place where sin was banished. I had never been anywhere like it and it was an overwhelming sensory experience.

It was a lot to take in for a new believer who was accustomed to a more traditional church. I was so naïve about religion that I didn't even know you could just go to a Christian bookstore and buy a Bible. I needed a new one desperately, and when my brother got baptized at a Christian church, they gave him a New International Version of the Bible, so I made an appointment with the church to be baptized, too, because I wanted the Bible. Operating from that level of ignorance, I was completely adrift on the stage at Four Corners Church, where everyone but me seemed to be privy to an intimacy with God that I simply had no clue how to access.

The singers seemed to be shouting each song at the top of their lungs. At some point, I realized it didn't matter what chords I played; no one could hear them anyway, so I just continued to pretend to play as I watched the carefully orchestrated chaos play out around me.

When the music was done, ending almost as abruptly as it had begun, the entire building was silent except for sobs that dotted the congregation. I don't remember the sermon.

I just remember how powerfully it was delivered. I had never heard anything like it. Following Sean's lead, I found myself saying "Amen" in the gaps in sound where Sean's grandmother paused to take a breath. I have never forgotten the power of that sermon.

I was in awe of her after that. I remember thinking, *this is the first truly great preacher I have ever heard.*

The entire experience had a gravity that demanded orbit. It was both overwhelming and inspiring. I had never been in a church service that seemed to operate in the miraculous. It wasn't that there were miracles—at least I don't remember anything like that—it was that the place just seemed to exude holiness, a reverence for God that transcended words, song lyrics or even the shouts and sobs of the congregation members. If there truly was a human way for people to have some sort of interaction with a sovereign God, I remember thinking that I had just experienced people doing it.

Sean's wedding was the next day, but I couldn't get the service out of my mind.

That night, Sean and I were staying at the parsonage where Sean's grandmother lived. The water, drawn from a well, was so laden with sulfur you had to set the glass down for a few minutes so the white flakes could settle toward the bottom before you drank it. It was then that he introduced me to the first Christian rock I ever heard, a tape by Jon Gibson, "Jesus Loves Ya."

"He used to be Stevie Wonder's backup singer," Sean said with that trademark smile. "He's working to win him to the Lord."

In Sean's religious faith, being a believer wasn't enough. You weren't a Christian until you "got the Holy Ghost," which meant you were filled with the power of God, as evidenced by speaking in tongues.

Without that experience, you weren't living the "full gospel," which meant that, even though Stevie Wonder had long proclaimed his faith in Christ, he wasn't a real Christian in Sean's eyes until he was "baptized in the Holy Ghost."

We stayed up most of the night listening to Jon Gibson, me soaking up the talented songwriter's music, Sean inexplicably not at all nervous about the next day's nuptials. Sean slept in a bed in his grandmother's guest room, its metal frame barely long enough to contain him. I slept on the floor at the foot of the bed, and it seemed as if sleep eluded us both for the longest time. I was obsessing over the church service I had just experienced, playing it over and over again in my mind, wondering how mere mortals such as Sean's grandmother could have been graced with such powerful abilities to preach, how the congregation must be the most holy, dedicated people I had ever encountered to react to the music and the preaching like that.

Sean, however, probably wasn't thinking about that kind of thing at all. Instead, he was tossing and turning about the journey he would embark upon the next day, when he married the young girl he had been wooing since before she was old enough to drive.

Chapter 4

ANTIOCH

S ean treated his young bride more like a daughter than a wife at times. Though they were loving and affectionate with each other, she naturally fell into a role of subservience as Sean flourished in the role of spiritual leader and head of the household. It was something he had dreamed about his entire life—not the marriage itself, which he largely saw as the means to an end; authority had always been his golden apple.

Growing up with three brothers who were bigger and stronger than him was difficult for Sean, whose family and friends call him "Bear" to this day. But as the smallest, weakest boy, "Bear" always got the short end of the stick, so he used his superior intelligence to even the odds—a difficult task, because his brothers are as brilliant as Sean.

When Sean finally did find something he could control—his young wife—he threw himself into the relationship with everything in him. Though people outside the marriage didn't know it yet, in Sean's mind, a husband's authority over his wife was absolute. And his wife, who was too young to protest, played along, feeding his authority with her submission as he tightened his grip on every aspect of her life, from what she ate to whom she hung out with—and when.

However, at Harbor of Praise, the church where they had met, trouble was brewing. A self-proclaimed "prophet"— nearly blind, balding and willing to speak up whenever he felt the Lord had so moved him—told the pastor that God had declared the church (which the pastor had paid to build) wasn't really *his* church.

The "prophet" declared that there was a change coming in the leadership of the church. The next week the pastor preached that he didn't care what anyone said, it was *his* church. For many congregation members that was the last straw.

Sean and a group of friends left Harbor of Praise, the church where he had met his wife, and formed a new church, The Antioch Ministry, giving it that name because Antioch, Greece (now in Turkey) had been the first place where Jesus's followers were called Christians. Sean's younger brother, who was attending OU by then, and his wife started attending the new church, as did several other families, including Sean's wife's parents and sister. Sean naturally fell into the role of the pastor.

At age twenty-two, Sean Goff became the spiritual leader for an entire church full of people. His powerful and engaging preaching quickly drew a large congregation, and the spectacle of one so young being so well-versed in the Bible helped, too. His preaching had the rare quality of appealing to the guttural Pentecostal sensibility while still engaging the cerebral. It was violent, explosive, yet well-thought-out and literate.

Sean asked me to be the new church's music leader. Though I knew only two or three church songs, I agreed. I was twenty-one. There were a lot of older people in the church, but the team in charge of ministry were all under the age of twenty-five. Such a group of people barely old enough to vote leading a church of course drew young people to the congregation, but older people also found themselves drawn there by the fundamentalist foundation of the ministry, a Bible-centric doctrine that appealed to wide swaths of people.

Sean and I developed a symbiotic style after a month or so. Taking a cue from the black churches we both loved and respected reverentially, we developed an idea that music enhanced preaching. After the congregational songs were over, I would take my Washburn acoustic guitar and sit down behind Sean, who was always dressed in perfectly-pressed khakis, a black, braided leather belt and a dress shirt and tie. His sermons always started slow, with him speaking amiably to the congregation, slowly building as his voice would catch between words while he gulped in air, punctuating his sentences, with the occasional affirmative questioning "Amen?" thrown in for good measure, his pitch rising as the cadence of the sermon intensified.

I would start playing riffs that sounded to me like the Hammond B-3 organ music in black churches, slow and mellow at first, but gaining in speed, power and intensity as Sean's sermon built, too. As his volume and cadence peaked, so would mine on the guitar. As his preaching lulled into a valley, my guitar would slow down and get quieter, too. It was as if we were both preaching the sermon together, he with words, me with music.

Sean even likened our dual style of ministry to the biblical King David, who had, according to the Bible, cast a demon
out by playing a stringed instrument for it.

"Man, I wish more people could have heard the way you
two flowed together," said Dwayne Williams, a guitarist who
played with a professional Christian musician named Kenny
Anderson who sometimes appeared at the church. "It was
really something. I remember when y'all let Kenny and me
join in one time, it just felt like such an honor to be in the
middle of that flow."

When his preaching would reach a fever pitch, Sean was
at his virtuoso best: his uncle Jake, his grandmother, Jimmy
Swaggart, Billy Graham and Paul the apostle all rolled up
into one skinny twenty-two-year-old prancing across the
stage with a grace and ease that belied the fire and brim-
stone pouring out of his mouth, exuding the power of God
to a congregation hungry for evidence of God's presence in
their lives.

Sean's preaching was truly amazing. If ever a preacher
was inspired by God, surely Sean was. The raw, emotional
delivery of the sermons was matched by the intelligence
behind them. It was at once both animalistic and sublime.
Like a caged beast, he would stomp from one side of the
stage to another, heel to toe, his lace-up Ropers pounding
the floor, microphone in one hand, floppy leather Bible
in another as the guitar and his voice swelled, ebbed and
flowed. When he really wanted to make a point, he would
leap off the stage and prance back and forth between the
rows of chairs or pews, microphone in tow, firing off scripture after scripture in a cadence that felt more like machine
gun volleys than a church service.

No one could come away without being captivated.
It was poetry in motion, theology for the common person

delivered with thunderous power that seemed impossible for the 140-pound body that delivered it.

It was a spectacle that almost immediately turned the church into a destination for believers starving for something vital and significant. Rather quickly, the church started to burst at the seams of the small storefront it had rented in Del City, just outside Oklahoma City. Many days, Sean would get up at five in the morning and drive from Norman to the church, fervently praying there for God to bless the church and the congregation members while revealing his power through signs and miracles.

Sometimes, I and others joined him at those early-morning prayer sessions. Other times, he went it alone. On Sundays, church started in the morning, stretched into the afternoon and in the space between services, many stayed to pray, sing and prepare for the evening service. In many senses, church went all day on Sundays. I was generally there from nine in the morning until nine or ten at night, and Sean usually was, too, except for a lunch break.

The hunger of the congregation seemed to draw it out of him and me. We were being pulled beyond the level we believed our own talents would allow us to achieve by the sheer power of the desire of the members of the congregation to reach higher toward God. As the group grew in number, word began spreading like a juicy rumor, and before we knew it, half of the people in each service were people we either barely knew or didn't know at all.

At the center of it all was a man barely old enough to drink—though he would never have dreamed of doing so. Eventually, the church had to move to a shopping center in Moore, Oklahoma, just north of Norman. The new storefront had room for more than two hundred people and, since it had been a church before, we didn't have to modify it to move in, except for a few cosmetic things. Almost immediately, the new building was packed with people and it became apparent that the Moore location would likely be temporary, too, as the church seemed poised to rapidly outgrow it. Though we were all working hard to make it happen, it also seemed like we were just along for the ride, as the power of Sean's charisma and preaching created a wake that drew everyone in behind him.

The new church's youth pastors moved just outside Oklahoma City to a ranch on a dirt road, where they took in troubled youths and tried to guide them back to the "straight and narrow" path of Christianity. Though no one knew it at the time, the ranch ministry was the beginning of a seam in the unity of the church that would later be unable to withstand the stresses placed on it by the explosive growth of the congregation.

We simply were overwhelmed by the exponential increase in the size of the congregation. Sean was a great preacher, but being a pastor required skills he didn't yet possess. None of us did. We had fooled ourselves into believing "the anointing" would take care of everything we needed to do to shepherd a congregation of believers, but preaching, music and desire weren't enough to face the realities of so many personalities gathering together in one place—especially when those personalities were each convinced absolutely of the correctness of their own belief systems to the exclusion of all others.

With Sean at the top of his game, Antioch was making noise in the Oklahoma City area, and it began to attract two types of people that Sean desperately wanted to keep away: "church hoppers" and habitual rabble-rousers.

The first were relatively easy to deal with: ignoring them caused them to "hop" on to the next church, where they might get more attention. At Antioch, we weren't prepared to give them the kind of attention they had come to expect from a pastoral staff, so when they felt neglected, they left. The second group of undesirables, however, proved to be the ultimate undoing of Antioch. Two self-proclaimed "prophets" with divergent visions for the future of the church began to roost in the congregation, each attracting followers and, before anyone knew what was happening, the church was silently divided down the middle, with Sean as the common thread in the division.

An older, more experienced pastor might have seen the rending coming and taken steps to head it off, but Sean was oblivious to the division until it was too late. We could see it developing but we naïvely believed that God would intervene to shake out the bad seeds, as we saw them.

One of the "prophets," the man who had told Harbor of Praise's pastor that the church wasn't his, saw a vacuum of leadership in the church.

In 2012, twenty years after Antioch, the "prophet" told me that he had liked Sean in the beginning. But it wasn't long before he was able to "see through him."

The "prophet" added that Sean just really wasn't what he was supposed to be. He suggested that he might have possibly seen what Sean would become. Asked for more specifics of what he thought he had seen in young Sean, he clammed up. "It was a long time ago."

The second "prophet," a younger man who was soft-spoken and resistant to attention being focused on him, saw a different vision. He saw a church where God was moving and blessing that needed little or no guidance from older ministers, a church heading toward a storm, but one it could weather if everyone banded together. At one New Year's Eve service, the younger "prophet" said that God had shown him Antioch as a tower with three men standing on it. Sean was one, I was another and the third was unidentified. That "prophecy" touched off a firestorm, with half of the church saying that the younger prophet had named himself as one of the three people on the tower, signifying that he saw himself as integral to the church's future. An audio recording of the service revealed that he had not, but it was too late for those who were upset at the idea that a self-proclaimed prophet might be trying to take over the church.

Sean was the lightning rod for each side's position. Some saw the confidence that had made him so attractive as a preacher as nothing more than arrogance, while others saw in him a youthful vitality sorely lacking in "dead" churches—which is what we called churches that were not as experimental. That vitality was absolute in our minds, even going so far as one of us asking the city if we could paint "BEFORE" underneath one of the handicapped parking spaces' icons, which portrayed someone sitting in a wheelchair, indicating that if they came to the Antioch ministry, they would no longer need their wheelchairs when they left. Those who saw Sean as arrogant tended to seek the older prophet for advice and leadership. The others gravitated toward the younger prophet.

Then, almost without warning, a large group of church members announced that they and the older prophet were leaving to form a new church. Among them were the youth ministers. Sean saw this as the ultimate betrayal—the family he had brought along with him to share in the ministry as youth leaders was now leaving to follow the new "prophet." Sean was gravely hurt by the youth ministers siding with the older prophet and he never got over it.

The female youth minister recently discussed with me why her family left Antioch. Sean had come out to the ranch-based youth ministry and strongly rebuked her, saying she wasn't submissive to her husband. She was twenty-two years old and was trying to do the best she knew. Sean compared her to Jezebel.

Jezebel, the woman known in the Bible for usurping her husband's authority—to the detriment of him and the entire kingdom of Israel—was a princess of Phoenicia who married into the royal family of Israel and became infamous for converting her husband, King Ahab, from the religion of the Jews to the Phoenician religion of Baal worship and then convincing him to allow temples of Baal to come into use in Israel, which considered Baal to be a false god. After Ahab's death, Jezebel worked to ensure that her sons would ascend to the throne of Israel. The prophet Elisha proclaimed that another man should be king; that man killed Jezebel's son and incited court officials to throw Jezebel out of a window and then leave her corpse where it fell. Her body was eaten by dogs, a serious breach of Jewish burial practices and a symbol of just how hated Jezebel was by the devout Jews of the time.

In fundamentalist Christian belief, there are few affronts as damning as calling a woman a "Jezebel," which portrays her as a pagan, sexually immoral, manipulative, scheming and ultimately unworthy of even a proper burial after her deserved death.

But Sean used the term freely, readily calling "rebellious" women Jezebels, both in jest and in earnest, depending on his tone of voice. The female youth minister saw it as a deep and abiding insult and an intentional attempt to injure her— one that ultimately worked, leaving a lasting wound.

She added that there was some question over the harsh-
ness of Sean's marriage, too. She remembers hearing about
an incident where he spanked his wife with a belt for something she had done.

Sean had spanked his young wife more than once. He
told me proudly that he had done it when she had gotten out
of line, but I hadn't known at the time whether to take that
statement seriously, since it was so inconsistent with my
understanding of how marriages were supposed to work.

The woman's husband also remembers when Sean's luster began to dim for him. He observed a lot of pride come
into Sean, especially at the Antioch Ministry. Sean appeared
to think he ran everything and he made end runs around the
church board whenever he wanted to.

One end run the youth minister was referring to was
that Sean bought music equipment for the church—a key-
board and a sound system—without seeking approval from
the church board first. But the older prophet went a step further when he described why he believes his group had soured
on Sean:

As he put it, the Spirit of God was in the process of being
withdrawn from Sean, and, in terms of Sean's ministry, "It
was pretty well over with" even before Sean left Antioch.

Whether or not he actually is a prophet, in this case he
was wrong. Sean's ministry, if anything, became much bigger after Antioch, as he became one of the most in-demand
preachers on the evangelism circuit that runs through
America's South and overseas to places like India, where Sean
found himself preaching to tens of thousands of people at a
time.

The Sunday after the church split, when Sean announced
that the Antioch Ministry, unable to pay for the larger storefront with so many members leaving, would close, he reached

out to me afterward for a hug. As he embraced me, Sean did something I never saw him do on any other occasion: he began heaving and sobbing with tears. He was completely broken by the demise of the church he saw as his baby.

It forever changed the young preacher. He would never be dumped again. Sean became an expert at reading the signals and reacting before he could ever get dumped.

Chapter 5

INDIA

After Antioch fell apart, those who found themselves on Sean's side scattered. Sean and I ended up at a church in Norman called MetroChurch that was pastored by a moderately successful Christian recording artist. Sean immediately started serving as an advisor to the pastor on all sorts of matters and I was playing guitar in the music group and leading the youth group.

Sean, who had gone adrift after Antioch, quickly found a calling when he was asked by an Oklahoma City missionary, originally from India, to go back to India with him and win souls. Sean threw himself into the task with the same dedication he reserved for every other endeavor, raising money for the trip by preaching in churches all over the Midwest.

In India, Sean discovered what he believed to be his true life's calling. Crowds followed him wherever he went, and so, apparently, did miracles. He proudly recalled stories of dozens of healings at the meetings, held in places as large as stadiums and as small as single grass houses in out-of-the-way villages few Westerners had ever heard of.

"I prayed for a woman with leprosy," he told me breath-lessly. "She came up and asked for prayer, so I laid my hands on her head and asked the interpreter what she needed prayer for. When he said 'leprosy,' my first instinct was to jump back and go wash my hands, but there were thousands of people there, so I just prayed for her."

The crowds were amazing, he said, as was the respect they showed for Americans.

"Everywhere I walked, it was like the Red Sea parting," he said. "Everyone just got completely out of my way, so even though there were these enormous crowds, I never had any trouble walking anywhere—except for Sikhs. Everyone gets out of their way, including Americans."

After the trip, Sean had a new purpose in life. He was reinvigorated. Everything was about India, the huge crowds, reports of miracles, the heat, the food, the culture—every-thing. He spoke at great length about how the caste system, which was supposed to have been done away with in India, was still alive yet underground.

Castes were essentially immutable social strata. If you were born upper class, you were always upper class. Brahmins always remained Brahmins, no matter what course their lives took. Untouchables, who were too low on the social ladder to belong even to the lowest caste, could never ascend above their classlessness. Most Indians, Sean said, could tell what caste other Indians were from simply by hearing their names. Even though castes were supposed to no longer exist, they were still in place in the minds of the people, he said, which infuriated many higher caste mem-bers, because people who had become Christians would abandon their Hindu names and take on new, Christian names, which essentially obscured their caste as well as their Hindu past.

"For example," he said, "I know a guy who took on the name Abraham when he became a Christian, and now all the high-caste Indians I know who are also Christians will still give him the cold shoulder because they can't tell what caste he's from."

More importantly, however, he said, was that Indians who converted to Christianity had to be thoroughly vetted to make sure they weren't just accepting Jesus as one of the gods they worshiped. Because Hinduism is a religion of multiple gods, it was somewhat difficult to explain that the Christian god wanted to be recognized as the *only* god.

"They have so many gods," Sean told me, shaking his head. "I was in the street in Calcutta and this guy came up to me and offered to sell me a god for what amounted to like sixty cents. So I went, 'don't you mean you want to sell me that *idol*?' And he said, 'no, this is a *god*, not an idol.' They have so many gods that they can sell you one for sixty cents."

Despite the obvious cultural differences, India firmly implanted itself in Sean's mind, and it did so as more than just a mission field.

"We should move there," he told me in his signature intimate way, leaning in and speaking quietly. "You can live like a king there on two hundred dollars a month. It's so backward over there. There were people with chickens on the plane."

He was more serious than it might have seemed at first about living in India. He began to research houses on the coast of the Indian Ocean, where Americans with support from churches in the United States could live in high style more cheaply than they could in spartan accommodations in the States.

"You could seriously get people to donate like five hundred dollars a month, and you could live in a huge house near the beach and still have enough money left over to hire servants," he said. "They'll work for five dollars a month."

He began seasoning all his food with Tabasco sauce to acclimate himself to India's more spicy palate, both for upcoming mission trips and a possible future move to the country. Once, when we were at a restaurant for breakfast, he was liberally dousing his eggs with hot sauce and I must have made a face.

"What?" he said, smiling. "You don't like hot food?"

"I do," I replied. "I just don't have anything to prove."

He laughed and acted like he was about to fling an egg at me.

For Sean, India was transformational. It even affected his speech. When he would have a conversation with an Indian national, he would speak with a very slight Indian accent. In his mind—and on his business cards—Sean became a "missionary evangelist," a preacher who travels between churches, particularly overseas, to minister to "the lost" who have never heard the name of Jesus. It seems strange to Americans, who live in a country where it's nearly impossible to reach adulthood without having multiple conversations daily peppered with Jesus and the Christian God, but in India, the world's second-most-populous nation, there are villages where residents still, in the twenty-first century, have never seen a Westerner.

To fundamentalist Christians, such a thing is one of the worst tragedies imaginable. Because the Bible states that there is "no other name under heaven whereby a man might be saved" than that of Jesus, those who take Jesus's command to "go ye into all the world and preach the gospel to every creature" literally believe it is their responsibility to bring the name and teachings of Jesus to the "unchurched" in those obscure and out-of-the-way places. In the most extreme of fundamentalist religions, the inhabitants of such remote places are doomed to hell by mankind's original sin, and if someone doesn't reach them with the message of Jesus they will roast for eternity because some missionary failed to put in enough effort to get to them.

In their minds, it is a tragedy almost beyond imagining: people perishing in flames for time without boundaries because Christians were too lazy or complacent to hand them the only lifeline that could rescue them from their otherwise-certain fate. It's a doctrine that makes raising money frightfully easy by simply playing on the emotions evoked by that mental picture. But for Sean, it was more than a mental picture or a good way to wrest cash from the wallets of complacent Christians in America. In his mind, the promise that the unchurched would burn in hell for eternity if someone didn't reach them wasn't metaphor; it was reality. With such a burden pressing on him, he invoked another scripture:

"For unto whomsoever much is given, of him shall be much required: and to whom men have committed much, of him they will ask the more." (Luke 12:48)

Sean knew that he was the target audience of that scripture. Though he never mentioned his mental superiority, he was keenly aware that he was smarter than the average person. Similarly, though he never compared himself to other preachers openly, he knew he was far better than the average preacher. It wasn't, in his mind, pride to acknowledge such talents; after all, they were gifts from God but gifts with a purpose. Much had been given to him but he realized that meant much would be required of him to account for how he had handled the gifts with which God had entrusted him.

That meant he took the responsibility of reaching "lost" people in India and other foreign nations very personally. This wasn't just an academic scripture to Sean; it was God speaking directly into his soul.

As such, his primary purpose when preaching in the United States was no longer to win converts here but to raise money for more missionary trips overseas to win converts there.

He began developing a mailing list and publishing a monthly newsletter, which he titled "On The Battlefield," named for one of his favorite songs, which proclaimed, *"I'm on this battlefield for my Lord/I promised him that I/would serve him till I die/so I'm on this battlefield for my Lord."* That song revealed a militaristic view of religion that Sean said was exemplified in a verse spoken by Jesus: "The kingdom of heaven suffers violence, and the violent take it by force." (Matthew 11:12) That violence was not physical, Sean maintained. Violent religion was explained as believers who vigorously pursued their faith, letting no obstacles stand in their way on the path to perfection. The devil was a vanquished foe to be trampled as a reminder of his defeat at the hands of Jesus. "The flesh," meaning the desires of humans to do things unpleasing to God, was something to be mortified, shunned and ultimately defeated as well. The "battlefield" Sean's song and newsletter referred to was the human mind—the central real estate in the struggle between God and Satan for souls. Sean was at constant war to win that ground for God—to "take the kingdom by force."

To him, that meant achieving knowledge and faith in God through prayer and personal mortification of the flesh, and it also meant in the real world actually going and personally delivering the "good news" of Jesus to people who had never heard of him.

And if anyone was going to win that two-front war against Satan and his minions, anyone who knew Sean could reasonably assume it would be him. From outside appearances, he was clearly winning. He was a respected and in-demand speaker, a family man, a trusted advisor and morally beyond reproach. He was a successful missionary, counting thousands of conversions to Christianity as a result of his ministry, not to mention the dozens of other Indian nationals who were able to attend Bible schools because of his efforts.

Sean's newsletter, too, was designed to elicit donations to finance overseas preaching jaunts and Bible schools, particularly in India. He packed it with evangelism reports but he was always careful to also include Bible lessons.

"It makes the newsletter valuable," he said. "It gives the reader a reason to open it."

It also gave Sean one more forum in which to disseminate the overwhelming passion he had developed for his religion and his particular theology over the years. For him, his uncle Jake's favorite song—Bob Dylan's "Pressin' On"—was a driving point of theology exemplified in another scripture:

"I press toward the mark for the prize of the high calling
      of God in Christ Jesus." (Philippians 3:14)

It was more than a scripture, much deeper than a song for Sean. No matter what plateau he reached in his personal Christianity or in his preaching, he was always seeking more, wanting to press further into God's presence and will.

"You know why none of you has ever seen the face of the father?" Sean preached in 1995. "It's because God doesn't want to kill you right now. Moses talked to God and said 'I want to see you, God, I want to know more about the God I'm serving. I want to know who my boss is.' But no man can see the face of God and live, so God hid Moses in the cleft of a rock and let him see the back, but not his face. We should all have that kind of desire to press in closer to God. We should press in to know the King of kings and Lord of lords."

That all-consuming desire led Sean to spend hours every day reading the Bible, researching different topics he discovered and discussing it at almost every opportunity with whoever would listen.

Behind closed doors, however, cracks were beginning to show. I saw Sean treating his young wife more like his child than his spouse but I didn't speak up, because I was told the woman's role was to submit to the husband unquestioningly. It was a view with which I didn't agree and one I could never have lived but it also wasn't my business, I thought.

For fundamentalist Pentecostals, there is an unwritten—but much preached-about—rule: don't oppose God's chosen one, often vocalized as "don't touch God's anointed." "Anointed" is a religious way of labeling those being used in ministry by God, and Sean's "anointing" was unquestionable. Not opposing "God's anointed" is based on the idea that mere humans can never truly understand the mind of God, so when he is using someone you may not understand everything he is doing, but trust that it is part of his plan and leave them alone.

That's a simplistic explanation, but it is hammered into the minds of the faithful: Don't mess with those God is using. To my shame, it's the flimsy explanation I gave for shutting Sean's wife down when, one day when we were driving to church together, she began telling me how Sean had cheated on her with an ex-girlfriend the first year of their marriage. I wanted to hear the details, but if anything is stressed harder in fundamentalist Pentecostalism than "don't touch God's anointed," it's that few sins are as insidious as gossip.

I desperately wanted to know more; it was the first truly bad thing I had ever heard about my best friend and those who are imperfect love little more than to hear how the seemingly perfect are just as flawed. I instantly felt guilty, but I thought about it a lot, creating the spiritual dissonance that keeps so many returning faithfully to church to seek absolution: the guilt over *wanting* to do forbidden things is just as powerful as that of actually doing them.

"I don't want to know," I told Sean's wife, trying to avoid seeing the look of isolation that immediately poured into her face. "That's between you and Sean."

I still feel guilty about it. She was reaching out to one of the only people she could—Sean generally didn't want her being alone with other men—and I closed off that door for her because of religious mumbo-jumbo that taught me to put the religion before the people it was supposedly serving. It would take me another decade to realize religion is useless if it keeps you from helping those who reach out.

Infidelity wasn't the only problem that began to peek out through the cracks. Sean's sixteen-year-old sister-in-law lived with Sean and his wife for a while in the spare bedroom of a condominium on Heatherfield Lane in Norman. Sean's dad had bought it for them while Sean attended college and worked on entering the job market. Years later, when I told the younger sister that Sean had said he would have chosen her instead of her older sister if she had been older at the time, she laughed and shivered and then she said, "Eww."

"He's so creepy," she said, shaking her head. "When I lived with them, he snuck into my bedroom one night and crawled into bed with me. I was just wearing a nightgown and I woke up when he put his hand on my breast. I freaked out and he jumped up and left."

Later, she said, he had apologized, saying he had mistakenly gone into the wrong room half-asleep. Just wanting the conversation to be over, she hadn't pushed it any further, despite the fact that the two rooms and their furnishings were so different that it would be all but impossible to make such a mistake, even "half-asleep."

But other women weren't the only problems that were beginning to surface in Sean's relationship. Many times, I arrived at Sean's house in the morning so I could accompany Sean to prayer at the church. During those early morning times, I heard Sean browbeat his wife so often that one time I felt the need to mention it to her.

"Don't be embarrassed," I told her. "I don't want to be here for that any more than you want him to do it in front of me. If you want, I'll say something to him about it."

Her eyes widened.

"Don't do that," she said, looking horrified. "That would only make it worse. I'm okay. I can handle it."

Sean was constantly criticizing her—in private—about the smallest things. She was naturally thin like her mother and sister and remained thin throughout her marriage to Sean, but that didn't stop him from riding her about every half ounce he perceived her to be overweight.

When she was pregnant with their son, Sean's wife once protested that she was eating for two.

"Yeah," Sean had said, then held his hand up, forefinger and thumb about a quarter of an inch apart. "But one of you is only that big."

Sean often talked about how women used bearing children as an excuse for being fat.

"My aunt says she's having trouble getting rid of the baby fat," he told me once. "But the baby is four years old. That's not baby fat; it's just fat."

It wasn't all bad, though. Sean and his wife often joked with each other. Once, when the three of us were driving to church together, his wife, who was driving, saw a full trash bag in the road and panicked when she mistook it for a human body. Once we all realized that it was just a trash bag, we laughed about it and moved on to another subject. It must have been trash day, because ten minutes later, out of the blue, Sean pointed to a house beside the road and shrieked, "Oh, wow, there are bodies just lined up by the curb at that house!" Sean's wife laughed and punched him in the arm.

It typically wasn't so lighthearted. Sean's wife usually got into trouble if she questioned or contradicted him in front of other people.

Writing it down years later, it seems obvious to me that I should have said something about it, but at the time, the admonition to not oppose God's anointed was all-encompassing, and though I saw a side to Sean that few others got to see, including his hair-trigger temper, I said nothing, because I believed he *was* God's anointed.

The only time I did say something, Sean realized he had pushed too far even for me. He was talking about "disciplining" his wife and mentioned that he had spanked her. And not in the fun, sexy way.

"You have *got* to be kidding me," I said. "She's your wife, not your child!"

He quickly changed his story, attempting to imply that he had been kidding about spanking her, but it was clear he had been serious.

The cracks in his armor were getting wider.

Chapter 6

"COME TO SAN DIEGO"

We languished for another year at MetroChurch in Oklahoma City before I decided to move to Dallas to take a job as the editor of a weekly newspaper. I was twenty-two; Sean was twenty-three. We didn't lose touch, however. It was 1991 and though the Internet existed few knew about it, so we kept in contact through letters and phone calls.

Sean was working at a quarter horse magazine and preaching to raise money for his trips to India. I had begun attending a raw, black Pentecostal church in a dilapidated building where it seemed that you could always smell the plumbing. Sean was jealous; he had always wanted to be a member of an all-black congregation (all black except for him, of course) but had never seemed to have been able to find one that suited him. The one I was attending, These Are They World Outreach in Ferris, Texas, was about as close to a black version of Jake's church as I had ever seen. The pastor was an amazing singer who should have been making millions of dollars with his voice, but instead was preaching at a small church, barely making ends meet. The congregation members started calling me "little Jimmy Swaggart" after they heard me preach and Sean made it a point to visit the church a time or two—and even preached there once.

Black churches and white churches of the fundamentalist Pentecostal tradition embrace different kinds of music. Many black churches feature call-and-response singing and, in just about every service, someone "gets the Holy Ghost" and starts dancing uncontrollably, screaming praises to God the entire time. Congregation members, who are used to the phenomenon, dutifully form a circle around the affected congregant, joining hands to form a human bumper table, preventing the enraptured person from hurting themselves or someone else while they're bouncing around in the spirit. After the person calms down, the members of the "bumper table" wordlessly slip back to their own seats, never missing a beat of the song that's playing at the time.

When Sean attended These Are They, it was he who was affected by the music. He, his wife and I were standing in the front row and the pastor was between Sean and me. About halfway through the song service, Sean bowed his head and his feet began to shuffle, arms thrown back behind him. He was standing next to a full-length window, and as he began to buck and dance more wildly, for a second I thought there was a very real chance he might just dive through the window and onto the ground outside.

The pastor, however, had it under control. Without even so much as looking Sean's way, he simply shot out his right hand and grabbed Sean by the back of his braided leather belt, and as Sean began to hoot, holler and hop around as he danced, he remained safely tethered to the pastor's arm until the excitement began to wane.

When he made his way to the stage, Sean was in rare form. It's hard not to preach loudly in a black Pentecostal church, and harder still not to find yourself half-singing most of your sermon as the Hammond B-3 organ (this one played by a man I only ever knew as Deacon) vamps in the background, almost forcing you to sing your sermon. Sean was no exception. He looked as out-of-place as it is possible for one to look, his skinny, white frame clad in flawlessly pressed khakis, fancy Roper boots poking out beneath.

But as he began to preach, he couldn't have been more at home, and as the congregation's encouraging shouts rose in harmony with Sean's sermon, their enthusiasm pulled more enthusiasm out of him, growing louder, more powerful, more lyrical as the congregation began to—as Sean later put it—draw the sermon out of him.

"Good preaching needs to be received by the congregation to become great preaching," Sean once told me after his These Are They experience. "It's like electricity. It's always there, but until something closes the circuit, it doesn't flow; it just sits there. Black churches let it flow. They draw it out of you."

And they certainly drew it out of Sean.

"Let me tell you something," he preached. "The problem with us not getting into the spirit today and worshiping God is because we are far too religious. You read in the Old Testament when the sacrifices came so often that soon God got sick of them. He didn't want to smell the burnt fat any longer. He didn't want to smell the perfumes they put on and all those things they did. He was *sick* of it, he was tired of it. He said 'these sacrifices that you make, they make me sick because they don't come from your heart but from that foul, stinking spirit of religion. It's all over you people and I don't want the sacrifices anymore!' It's time we go ahead and take off that cloak of religion too and find out whether we want to serve God or just come to church for social purposes."

That kind of preaching resonated with the congregation, and they were on their feet most of the sermon. Later, Sean confessed that the experience, which should have been exhausting, was instead rejuvenating. He and I often discussed ways we could get the passion from black churches to somehow transfer over to white churches—or better yet, to find a way to integrate the two—but we were unable to settle on ways to make that happen.

Two years later, I moved back to Muskogee, Oklahoma, and took a job as a copy editor at the daily newspaper there while pastoring a small church furnished with pews donated by Jake, Sean's uncle who pastored the church in Locust Grove. When I had first moved, I had absolutely no money and I moved into the back room of the church, where Sean's father came to install a shower.

I thanked him profusely; he pretended it was nothing.

"When you're rich, just let me be your limo driver," he said with characteristic deadpan Goff humor. The entire Goff family have always shown themselves to be generous nearly to a fault. Anytime someone was in need, some member of the Goff family was there to reach out to them and help in any way they could, never asking for accolades or any physical thing in return. They did it out of what I perceived to be the true Christian spirit: simply because it was the right thing to do.

Sean came to Oklahoma and preached at my church, leaving a lasting impression on some of the congregation members.

"He was just so anointed," Moya Barnoskie said years later. I had known Moya since high school, when her father had been my martial arts instructor, and now her husband was moving quickly to become my assistant pastor. "Sean's preaching was amazing. He was just incredible, so loud, so powerful."

She also remembered Sean's young wife, who was "so quiet and nice."

Over the years, the Goffs and the Barnoskies kept in touch, Moya said, and Sean would fill them in about the ministry trips he was taking, the preaching he was doing, the healings that were happening through his ministry and other details. They became friends with Sean's younger brother too, and still visit with him to this day.

But it was Sean who left the most lasting impression, Moya said.

"I couldn't tell you what he was preaching about now," she said. "But I still remember how powerful the sermon was. It wasn't something you could just forget."

Even with the preaching help, my tiny church struggled to survive; the congregation members were desperately poor and had no extra money to give to a church, so even as attendance swelled, money was scarce.

Sean, meanwhile, had been hired as a writer for Morris Cerullo, a big-time televangelist, and Sean had moved to San Diego, where he was making more money than he ever had before. He telephoned me one day when I was thinking about closing the church for lack of money.

"We don't have a church here in San Diego," he said out of the blue, "so we will send out tithes to your church."

"Tithes" means 10 percent, and true to his word, Sean sent a check for 10 percent of his income every time he got paid. It was the difference between my little church making the rent so it could continue to reach out to the poor or having to close the doors for good. It was above and beyond the call of friendship—he could have found somewhere else to give the money, had he been so inclined, but he reached out to help me on something we probably both knew wouldn't last. The vast majority of the time I knew Sean, that's who he was—a compassionate man who helped everyone he could every time he had the opportunity.

It was a lesson I never forgot: generosity for generosity's sake is a virtue to be aspired to. Sean never stopped reaching out to me. At the newspaper, I was making three hundred and fifty dollars a week, which added up to just eighteen thousand dollars a year. I had married in the early fall of 1995—Sean had flown in from San Diego to officiate at the wedding—and money was tight. My wife and I celebrated the infrequent times we had enough money to eat out at a fast food restaurant, and even then, we often could only order off the children's menu. The house we were living in had very little insulation, so in the winter we had to stuff blankets in the cracks in the walls to keep the cold air out.

In the late fall of 1995, I asked for a raise, but the editor said the money just wasn't there. I didn't feel guilty, therefore, using the newspaper's long-distance service after deadline late at night to dial up to the Internet and e-mail my friend in San Diego.

"You have to come here, Leif," I read in Sean's message after the characteristic "You've Got Mail" chime. "San Diego is paradise. And the ministry is starting a newspaper; it needs an editor."

I gathered up clippings of my work and typed up a résumé to send to San Diego. A week later, I was hired for thirty thousand dollars a year—plus a two-thousand-dollar moving stipend, which was more money than I had ever seen at one time in my life.

At the time, I considered this salary to be rock star money, so I put in my two weeks' notice—maybe a little more smugly than I had intended—sold my old pickup truck and rented a truck to drive to San Diego for my new job, editor of Morris Cerullo's new newspaper, *GVA Today*, shamelessly fashioned after *USA Today* (the styling got a quick makeover after Gannett, *USA Today*'s parent company, sent a sternly-worded letter to the ministry).

When I arrived in San Diego, Sean offered to carpool to work with me if I could find an apartment in Chula Vista, a bedroom community just north of Tijuana. We began to commute together daily. I immediately noticed a change in Sean.

The strict moral absolutism of his Midwestern Pentecostal upbringing had changed in subtle ways. Suddenly, Sean liked to talk about sex, something I had never heard him mention in all the years I had known him. On one commute, out of the blue, Sean said something that left me speechless.

"I gave her two orgasms last night," he said, matter-of-factly. "That's a personal record but I'm not going to stop there. I'm going for three next time."

I had absolutely no response. Sex had always been an intensely personal subject, strictly forbidden in fundamentalist thinking. Though husbands and wives were expected to engage in sex, they were definitely not expected to talk about it with other people. There were still arguments going on in theological circles about whether oral sex between a husband and wife was okay, about whether condoms were thwarting God's will and whether masturbation—even that word was deemed too risqué and never used—was a sin. In that kind of repressed environment, two buddies talking about sex was unthinkable, yet almost from the beginning of my time in San Diego Sean made it one of his favorite subjects of conversation.

Sean's relationship with his wife had started changing as well, with his "disciplining" of her becoming more public, less shielded behind closed doors.

One Sunday afternoon, my then-wife and I had eaten lunch with Sean and his wife after church. Then we decided to go back to their apartment in Chula Vista to watch football. As we were ascending the stairs to their third-floor apartment, Sean and his wife began tag-teaming the telling of a story. They were disagreeing mildly on some of the details and finally Sean's wife said, "Sean, just shut up and let me tell the story."

And, shockingly to me at the time, because I had been the only one who had seen firsthand the way Sean and his wife truly interacted with each other, Sean did "shut up" and let her tell the rest of the story. But when we got to the apartment, the storm clouds converged.

Sean pointed his finger dramatically back toward the master bedroom of the tiny two-bedroom apartment, which, though furnished almost spartanly, was still chock full of the trappings of an Oklahoma house crammed into the compact lifestyle of the super-crowded beach communities of the West Coast. As he gestured toward the bedroom, he said to his wife with a pinched, barely controlled fury: "Go to your room!"

The expression on her face fell and her porcelain complexion drained. Her shoulders slumped, her head bowed and she immediately cast her eyes down to the floor, turned and slinked off.

"Excuse me for a second," Sean said, and bounded in gazelle-like strides toward the bedroom, slamming the door behind himself when he reached it. Uncomfortably, we stared at each other in silence as muffled sounds—overwhelmingly Sean's voice—emanated from the closed room.

Then silence.

Finally, after several beats too long—we had been quietly debating sneaking out of the apartment so they could handle their marital issues in privacy—Sean came out of the bedroom, the weird smile/grimace that always adorned his face when he was angry displayed in full effect. Behind him, shoulders still slumped, face still drained, his wife followed silently. Her eyes were red, as if she had been crying.

"My wife has something she wants to say to you," Sean told us through the grimace/smile.

"I'm sorry I put you two in such an awkward position," she said. I'm not sure if my mouth dropped open, but it felt as if it wanted to. "I shouldn't have disrespected my husband like that."

What do you say to something like that? "It's okay" seems like you might be agreeing with the chastisement she had just endured at the hands of someone who should be just fine with his wife wanting to tell a story. In pained silence, we simply didn't respond to her apology for putting us in an awkward position.

"Awkward" was the right way to describe the rest of the afternoon, and after we left, we talked about nothing else for days. For the first time that I could remember, Sean had let his inner controlling anger show to someone besides just me.

But displays like that were still rare in the early days after I moved to San Diego. Soon, Cerullo was demanding that Sean and I always attend the monthly creative meetings in his office, which were where the ideas, plans and directions for the worldwide ministry were generated. It was an honored position to be in.

"There are people who have worked here for twenty years and have never even met MC in person," Sean said at lunch during a break in one of the all-day meetings, where we were eating Thai food. "MC" is what people around the office informally called Cerullo. "We have just been here a little while and we are in his top advisors' meeting."

Cerullo counted on us for ideas and it became quickly apparent that the ideas had better be fleshed out before the meeting. Amateur hour was for other people. MC did not appreciate his time being wasted. Sean and I both thrived in that atmosphere. We became closer than we had been in Oklahoma and our daily commute gave us time to grow even closer.

Chapter 7

WORLDWIDE MINISTRY

T elevision ministry is a strange animal. The phenomenon, popularized by Tulsa evangelist Oral Roberts
in the 1950s and 60s, has created superstars out of
otherwise obscure ministers and has spawned a litany of
scandals, from the Jim and Tammy Faye Bakker embezzle-
ment scandal of the 1980s to preacher Peter Popoff using
wireless radios to "prophesy" to believers who came to him
to hear from God.

Then there are the sex scandals, such as televangelist
Jimmy Swaggart's penchant for hookers and anti-homosexual
crusader Ted Haggard's closet gay lover exposing his secret
life to the media.

Through television, ministers believe—correctly—that
they can reach a much larger and more diverse audience than
if they preached every single day of the year from coast to
coast. With one well-chosen sermon, a mid-level minister
can become a superstar almost overnight by broadcasting
that sermon on the many Christian networks that seem to
inhabit every other channel on late-night television. But

those time slots aren't free or cheap. Most ministers must pay the networks that broadcast their shows, and therein lies the inherent problem.

Moderately successful ministers embark optimistically on their first tentative broadcasts with well-intentioned hopes of reaching the masses with the message they believe God has put in their hearts to share with the world. If the message is good, feedback starts coming in from people all over the nation requesting prayer, more information or both. Encouraged, the minister knows he needs a follow-up message to transmit but that means paying the broadcast fees again.

So he raises money by encouraging listeners to donate to the ministry to help ensure it reaches as many viewers as it can possibly reach. Soon, the money that viewers mail in from the appeals on the TV broadcasts isn't enough to pay the ever-increasing broadcast bills; the minister needs a steadier, more predictable income to ensure future broadcasts can safely be embarked upon, so he starts a newsletter to be periodically distributed to those who have already responded. But the minister is busy ministering and he doesn't have time to write the newsletter, so he hires people like Sean and me to write the newsletter for him.

But then he needs to raise enough money to pay for the broadcasts *and* pay for the writers' salaries. Then he needs graphic artists. Printers. Postage. Mailing lists. People to open the letters sent from people who agree with the messages. People to count the money. People to assemble the prayer requests. Accountants. So, to raise more money, he starts sending out a monthly letter to all his "partners"— the people who have responded—expressing the need for more funds. To maximize the return from those letters, he personalizes each one using complicated programs that reach deep into databases that store information about the "partners" and enable the letters that get sent to each one to be personalized enough to touch on their hot-button issues. Usually, the big companies that write such letters charge a percentage of the return on the letters, plus, now that the minister has gotten so busy, he needs extra incentives to encourage people to give to support the vast infrastructure that seems to have sprung up around him from nowhere. So he starts offering trinkets—a "prayer cloth," water from the Dead Sea, "anointing" oil—that promise to carry miracles directly from the minister's hands to the hands of the partners after they have sent in a gift that reached the predetermined threshold amount to trigger the sending of the trinket.

Before he knows what has happened, the ministry is a big business, running with the daily purpose of raising enough money to keep itself going. And somewhere in the jumble of newsletters, glossy "crusade" posters, personalized letters, DVDs, maps, oil, water, cloths and other junk, the message the minister initially felt so moved to preach becomes lost. Now he is responsible for all these people and that means he needs to raise money almost all the time. And as the head of such a big, successful business, shouldn't he reap some of the benefits of all his hard work? Of course. So he buys a luxury car—but nothing too flashy, because he doesn't want the partners to think he's living high on the hog. He buys a big house through a shell company. Then a vacation house. Then, because he's well-known, he can't fly commercial airlines anymore for fear that the partners who have fostered his lifestyle might actually corner him and force him into talking to them. So he issues an appeal to the partners: we need to be good stewards of God's money and flying commercial is too expensive; it's a waste of God's money, so he needs to buy a private jet. If you believe in the message of this ministry, won't you donate for God's jet so we don't waste his precious money?

It all becomes a self-feeding machine, a vicious cycle that has to be nourished. And the cadre of companies that have sprung up around the industry suck on the teat of that vicious cycle, helping preachers "reach the next level" of big-time ministry.

Sean and I quickly became cogs in that all-consuming machine and, before we knew it, we were integral members, swallowed whole and deeply involved in churning out the vile brew that constantly emanates from such ministries to feed the machine. Our primary gig was always working with Morris Cerullo, who pioneered many of the techniques used by big-name ministries today.

Cerullo has been able to keep his reputation much less known than it should be—at least in the United States. He is huge overseas, but in the United States, he prefers to keep his name out of the media altogether.

Cerullo has managed to avoid any major scandals, unlike many of his contemporaries. His 12,000-square-foot home is estimated by critics to be worth more than $12 million. He also owns a Gulfstream jet worth more than $50 million, employing two full-time pilots. His defenders have said that Cerullo's great wealth—estimated at more than $100 million—did not come from defrauding donors, but from wise investments in real estate and other holdings.

My own experience in his ministry was mixed and Sean and I discussed it at great length in the beginning. We both had a distaste for Cerullo's fund-raising techniques, but unlike some other televangelists, we could get on board with the actual ministry that Cerullo performed around the world almost constantly. We could see where much of the money

Cerullo raised through his television shows and various ministry publications went, and we believed that the bulk of the money was truly being used to minister to people all over the world.

That belief led us to something that both of us had condemned before we moved to California: an end-justifies-the-means belief that, although we were uncomfortable with how the money was being raised, we were very comfortable with *why* it was being raised. And it was that dissonance that played out as Sean and I both found ourselves stretching the truth, glossing over moral compunctions and side-stepping our former reluctance to communicate what amounted to untruths.

"We would write about events and report their results before the events even happened," recalled a man who used to run Cerullo's communication department. "We would base our reporting of the results on what had happened at events in the past, and then we would justify it by saying we had to meet printing deadlines, so lying was OK, because we believed that in the end the lies would be made true by what was going to happen."

Ultimately the means began overshadowing the ends so much that we found ourselves helping to plan new ways to raise money regardless of the reason. The raising of the money became the goal, and we ceased being concerned with why. Sean was clearly impressed with Cerullo's personal ability to raise money at his week-long conferences, during which it was not uncommon for him to raise $100,000 in a single offering simply by demanding that the ten thousand people who were in attendance reach deep and give according to the blessings God had bestowed on them through the ministry.

"He's a heavyweight," Sean said one day when we were standing in the front row of such a meeting—the front row being a place of honor reserved only for the highest donors and most-respected ministers. "All these other guys are amateurs. I have seen MC ask everyone to hold up the offering envelopes to pray, but what he's really doing is letting the light shine through the envelopes so he can see inside them to be sure there's money in there. I saw him call out Tim Storey one day for having an empty envelope."

Tim Storey, who has been called the "pastor to the stars," runs a ministry in Los Angeles attended by many major celebrities. But Cerullo was never one to be starstruck. As far as he was concerned, no matter where he was, *he* was the luminary in the room. Other ministers, no matter how big their ministries were, played second-fiddle to Morris Cerullo. Even Oral Roberts found himself doing what Cerullo told him to do one day when Cerullo assigned me to secure a book endorsement from Roberts. He gave me Roberts' home phone number and told me what Roberts was to be told to say in endorsing a book he hadn't even read—since I hadn't written it yet.

And Roberts did exactly as I told him to, offering the endorsement exactly as it was presented to him.

Almost immediately after arriving at Cerullo's ministry, Sean was called upon to author Cerullo's Bible study magazine, *Victory Miracle Living*, which had formerly been penned by the woman who had hired Sean. Each month, Sean would spend most of his time carefully researching and writing lengthy Bible studies. Cerullo's ministry then distributed them to tens of thousands of donors who were led to believe Cerullo himself had authored the studies.

"Almost immediately, it was clear how talented and gifted Sean was, and I had to have him," the head of Cerullo's communications department said. "I took him right away and brought him into communications."

VML, as *Victory Miracle Living* was called, was the cor-
nerstone of Cerullo's mailings each month—other than the
ministry letters, which were the chief raisers of funds. Those
were most often authored by a man named Dave Rostell,
who had started at Cerullo's ministry but had gone on to be
a partner in a large company that wrote letters for dozens of
ministries. In San Diego, Sean's goals changed course from
just being a world-traveling evangelist to being something
more akin to Rostell. He envisioned a time when he would
have a company that did the same types of things Rostell's
company did. Though he never gave up the idea of being a
world-famous evangelist, he actively pursued the second goal
of becoming a wealthy consultant to big-time ministers at
the same time.

He bided his time writing *VML* and authoring the
monthly book that was the "hook" at the end of *VML*
designed to get its recipients to send in donations. If their
donations reached a certain threshold (usually twenty or
thirty dollars), the ministry would send them the book Sean
had authored as a gift to thank them for their donation. The
book, of course, always carried Cerullo's name as the author.
Sean, the woman who hired him and I ghost wrote Cerullo's
books at that time, with the woman who hired Sean focusing
on prayer, Sean focusing on theology and me focusing mostly
on prophecy.

Any "partner" who was paying attention could have
easily realized Cerullo could not possibly be authoring all
the materials credited to him—it wasn't humanly possible,
especially for a guy who was spending two hundred days out
of every year either ministering somewhere or traveling to
minister somewhere. And we weren't the only writers; we
were simply the top three. Sean thrived in the role of Bible
study author. It played directly into his strength, which was

reaching deep into the sometimes confusing scriptures and pulling out lessons that appealed to common people on a powerful, emotional level. For a guy who disdained the idea of being governed by emotions, he was a master at using emotions to control people and to get them to acquiesce to his desires, whether they were for prayer, donating or obeying his husbandly commands.

Deadlines at Cerullo's ministry were regimented, militaristic and unassailable. The ministry had honed mailing down to a science. It knew how long it took a piece of first-class mail to reach Louisiana or Kentucky. It knew how much four pieces of paper would cost to mail as opposed to five pieces. Cerullo himself could easily calculate whether a particular letter or newsletter would be successful in generating donations, and he could look at the proposal for a letter, newsletter or magazine and know what it would cost to produce as opposed to how much money it would raise. We had to have those numbers and estimates ready when we approached him with those ideas but they weren't really necessary, because he was such an astute businessman that he could accurately estimate the numbers off the cuff.

And the *VML* that Sean authored was consistently a good moneymaker for the ministry, as well as drawing rave reviews from the people who actually read the messages and applied them to their lives. Sean's view of those partners, however, quickly became jaded.

"People don't read the books we write," he said one day, smiling humorlessly. "They just want to have them on their bookshelves. We could write anything we wanted in there. MC doesn't read them either. He's just lucky we aren't unscrupulous."

They did, however, read *VML*—and so did Cerullo—and they loved it. Sean's ability to put new spins on words and phrases that were thousands of years old was unmatched, and ultimately the lessons he taught through *VML* breathed new life into that publication, making it relevant, fun to read and useful.

Cerullo loved Sean's work.

"Sean was a very good employee," Cerullo told me in 2012. "How can someone go from a deep, spiritual experience to one losing control of his life?"

The rhetorical question went unanswered, but it was clear, even after everything that later came to light about Sean, that Cerullo still respected him deeply.

Sean, however, didn't respect Cerullo after a year or so at the ministry—except maybe as a businessman. As members of the inner circle, we were privy to all the workings of the ministry and we were counted on to not be starstruck by Cerullo or the other ministers he would draw to himself. We also were supposed to understand that the man behind the curtain was neither a wizard nor God. The ministry was ultimately a business, and while lower-level workers were expected to believe everything it did was ordained by God, the very few of us who were behind the curtain were expected to understand the inner workings. Many employees at the ministry were there because they were true believers in Cerullo, people who would be loyal to him and work for less-than-standard wages because they believed in what they were doing. But you get what you pay for and those people weren't counted on to generate ideas; they did what they were told and that was enough for the kind of money they were making. But Cerullo paid us what then was considered good money and he expected us to earn that money by seeing beyond the veneer he had created around himself. We were supposed to understand the business side of the ministry—but never mention it.

And we were expected to accompany Morris Cerullo to his domestic meetings and crusades and do whatever it took to make sure the events ran smoothly, which might be standing on stage with him and dutifully "Amen-ing" one day or grabbing unruly congregants by the collars and escorting them out the next.

Initially, Sean was put off by the morality—or lack of it—that he saw in the household-name preachers we were meeting and working for.

"Let me tell you something," he preached in 1995, after he had been at the ministry for a year and a half. "If you have enough money, you can draw hundreds of thousands of people in foreign countries and thousands in the U.S. In fact, I could take anyone in this building and I could spend enough money and you could preach to ten thousand people in two months. If you have enough money, you can do it, and the momentum would grow and in six months, your name would be a household word. You'd be doing crusades with Kenneth Hagin or Rodney Howard Brown and whoever you wanted to, if you had enough money in the beginning. These men have grown and built multi-million dollar ministries and millions come in every year, sometimes hundreds of thousands in a day—but they're bankrupt spiritually."

Already, he knew the ministries of big-time preachers had become those self-feeding machines, and he understood that the machines themselves could trap the ministers who built them.

"What happens if you backslide while you're out on the road on your Christian tour?" he asked in the same sermon. "What do you do? Do you come out the next day and say, 'Sorry guys, I backslid; I'm not going to do this anymore. I'm going to go down to the [convenience store] and start selling gas.' What about a man who has built a multimillion-dollar-a-year ministry? What happens if he backslides? Does he quit? No. He tries harder and he does everything he can to keep the momentum going."

For Sean, it was an eerily prophetic statement. When he found himself in a situation that later turned out to be as far from what he would have earlier considered God's will as possible, Sean didn't just quit and say, "Oops, I've made a mistake." Much like the ministers he was chiding in that 1995 sermon, Sean instead just kept pushing forward, kept trying harder.

Sean saw the big-time ministries he was working for as a springboard to his own ministry. He focused on learning from them, learning how to transition from mid-level ministry into becoming a marquee name. He analyzed every aspect of big ministry and, as was his gift, he distilled ways to make it better, to do it more efficiently, to bend it to his own will. He could, he understood, apply the principles of what he was learning to bring something to a mass audience that had never been there before: holiness. Instead of fake miracles, Sean confided, he would broadcast real ones. Instead of preaching about prosperity and ways to achieve your goals in life, he would preach an uncompromising Gospel of repentance and fidelity to God. He would bring the kind of church he had grown up in—his uncle Jake's, the Four Corners church, the Antioch Ministry—to a mass audience.

But those days had already slipped beyond his grasp, even though he didn't realize it.

"When you're in deception, you never know it," Sean's boss at the ministry said. "It's only later that you can look back and go, 'Wow, I can't believe what I was doing.'"

Sean, whose preaching had taken a downward turn along with his morality, still used his connections in the Christian world to get speaking gigs, to hone his own marketing skills and position himself to create momentum for his true dream: to make a living as a minister, both preaching and through the written word. He was still a good preacher and those who hadn't seen him preach before would have thought he was probably the best preacher they had ever heard. But Sean's preaching wasn't what it had been when he was younger. It was following the same downward trajectory as the rest of his Christianity.

During our time with Cerullo, Sean's young sister-in-law had moved to San Diego as well and she was living with them again. It was through her that I met Joy Risker, the always joking, always laughing, always smiling girl who seemed to always be around from that point forward.

Joy, who attended the youth group where Sean was assisting as a leader, was gregarious, funny and just wild enough to be unpredictable. Sean had encouraged us to visit the church he attended, which was pastored by former televangelist Larry Lea. We attended for a short while, but it wasn't for me and we ended up finding a small, predominantly black church—I was generally the only white person in whatever church I attended—to go to because it felt more like home.

Sean, however, thrived at Lea's church, working with the children's pastor, a wickedly funny man who loved to poke fun at everyone, including Lea. He told us about a dinner he had attended with Lea and his wife, who was in the habit of standing up at church and singing the "Hallelujah Chorus" in a serious and over-the-top operatic voice. When the waiter asked the children's pastor what he wanted on his salad, he had stood up, raised one hand and in an operatic voice, sang "Jalapeño!" Lea apparently had snickered. Lea's wife had not.

Sean loved to hang out with the children's pastor, who also was finding his way out of the moral strictures of fundamentalism. He told one story of being cornered by a group of people who thought everyone could stand to have a demon or two cast out of them. They had surrounded him in a chair, and after an hour, it became clear to him that they weren't going to let him leave unless they were satisfied they had cast a demon out, so he began to chant "fuck you, fuck you, fuckyoufuckyoufuckyou."

"They went wild," he told me, laughing. "They cast the demon out of me and I got to go home."

I was both amused and shocked. I had never heard a Pentecostal cuss like that, but I respected the children's pastor implicitly, so I wanted to know more. It was that incident more than any other that started me on the path away from fundamentalism. But for Sean, the influence was something more. He could not say enough how attractive he found the children's pastor's wife to be and although I have no reason to believe he was ever inappropriate, it was shocking to hear him so openly admiring a woman to whom he was not married. Little did I know it was just the beginning.

Maybe the reason Joy Risker always seemed to be around had nothing at all to do with Sean's young sister-in-law.

Chapter 8

"LIKE WATCHING THE SUN"

I f there was one thing you could say about Joy Risker, it's that she wasn't a follower.

Most teenagers are intensely concerned with what everyone else thinks about them every second of every day, but Joy wasn't that way, according to a high school friend.

Joy attended Grossmont High School, which was on the border of La Mesa and El Cajon in east San Diego, an area that used to be known as "the boondocks" because it was isolated from the rest of the city. El Cajon and La Mesa are considerably less affluent than the rest of the area and, being inland, they get the desert heat more than San Diego's trademark ocean breezes. With an average annual rainfall of less than twelve inches, the locale isn't considered as desirable to live in as the wetter, more scenic coastal areas, so it attracts residents who can afford the less expensive housing in the area—"less expensive" being a relative term, since the average price for a two-bedroom house in the area is still a third of a million dollars.

Several of Grossmont's alumni went on to storied careers, from Indian chief Anna Prieto Sandoval, of the Sycuan Band of the Kumeyaay Nation, to broadway actress Karyn Overstreet, CNN producer Jack Hamann, Naval admiral Gregory R. Bryant and even the 1980s' most notorious TV spokesman, Joe Isuzu (actor David Leisure), who graduated in 1968.

"Our high school was almost completely segregated," said Rino Ortega, who now does IT work for a Navy contractor. "All the white people would hang out in one section, blacks in another section, Mexicans in another. It was real separated like that, but our group had a good mix of white people, black people and other minorities. [Joy] kind of gravitated to our group and right from the beginning she was always just around."

Rino was a junior; Joy was a freshman. But immediately, the group gelled around the self-confident jokester who always seemed to know what she wanted out of life and if other people were okay with that, fine, but if they weren't, Joy didn't seem to care.

"She was never off," Rino said. "She was always smiling, cracking jokes, being happy. I never saw her stressed out. I mean, when I was a freshman, I was real nervous about high school, but Joy wasn't. She was just *there*, in the moment."

The Joy he knew wasn't particularly religious, Rino said, though she did attend church at the time with her mother. But religion didn't dominate her entire life. In fact, Joy would join with all of her and Rino's other friends, going to raves and parties, enjoying herself just like everyone else.

"She believed in God and things like that," Rino said. "But she wasn't like married to a certain type of religion."

Joy was open about the fact that she was a Christian, he said, but she wasn't really attached to any particular sect of

Christianity at the time, and she certainly wasn't what folks would call "religious."

All Joy's friends knew was that she was fun to be around, the kind of person who makes you want to be involved in whatever she's doing. If she was serving God in high school, she wasn't putting that in her friends' faces, and she certainly wasn't trying to push her religion on anyone. Just the opposite; it seemed Joy was all about being in the moment, not waiting for some far-off heaven.

"Joy...man, that name probably fits her dead-on," Rino said. "She was always so fucking happy. People wear different masks all the time, and I know with us, Joy never did. She was always the same person...until she got together with *him*."

Rino's Joy, the high school Joy, was always the center of her own universe, unconcerned with outward appearances. She dressed in a bohemian style, listened to a wide variety of musical genres, from the soul of the 1970s that her mother so loved to the grunge and candy pop of the 1990s that she identified with. Joy was who she was, and that person was happy, friendly and always ready to poke good-natured fun at someone.

"I'll give you an example," Rino said. "My name is Rino and I'm just not the friendliest person all the time. I'm not an asshole or anything, but I don't just reach out and say hi either. Joy would make fun of me and go, 'you're such a dick.' And after a while, she'd be like, in a situation where she couldn't say 'dick' and she'd say, 'you're a penis.' And then she combined my name and 'penis' to 'Renis.' And that was my name from then on. 'Oh, hi, Renis!'"

Jokes weren't all Joy had up her sleeve, he said. She was up for just about anything, and whenever she did something, it didn't matter what everyone else was doing; Joy did her own thing, and more often than not, everyone else ended up joining in, because Joy made whatever she was doing become the thing to do. The entire group would go dancing from time to time, whether to private parties or wild raves, which were events that featured electronic and techno music—and lots of times psychedelic drugs, though no one seems to recall Joy partaking in the drugs. Joy just loved to dance at those parties, and she went as often as she could, Rino said.

"She was one of the best dancers I've ever seen," he said. "And I'm not just saying that. I know people like to talk good about people when they're gone, but I'm not just being nice. Joy was an amazing dancer. She was real graceful. She was really into music. We'd all dance together in a big group, but Joy would always be at the center of that. She'd be in the middle, and everyone would dance around her. It was kind of like watching the sun."

That metaphor didn't just apply to people orbiting her when she was dancing, either. When Joy talked to you, you knew for that moment you were the center of the solar system.

"She really had a way to tunnel vision on you and focus on you," Rino said. "Some people look through you; they don't care what you say. If you were in a bar, she would lean in to make sure she could hear what you were saying. When you were talking to her, you were talking only to her. Everything else blurred. It's really hard to find people who do that to you, make you feel like you're the only one there. It's really rare."

That ability to make people feel as if they were the only one important in a crowded room endeared Joy to those who knew her. The feel-good, happy-go-lucky, wonderful dancer and hilarious jokester was more than the surface woman those things described. When she was your friend, she was your *true* friend. You got the feeling that you could tell Joy anything and not only would your secret be safe with her, she would do whatever it took to help you solve whatever problem you were having.

Maybe it stemmed from Joy having to be the one her single mother leaned on when she had troubles—and troubles abounded for Gwen Risker, raising a young daughter by herself in one of the most expensive places in the world to live. After Joy's father, Charles Risker, left Gwen, she had to lean on Joy for moral support as much as Joy leaned on her to provide a roof over her head and food to eat. The two developed a symbiotic relationship, becoming something far more akin to best friends than mother and daughter. Joy knew she could tell Gwen anything, and Gwen knew Joy was a good girl who would tell her anything and everything.

And Joy's friends knew she was the real deal: someone they could count on, someone they could always turn to for both confidence and footloose fun.

But when Joy was seventeen, coincidentally at the same time Rino was graduating from Grossmont, she met Sean Goff. Her core group of friends, the ten or fifteen people who circulated in and out of the motley group, stayed in close contact. Except for Joy.

"She just kind of dropped out," he said. "Looking back on it, it makes sense that she was with him."

That later Joy, he said, still had the core of the Joy he knew but she changed in subtle ways, ways that were hard to define yet noticeable. After she met Sean, Joy's luster, still discernible, dimmed somewhat.

"Something was a little bit off," he said. "I remember that."

Her friends didn't know it, but the handsome young preacher Joy had met whose piercing blue eyes and encyclopedic knowledge of the scriptures, combined with the powerful and authoritative delivery of his sermons, appealed to her on a level she hadn't known she was missing: a father figure. Joy hadn't known the absence of Charles in her life had left a gaping void until Sean came to fill it.

Gwen and Joy collaborated on Joy's development and their relationship grew closer because of that cooperation. Gwen didn't boss Joy around; she instead involved her in all the decisions that affected her life. Joy never really got in any serious trouble and she leaned on Gwen with all the things that most teenagers try desperately to keep secret from their parents. She could, after all, tell Gwen anything. Sean burrowed himself into both Joy and Gwen's lives like an Oklahoma deer tick, offering advice and assistance wherever Gwen felt it was necessary, giving Joy an anchor to guide her away from the influences that were slowly pulling her in directions Gwen didn't approve of, including the club scene, which Gwen thought was probably riddled with drugs and crime.

Without officially doing so, Sean became a counselor to Gwen on how to raise her daughter and on matters both practical and spiritual. Gwen was a single mom who worked for a school district in San Diego. She struggled daily with bills and trying to carve out enough time to meet all her responsibilities. In Sean, Gwen found a sympathetic ear, a man who would give her the information she had been so lacking since Charles had abandoned her and her daughter so many years ago.

Sean was never romantically interested in Gwen but it would have been easy for an outsider to make that mistake, because Sean had a way of integrating himself into people's lives so deeply that you couldn't escape the impression that the involvement had to be more than just platonic. That's just who Sean was, though. If he was interested in helping you, he was obsessed with it. He would do anything he could to make sure he was making a positive difference in your life. In the case of Gwen Risker, Sean had a double motive: he truly cared about what happened to Gwen but he was also starting to become interested in her daughter.

Because Sean was so deeply and helpfully intertwined in Gwen's own life, she had no reason to suspect that he was anything more to Joy than that—a mentor, a pastor, a helper. In fact, Joy and Gwen both knew that Joy told her mother *everything*, even when the things she told were hard to stomach. In the beginning at least, there was nothing to tell. Sean was just who he appeared to be in Joy's life: a concerned and helpful pastor and friend.

When I first met Joy, she was a member of the youth group with which Sean was helping the children's pastor. Sean and the children's pastor called me up to the stage to play guitar during one service, so I played a familiar tune that has only one word as its sole lyric. As I played the riff from the song a few times, the youth group began to smile and groove to the music, and when the music paused, Joy threw her hands up in the air and shouted "Tequila!"

For a few seconds, the room was enveloped in silence and then the entire group burst out in laughter at the absurdity of shouting "Tequila!" during a church service. For the duration of our friendship, I periodically teased Joy by randomly shouting "Tequila!," to which she always gave me a scornful look before breaking into a smile.

But Joy's friends had begun to notice that their friend was changing, though not significantly enough to be worried about it.

Then, when Joy turned nineteen, her friends mostly lost all contact with her for several years.

Chapter 9

THE MORMONS

Fundamentalist Pentecostals will deny that they believe that only Holy Ghost-filled believers will go to heaven, but my experience has been that most believe that very thing, not maliciously but simply from their inability to imagine how anyone could make it through life and into heaven without a "baptism in the Holy Ghost."

Their teaching and preaching is not mean-spirited; it's more pity than self-congratulation. Pentecostals, especially fundamentalists, call themselves "full gospel," implying that those who are not Pentecostals do not have the complete message that God intended for them to have. Specifically, they believe there are certain signs that accompany the Holy Spirit as he inhabits believers' hearts. They believe that those who "have the Holy Ghost" will speak in tongues, pray for the sick and generally live holier lives than those who have not entered into the "full gospel."

Such exclusionist thought is not unique to Pentecostalism. Most fundamentalists have trouble seeing how anyone else can possibly make it to heaven. It's a function of the conviction that what they're hearing in their churches and Bible studies is absolutely inspired by God and therefore unassailable. How could others be correct when they disagree with what God himself revealed?

Almost all of them, aspiring to being living examples of humility, would balk if the direct statement were made to them that they believe their group is going to heaven and that other groups are not, but that's exactly what they preach in so many words.

So a great deal of Sean's and my discussions revolved around "false" religions, which counted as both the non-Christian religions such as Islam and Hinduism and what we saw as fringe Christian religions such as Mormonism and the Jehovah's Witnesses. Sean relied on me for information, because I had read the other religions' foundational documents, from the Quran to the Book of Mormon to the Bhagavad Gita and could thus converse with some level of proficiency with the adherents of those religions.

In general, it's frowned upon for those considered to be novices in the Pentecostal faith to read the foundational documents of other religions, because the fear is that the readers will be "deceived" and "fall away" from the true religion because of the "deception" they received while reading the "demonic" documents on which other religions were based. But because I was considered strong in Christianity, it was acceptable for me to have read those documents, especially because I could then use them to criticize the religions that had grown from them.

It was in that context that I got a call from Sean in 1997, after he had moved from Chula Vista to Seaport Village and I had moved to downtown San Diego.

"Leif, I have some Mormon missionaries coming over," he said. "This is their second visit and now they're bringing their bishop. I need you to bolster my knowledge. Can you come over?"

The Mormon church—officially known as the Church of Jesus Christ of Latter-day Saints or LDS—is an offshoot of Christianity that was founded in the 1820s by Joseph Smith in Palmyra, New York. Smith claimed he had been directed by an angel to find several golden plates that contained the account of Jesus Christ coming to America after he had ministered in Israel. Smith, using the assistance of mysterious stones he called the "urim and thummim," translated the plates he had found, and the translation became known as *The Book of Mormon*, named after one of the main characters. Smith was as surprised as anybody when a religion sprung up around his book and he quickly scrambled to have more "revelations" from God, the bulk of which became two additional books called *Doctrine and Covenants* and *The Pearl of Great Price*. It was those extra books that contained most of the doctrines that outsiders find strange about Mormons, including polygamy, which Smith said God had revealed to him as being necessary for salvation:

"For behold, I reveal unto you a new and an everlasting covenant; and if ye abide not that covenant, *then are ye damned; for no one can reject this covenant and be permitted to enter into my glory*." (Doctrine and Covenants 132:4) "If any man espouse a virgin, and desire to espouse another, and the first give her consent, and if he espouse the second... then is he justified; he cannot commit adultery for they are given unto him; for he cannot commit adultery with that that belongeth unto him and to no one else. And if he have ten virgins given unto him by this law, he cannot commit adultery, for they belong to him, and they are given unto him; therefore is he justified." (Doctrine and Covenants 132:61-62)

Sean and I hadn't yet discussed the Mormons' history of polygamy, but it represented a key plank in my plan to "win" the Mormon missionaries away from their religion.

I drove over to Sean's apartment, which was always meticulously clean, utilitarian and small. The couches were dainty, as was the kitchen table, chairs and even the computer Sean used. Everything looked as if it matched Sean, who had always been thin and understated, perfectly.

Everything felt fragile. Even Sean's guitar, an Ovation Adamas, felt like a display piece. It wasn't that he didn't play it; he did. But when he did, he used the flimsiest picks he could buy, and his strumming was almost ethereal. I always just beat my guitars, breaking strings almost every performance, so I was reticent even to pick up Sean's guitar for fear of injuring it.

Everything in his apartment was similarly fragile. His couch seemed like it might buckle under the weight of anyone weighing more than Sean, and I was always careful when I sat on it.

The Mormon missionaries began their pitch almost immediately. According to their view, Jesus came to America after he rose from the dead but before he ascended into heaven, to preach to the lost tribe of Israel, which inhabited the Americas. Pray and ask if this testimony is true, they said, and the Holy Spirit will give you a burning sensation in your chest telling you that Joseph Smith was a prophet of God.

Sean took a dim view of such methods of discernment.

"It's demonic," he had once told me. "Some of them get the burning so strongly that it's painful. When you open yourself up to that kind of thing spiritually, you're just asking a demon to come possess you."

Our religion at the time did not leave any room for acceptance of any others, so when the missionaries spoke of a confirmation of the truth of Mormonism coming by way of a burning in the bosom, I was not inclined to accommodate their assertion. They believed the very real burning they felt was the Holy Spirit. Since Sean and I believed such a thing could not possibly be the Holy Spirit, which had revealed to us a completely divergent view of religion, it had to have some other source and psychosomatic wasn't an option for us. It had to be demonic, which was the power to which we ascribed anything supernatural that we didn't believe came from God.

And when the Mormon missionaries pronounced Joseph Smith a prophet, that was my opening.

"If he was a prophet, why don't you do what he says?" I asked, setting a familiar trap. I had had the very same conversation with dozens of Mormon missionaries. They, predictably, were shocked—they were, after all, giving up two years of their lives to deliver the good news of another testament of Jesus Christ, and Mormons are renowned for their moral virtue. It was a particularly offensive affront to suggest that they weren't following the teachings of Joseph Smith.

"We do follow the teachings of Joseph Smith as well as the Bible," the lead missionary said. "Of course, everybody falls short, but we never intentionally ignore his teachings."

I smiled.

"What about polygamy?" I asked smugly, watching their faces as they started to mentally rehearse the 'we don't do that anymore' answer they had been taught to give to that question. I headed them off at the pass. "Joseph Smith said salvation depended on polygamy, but the LDS church later rescinded that revelation from God, saying essentially that God had changed his mind. The Bible, which you claim to follow, says God is the same yesterday, today and forever. If he revealed to your prophet that polygamy was necessary for salvation, why did he change his mind when the American government said that Utah couldn't become a state unless the church renounced polygamy? When has God ever bowed to pressure from men?"

They appeared dumbstruck. Mormons are accustomed to questions about polygamy, which they view as a dark chapter in their church's history, and mainstream Mormons not only don't practice polygamy, but they are almost pathologically opposed to it. The discrepancy they were not prepared to discuss was that Smith said God had shown him that polygamy was necessary for salvation. Without plural marriage, he had said, there was no eternal life in the celestial kingdom—Mormons' version of heaven. Each man had to have at least two wives "sealed" to him in order to progress through the plan of salvation, which they viewed as a teaching program for gods-in-training, who couldn't possibly populate the worlds they would eventually be given to rule without multiple wives.

Later, when Utah was seeking statehood, the federal government, in an attempt to avoid a "Mormon state," outlawed polygamy and said Utah would never become a state as long as it tolerated polygamy. In a surprise move, the church's then-prophet, Wilford Woodruff, announced that God had spoken to him and forbidden polygamy:

"I, therefore, as President of the Church of Jesus Christ of Latter-day Saints, do hereby, in the most solemn manner, declare that...we are not teaching polygamy or plural marriage...and I deny that plural marriages have during that period been solemnized in our Temples." (from *The Manifesto*, issued by Wilford Woodruff, 1890, later canonized as part of the church's Standard Works and accepted as divine revelation)

The move, politically savvy, had enabled Utah to attain statehood but it also created a giant rift in Mormonism, with some saying the church had become apostate, trying to change the will of God. Ultimately, that split led to the Fundamentalist LDS church, which still practices polygamy to this day in defiance of federal and state laws, and which has become infamous because of the excesses of "prophet" Warren Jeffs, who both married multiple underage girls and gave other underage girls to aging men in the church for them to marry.

Many in the LDS church (mainstream Mormonism) are embarrassed by both the fundamentalist LDS offspring and its own polygamous past, seeking to distance themselves from plural marriage as much as possible. But the polygamy legacy also called into question the nature of the "revelations" that guided the church and provided a vector for me to challenge whether the missionaries had even fully considered who was right: Joseph Smith, the church's founder, or Wilford Woodruff, the later "prophet" who rescinded the founder's prophetic teaching. Both couldn't be right, because Mormons also followed the Bible, which said the nature of salvation was unchanging.

I pressed the matter further; this was where my actions triggered unintended consequences. Wanting to set them at ease that I wasn't judging their religion because of its past, I said the fatal words: "I don't have a problem with polygamy. Most of the patriarchs in the Bible were polygamous, so I'm not criticizing it. Polygamy is fine. I'm just wondering how it is you reconcile a belief in an unchanging God with such a clear change in what your prophet said was necessary for salvation."

Because polygamy had been declared necessary for salvation by the man who had founded the church, it presented a big problem for them when the church later said God had changed his mind. That was really the only reason I had brought polygamy up and it worked: the missionaries didn't have an answer for me. They promised that they would ask higher-ups and return with a reply, but they never did.

I didn't think for even the tiniest moment that my words might touch off a chain reaction in Sean's mind; I was focused on my misguided desire to "rescue" these good people from their religion. I'm not proud of it, and if I could, I would apologize to Mormons everywhere for my former prejudice against their religion. It was the height of arrogance to assume my religion was so superior to warrant that I "rescue" others from their own religions.

But my words took up roost in Sean's mind and, over the next several weeks, we had numerous academic conversations about polygamy, the gist of them being about how and why polygamy was discontinued in Christianity itself.

We could find no line of demarcation. Polygamy just disappears from the Bible after the period of the patriarchs, with no explanation given. It briefly reappears during the time of the kings, with Solomon notoriously having 800 wives and concubines, some of whom he apparently never even met. But then, from the early kings period through the rest of the Bible, polygamy simply disappears and is never again practiced. Though the Bible never condemns the practice, the experiences of those who participated in it in the Bible are generally reported negatively.

My grasp was that polygamy was based on the outmoded belief that women were the property of men, and therefore it had rightly been dropped when humanity largely came to the understanding that men and women were equals. In early biblical times, I contended, the more children you had, the wealthier you would become, because you would have a built-in free labor force to work the family farm, so it made sense to marry as many wives as possible to generate as many children as possible. Technology had eliminated the need for so many children, so the idea had been dropped. The matter was over in my mind but Sean kept thinking about it, researching it online and reaching out to non-Mormon polygamists he found online during his research.

For him, polygamy solved several problems. It filled a gap between the miraculous lives of the Bible's patriarchs and modern Christianity and it provided a solution to a problem that had bedeviled Sean his entire life: sexual attraction for women he wasn't married to in the face of Bible restrictions forbidding him to act upon it. Why had God approved— even endorsed—polygamy in the Old Testament but now Christianity considered it disallowed? Sean found that the Bible had in fact never forbidden polygamy. If it had never been forbidden, in Sean's mind, that meant it wasn't a sin, and therefore he could—at least in the eyes of God—marry as many women as he wanted and not be askew from God's commandments.

Using a scripture that describes Jesus as a groom and all believers as brides, Sean even went so far as to say the Bible portrayed Jesus as a spiritual polygamist, because he was married to millions of believers.

I didn't share Sean's intense interest in the subject and he stopped mentioning it to me. But in secret, he had already set his eyes on a second spouse and he had already begun pressuring his wife to comply with his desires, though at that point he was simply laying the groundwork for the demand he would later make. He went out of his way to "teach" her that polygamy was God's plan. Using his classic collabora- tive style, he would point to a scripture and say, "Hmm. Isn't that interesting?" and then let the listener—in this case, his young wife—discover what he had already planned for them to discover. Polygamy wasn't in the Bible for the purpose of pleasing Sean; it was the way God wanted his "anointed" to live, just like the patriarchs—it was God's plan that had been somehow lost and had fallen into disuse over the years.

Sean's wife was busy with the couple's newborn son, vulnerable because pregnancy had made her feel fat and she knew that Sean hated fat women. As his plan to get her to comply advanced, he exploited her fears that he would leave her and take their son with him if she didn't comply with "God's will."

Chapter 10

SECRET MARRIAGE

After I moved back to Oklahoma, my salaried job with Morris Cerullo having turned into a more lucrative freelance gig, Sean began getting everyone accustomed to seeing Joy around, even finding her a job at the ministry with him and taking her with the family wherever they went.

Joy told co-workers she had a boyfriend named Sean—but not *that* Sean, the one she rode with back and forth from work every day. That would be *crazy!* He was *married!* He and his wife had just taken her in because her mother couldn't afford to pay the rent for both of them. They were simply being good Samaritans. There was nothing more.

And people bought it.

"It all seemed so innocent and nice," Sean's boss at the ministry said. "They took in this young girl who had no place to go. It looked like a nice, beautiful, Christian thing to do."

"I hate every second of it," Sean's first wife told me one day when she was giving me a ride to the airport so I could return to Oklahoma. "I don't believe in a polygamous lifestyle, but I love my husband and I'm not going to leave him."

Later, she felt comfortable sharing more details.

"I was terrified he would take my son," she told me when I asked why she had acquiesced. "I knew if I didn't go along with it, he would take [my son]."

That fear was a powerful motivator that Sean gladly exploited to force his first wife to let him marry Joy Risker, his new girlfriend.

I didn't know anything about it, but Sean and Joy had gotten "married" in a ceremony on the beach. To avoid trouble with the law, they signed no official marriage license but, in the eyes of God, Sean told his first wife and Joy—and later anyone who would listen—that Sean and Joy were just as married as Sean and his first wife were. At the time, however, the marriage had to remain their little secret. Sean and Joy were still working for Morris Cerullo and Sean was beginning to get some television airtime as one of Cerullo's ministers.

Because no one could imagine Sean taking a second wife while he was still married to the first, most people at the ministry who might have doubts about the arrangement just shrugged and went on about their lives. After all, Sean was just living the same stuff he was preaching as chaplain at the ministry. He was opening his home to someone who had no other place to go. He had gotten her a job and he was doing everything he could to make her life better. It was "loving thy neighbor," just as the Bible had commanded. Almost everyone was fooled.

Though there is no Bible prohibition against marrying more than one woman at a time, Sean was savvy enough to know that mainstream Christians would have violent reactions to the news that he was a polygamist. In my experience, he was right about that. Sean's own mother, his chief cheerleader and promoter, told her son he was going to hell when she heard the news that he had taken another spouse in addition to his first wife. Every time someone found out, their reactions were universally negative, and they all went to the same place mentally: Sean wanted an excuse to have sex with women other than his first wife, so he found a loophole in Bible law and exploited it.

Most people assumed he had started collecting wives to satisfy the wicked lusts of his flesh, not in response to a spiritual prompting by God. He was still working at churches across the country to raise money for India and other mission trips and he knew those doors would slam shut if his family situation came to light, so Sean's polygamy was, by his own description, "in the closet."

Little did he know, the changes in him that appeared subtle to those of us who knew him well and saw him often were jarring to those who hadn't seen him in a while, and his preaching gigs in holiness and fundamentalist churches were in danger of drying up even without the polygamy problem. The minister who had originally invited Sean to India wasn't too sure he wanted Sean back anymore after what turned out to be Sean's final trip there—and his reticence had nothing to do with polygamy.

"He was inappropriate with some of the girls," the minister told me. "Just paying them too much attention. He didn't touch them or anything. But it did seem like he was treating people more like servants."

It was a stark contrast from the humble man willing to do anything to help that the minister had first encountered and invited to preach in India. This preacher had morphed into something more like a televangelist than a man hungry for intimacy with God. Sean had grown accustomed to the deference that televangelists receive from everyone around them, and that attitude showed through to the point that it offended the man whose invitation had touched off Sean's zest for missionary evangelism. The shifts in Sean had finally leaked into what he viewed as his life's calling. Sean might have found that his life changes were closing doors for him even when it wasn't clear why. Accepting polygamy was only the most obvious outward sign of the changes that had turned Sean inside-out. He had pulled anchor and floated away from the foundation that had served him so well for two decades: he had almost imperceptibly abandoned the holiness of his grandmother and uncle and had embraced the relativistic morality of the West Coast televangelists he so wanted to imitate. And people were starting to notice.

But in his mind, being discovered as a polygamist was still the greatest threat. He talked at great length in an e-mail to a polygamist friend about the dangers of "coming out of the closet" as polygamous. Of course, most of the legal danger was imagined; the "marriage" wasn't official, so he wasn't breaking any bigamy laws. Joy wasn't telling anyone she was married, and she wasn't filing her taxes as married, so they weren't awry of the IRS.

No, the danger Sean and his polygamist friends imagined so vividly was mostly in their minds. But that didn't make them any less paranoid that they might be discovered.

I had some inkling that Sean was starting to develop inappropriate feelings toward Joy because of an accidental discovery I made at his apartment. The first year that I flew back and forth to San Diego monthly for my meetings with Morris Cerullo, Sean offered to let me stay at his apartment overnight to save me the expense of renting hotel rooms when I was in San Diego. Though sleeping on couches has always bothered me, I accepted, because I'd always been very careful about spending money needlessly.

On one of those trips, I nearly missed my deadline for having all my materials together for the meeting with Cerullo, so I called Sean before I left and asked if I could e-mail the unfinished documents to him and then complete them on his computer before I went to the meeting the next morning. I couldn't use my laptop, because it had died. Sean readily agreed and after he and his wife had gone to bed—and Joy had gone to bed in her room, ostensibly as simply a needy soul they were helping out by giving her a place to stay, which was completely plausible—I sat down at Sean's computer and began working.

My way of writing is both feverish and disjointed. I can write very quickly for long stretches of time, but occasionally I need a brief distraction completely unrelated to the subject I'm writing about to clear my head and let me see the project from a new perspective when I start again. At about 1:30 A.M., I closed the document I was working on and rubbed my bleary eyes. On his computer's desktop, I saw a document titled "novel idea," so without thinking, I clicked on it. The document was a set of character outlines for a book Sean was working on, to my surprise.

One character was titled "Beautiful, exotic woman in love triangle" and beside the title was a parenthetical: "(Joy)." I looked at it for a while, wondering what, if anything, the title could mean. It was clear that Sean considered Joy beautiful and exotic, but did that mean anything inappropriate? I decided probably not. Sean was probably attracted to Joy in some mild way but he was in love with his first wife, the mother of his son, and I didn't think there was any way some character outline in a novel idea meant he was inappropriate toward her.

Then I saw the next character: "Funny mooch," and beside the words, I saw a parenthetical "(Leif)." My first reaction was to be annoyed but then I was just hurt. It was probably true, I thought, from Sean's perspective. I had been incredibly poor for most of our friendship and now that I finally was making six figures, my habits from being poor had persisted. It was hard for me to reject the "mooch" label when I was sitting there, staying rent-free in his apartment, borrowing his computer to finish my work. I could afford another laptop, but I was using my friend's because it was cheaper. Mooch? Yeah, it was probably true, and I didn't think anything else about the character outlines, except that I occasionally would wince when I recalled that was how my friend saw me, at least part of the time—and that his opinion was justified by my own actions.

After the meeting with Cerullo, I went home, still smarting from realizing the verity of the platitude "the truth hurts." And I vowed that I would try to change my ways, with mixed success, I'm sure. But I also couldn't shake the feeling that maybe Sean was playing with fire by having a woman he was clearly attracted to living in his house.

Sean admitted he was polygamous to me a few months later.

Computers allow you to copy things from one place and paste them to another. When you copy something, the computer stores it in a special area called the clipboard, where it stays until something else is copied and replaces the original thing in the clipboard. When you go to paste something, the computer doesn't care what is currently in the clipboard; it assumes you know what's there and you want that thing pasted into whatever you're doing.

Sean and I e-mailed frequently at the time and the conversations were usually quite long. He would often copy small portions of my e-mails and paste them into his response so it was easier to keep track of what we were talking about as the e-mails got too long to be convenient to read. This time,

Sean pasted the wrong thing at the bottom of one of our exchanges and I got a full accounting of a conversation he had been having with one of his polygamous friends, including a description of his wedding with Joy.

At first, I had to re-read it to be sure it wasn't an elaborate joke. But as I re-read the e-mail, I realized it wasn't a joke; Sean had really entered into a polygamous marriage with Joy while he was still married to his first wife. Everything made sense now. But my anger was roused. My primary concern was for Sean's first wife, who at that time always seemed to me like a person who needed to be looked after. She had married Sean with the expectation that, until death did they part, she would be his only wife.

It wasn't difficult for me to believe Sean had talked her into allowing him to marry a second wife; after all, it had been clear for years that Sean could talk his wife into anything because of the almost total control he exercised over every aspect of her life. I was angry for her. She had just given birth and was navigating one of the most insecure times in a woman's life just as her husband had added a younger, more fit woman to the relationship. And then I was angry with Joy. How could she have done that to Sean's first wife, who had taken her into her home? My anger with Joy was short-lived, however, after I realized she was still basically a child and had no idea of the repercussions of her actions.

No, this was all Sean. He had found a loophole in the Bible and used it to do something I considered abhorrent— and at the expense of his faithful and dutiful wife. I was furious.

The unintentional revelation also thrust me into a moral quandary. On one hand I had my longtime best friend, who was lying and keeping a pretty big secret from me. On the other hand, if his secret became known, he was putting a

major international ministry at risk for ridicule and exposure. Television journalist Diane Sawyer had just done
damning stories on several big ministries—including Sean's
pastor, Larry Lea—that had shut those ministries down
almost overnight, and although I was already souring on televangelists, I didn't think Sean had the right to expose them
to unnecessary risks because of his secret marriage.

I turned to someone whose moral compass I had always
trusted—and who I knew loved Sean and would be able to
help me navigate the twists of the situation: Sean's younger
brother. I called him at his house in Oklahoma, about twenty
minutes from my home, and told him what I had found out
and what my dilemma was now.

He didn't hesitate.

"You need to call Sean and confront him," he said. "Then
say to him that he needs to tell Morris Cerullo or you'll tell
him, because Sean has no right to risk another minister's
ministry like that."

Sean's brother was furious and disgusted at what he saw
as a technicality being exploited by Sean to satisfy immoral
sexual desires. At the time, I agreed with him, to the point
that we both decided Sean had gone off the deep end. We
had a long conversation about it. Sean's brother insisted
that I forward the e-mail to him so he could show the rest
of his family. I did, and when he received it he was appalled.
He reiterated that I needed to call Sean and force him to tell
the ministry that he was exposing them to possible jeopardy
because he was living with two wives.

Finally, I dialed Sean's number.

"I have an e-mail from you that talks about your marriage to Joy," I said. "You accidentally sent it to me."

Sean was shocked. But he barely missed a beat. Almost
immediately, he launched into a clearly rehearsed spiel about

the patriarchs of the Bible and how polygamy was God's original plan for marriage.

"Romantic love is a lie, Leif," Sean said. "The Catholics invented it. It's even in the name, '*Roman*'-tic love. It doesn't exist in the Bible; in the Bible, marriage was arranged and almost no one ever got divorced. Today, people feel this *Roman* need to fall in love and then get married. That puts unreasonable expectations in people's minds that the initial feeling they call 'love' will always continue, but you and I both know that feeling is a chemical reaction in the brain designed to get us to procreate. So when that '*roman*'-tic feeling goes away, people get divorced and remarry. It's serial monogamy. How is that different than me marrying two women without forcing one to live with the stigma and problems of divorce first?"

In Sean's mind, the Roman Catholic Church had corrupted true Christianity with pagan beliefs, of which monogamy and romance were two of the worst examples. That concept of romance was part of the problem with traditional marriage, he said, and if people would just go back to the unadulterated religion of the patriarchs, most of the world's problems would be solved.

"There are more women than men in the world," he said. "Without polygamy, millions of women will never have a husband."

I was in no mood to hear one of Sean's convoluted explanations.

"All of that may be true, Sean," I said. "But it doesn't change the fact that you're putting MC's ministry at risk and you don't have the right to do that."

Sean tried to deflect me from that conclusion, saying his marriage was nobody's business.

"That may be true too," I said, "but it doesn't change the fact that people dig in other people's business all the time.

This *will* get out, and when it does, all anyone will say is 'hey, that guy was on TV for Morris Cerullo, and didn't he also write all those Bible studies for him?' You don't have the right to do that. You need to tell him and let *him* decide if he wants to take that risk. And if you don't, I will."

Sean sighed.

"Give me a week," he said. "You're forcing my hand here. I don't want to tell him, but I will because I don't have a choice."

A week later, he called me. He sounded tired.

"It's over with Joy. It was the toughest thing I have ever done, but I told MC," he said. "He thinks I'm crazy, but he said as long as I end it with Joy, it's okay."

That didn't sound like the Cerullo I knew, so I pressed him.

"He's not worried about the exposure to his ministry?"

Sean laughed.

"He said he has lawyers that eat other lawyers for lunch, and they can bring it on if they want to."

That *did* sound like the Cerullo I knew, so I told Sean I was glad he got it off his chest.

"You're going to break it off with Joy?"

"I already did," he said. "I had to."

I apologized for putting him through such a mess but I reiterated that I had done it out of the best intentions. The next time I visited San Diego, Joy wasn't at Sean's house, and I thought everything had been taken care of.

About a month after that, however, I was back in San Diego, at the house of a friend who had worked with us at the ministry, who had left to go into full-time ministry himself, teaching Bible prophecy.

He pulled me aside in his home office.

"Brother, can I ask you a personal question about Brother Goff?"

I closed my eyes. I knew what was coming.

"Of course," I said.

"Lots of people who know I know him are asking why he's running around town with this young girl like they're man and wife," he said. "One pastor said he saw them kissing. They're worried, because they don't want him preaching in their churches if he is immoral."

"Is the young girl black?" I asked. My friend nodded. "That's Joy Risker."

I told him the whole story.

"You need to call Sean's boss at the ministry and tell him," my friend said. "People are starting to talk, and this isn't good. It's going to cause a lot of problems, and it has to be stopped now."

Sean's boss had recently been promoted to executive vice president at the ministry and Sean had been promoted to vice president of communications. The day after the talk with my friend, I flew home. The minute I got to my home office, I called Sean's boss.

"Sean is married to both his first wife and Joy," I said. "I told him he needed to tell MC or I would, and he lied to me and said he had."

Sean's boss was dumbstruck. Sean's office was next to his. For a minute, he was completely silent. Then he asked me if I was joking. I assured him I was not.

"When you first called, I didn't believe you," Sean's boss told me years later. "I thought, 'Sean is a third-generation preacher's kid. He knows better than that.' So I called him in and said, 'Sean, I have Leif on the line, and he's making some pretty outlandish claims and you need to tell him he's crazy.' At first, I thought you two had had some kind of big fight and you were trying to smear him."

Sean's boss put me on hold to talk to Sean in his office. A few minutes later, hold turned into speakerphone.

"Leif, I've got Sean in my office and he says you're lying because you want to get him fired so you can take his job," Sean's boss said. I was amazed. Nothing could have been further from the truth. I was making more money than Sean where I was and I had no interest in being in charge of Morris Cerullo's communications department. In fact, years later, after Sean's boss at the ministry had left, they offered me *his* job and I turned it down. But Sean had been caught by surprise and he grasped at the first branch he could, which meant accusing me of lying. "He says you made all of it up."

I was furious. It's one thing to be lied to by your best friend, another altogether to be accused of making up lies to take his job.

"Let's call his brother," I said. "He has a copy of the e-mail that will verify that I'm telling the truth."

"That's stupid," I heard Sean say. "Why involve him and just let this craziness get bigger?"

"If I made it up, you have nothing to fear," I said. "Call Sean's brother. I'll give you his number."

I heard a hand being placed over the phone's microphone, and then I heard mumbles. Sean's boss came back on the line.

"I'm going to call your brother, Sean," he said. "I'll call you back, Leif."

An hour later, Sean's boss called me.

"Sean resigned," he said. "Before I could call his brother, he left me a voicemail saying everything you said was true and he was sorry for lying to me."

Sean resigned and then had some time to think about how I was ruining his life after all he had done to help me with mine. It's easy to see where he was coming from, being angry with me. He had done nothing but help me time and time again, and I had betrayed him and ultimately caused him to lose his family's sources of income, since Joy was also employed by the ministry and had to leave, too.

I would have been angry, too. I have regretted my actions many times since then, not because I took a moral stand, but because the stand wasn't mine to make. Butting into Sean's business placed his family in a precarious position and it wasn't my call, I decided much later.

The bad got worse when the children's pastor at Sean's church, who Sean so respected, heard that Sean was polygamous and called me.

"We should launch a commando raid and rescue her," he said, laughing. In the beginning, everyone's concern was for Sean's first wife, who everyone assumed had been brainwashed into accepting her husband sleeping with another woman. Then, realizing how silly a commando raid sounded, he started to giggle more and expand the scenario. "We could rappel down from a helicopter right into their living room. You hold off Sean and I'll grab her and we will signal the helicopter and fly away."

Somehow the story got back to Sean, who thought the idea had come from me and that I was seriously considering breaking into his house, beating him up and kidnapping his first wife to save her from him. He called and threatened me and said his first wife now hated me for suggesting such a thing and if he ever saw me, he would kick my ass.

At the time, I found that thought funny; I was always bigger and stronger than Sean, and as far as I knew, I had a lot more experience fighting. The thought that the wispy preacher could beat me up was laughable. At least I thought so. Of course, others had seen pure violence in him that I had forgotten was there.

Trevor Whitken, an affable British import who was one of Morris Cerullo's go-to on-stage musicians, once went on a preaching crusade with Sean, where he saw Sean's dark side manifest itself at a restaurant, in a situation eerily similar to the one where I had first seen Sean's temper at the University of Oklahoma's dorms.

"We were just sitting and eating in the restaurant, me, Sean and his wife," Trevor said. "And this whole table of kids was sitting behind us, talking loudly. They kept cussing, and Sean got really mad that they were cussing in front of his wife, so he turned around and started screaming at them. I thought he was going to jump up and take the whole table on and at that moment, I was sure he could do it."

That violence was always brimming beneath the surface of Sean's personality and it served him well in his preaching, which certainly fit the bill as "violent," but then it spilled over into his daily life.

After all those years, when he finally turned his anger on me, it only exposed how blind I was to the truth that lay just beneath the surface of the friend I had been closer to than anyone else for more than a decade. Instead of being frightened, as I now know I should have been, I laughed at the thought of Sean doing any kind of real, physical violence.

And then Sean didn't speak to me for several years.

Chapter 11

SULIMON

I called Sean in late 2002 and apologized for forcing him to quit his job at Morris Cerullo's ministry, which I had come to see as an overreaction on my part.

Sure, I was still a bit freaked out by the polygamy, I said, but it hadn't been my place to put a stop to it. I had overstepped my bounds by forcing him to tell the ministry what he was doing, and had gone even further by calling them myself and telling them what Sean was up to. It was an honest apology, and I had done it out of an intense feeling of regret over how I had ended our friendship.

Sean's forgiveness was immediate. It was another sign of his character that many people overlooked. When Sean was wronged, he didn't hold a grudge. He saw that as a waste of energy and time. Though I had been his closest friend and had betrayed him by telling both his family and his employer about his polygamy, Sean let bygones be bygones and we picked up our friendship almost from where we left off.

Sean, as ever, was gracious. He forgave me, he said, though he wasn't sure his first wife would ever see me the same way after she had heard I was telling people she had been "brainwashed" by Sean. She had been offended that I could think she was so weak-minded that she could be brainwashed. The "brainwashed" statement had actually come from the children's pastor but I wasn't going to argue the point as Sean and I worked on repairing our friendship.

Most people who knew Sean had difficulty believing he had become a polygamist, and those who knew Joy or Sean's first wife also were dumbfounded—even those who had observed the family together.

"I heard it," said Tara Walzel, who was Morris Cerullo's official photographer at the time, "when we were at a conference in Palm Springs. Somebody asked 'did you hear?' and I thought, 'no way; I've been to their house and never seen anything weird.' I mean, I had been there a few times while they were claiming to be roommates. I had a jazz dance class with Joy and when I would drop her off, it always seemed like what she said: a roommate situation. The apartment had two master bedrooms on opposite sides of the place, and I didn't notice any pictures with her and Sean or anything weird like that. It just looked like what they said it was: roommates."

After Sean and Joy were exposed as polygamists, Tara maintained her friendship with Joy, even after Sean and Joy were forced to leave the ministry.

"We kept going to the class," she said. "Joy was a very good dancer. The teacher was the same guy who had taught her in high school and he was really hard on her, but she was just amazing at dancing. After we all found out about the polygamy, I sat with her in the car and said, 'Are you sure you know what you're doing?' I wanted to maintain our friendship in case she ever decided she wanted out."

Work wasn't the only aspect of the Goffs' lives that was curtailed by the polygamy.

The lifestyle kept Sean from regular church attendance for fear that his family structure would be discovered. Where formerly he had preached exhaustively on the need for ministers to submit to a local pastor somewhere, he found himself now without one and, much like the ministries he had derided, he came up with letter-of-the-law excuses to say that he had one.

Big-time ministries can't really be tax-exempt unless they're based in a physical church. To get around that IRS restriction, many of them—including Morris Cerullo's—declare themselves to be brick-and-mortar churches, enabling them to gain tax-exempt status. To do that, they have to hold regular church services, so Cerullo's ministry had chapel services on Friday mornings, which the entire staff was required to attend. Cerullo himself didn't usually minister at the chapel services, which were held in the cafeteria. Instead, he appointed a chaplain to run the services, the chaplain serving as "pastor" of the "church." When Sean was the chaplain at Cerullo's ministry, he had often privately bemoaned the fact that Cerullo himself did not submit to a pastor.

"It's unbiblical, Leif," he'd told me years earlier. "Without the covering of a church, he's out on his own and he can be tossed about by any wind of doctrine. I believe he's solid spiritually for the most part, but he's got some weird ideas, and I think most of that stems from the fact that there is no one to hold him accountable. He can do and say what he wants, and there's no pastor to call him onto the carpet."

By the time Sean, his first wife and Joy were being relatively open about their polygamy, Sean himself had no pastor, no church covering and no accountability and it began to show in his beliefs. He told confidantes that the man he had been corresponding with in Utah—the one whose e-mail I had accidentally been sent—was his pastor.

Polygamy put Sean doctrinally into the midst of some strange bedfellows. Though he vigorously opposed homosexuality as a fundamentalist holiness minister, he found himself on their side politically, because he wanted the government to get out of marriage altogether.

"If I want to marry two or three consenting adults, why does the government care?" he asked. "Marriage is God's jurisdiction. Why is the government involved at all?"

Sean told me that the same should apply for homosexuals, though he was dead-set against their orientation. Because he believed the government shouldn't be involved in marriage, he supported the idea that the government shouldn't oppose any kind of marital union. He opposed homosexuality on religious grounds, but he believed that should be the extent of it; the government, he said, should leave homosexuals alone and let churches do their best to try to "convert" them.

Sean's foray into polygamy led him to sympathy for another religion: Islam. Morris Cerullo had spent thousands of pages—many of them written by Sean—talking about how Islam was the enemy of pro-Israel and God-fearing Westerners and how there could never be peace in Israel as long as the Muslims believed that Christians (who believed the same about them) were infidels.

But Muslims, particularly foreign Muslims, support polygamy. So Sean found himself with odd allies: Muslims and homosexuals, both of whom had previously found themselves on the business end of his writing and both frowned upon by every other aspect of his religion.

One of the things that made Sean so effective at evangelism was the way he could immerse himself in the culture of the group he was trying to reach. Islam was no different. Sean read up on Islam and its adherents and began developing friendships with Arabic people online with whom he could discuss polygamy.

"The Quran limits you to four wives," he told me after he and I had reconciled. "I don't support the limit, but it also says if a wife is disobedient, you are to beat her soundly on a couch." He laughed. "I'm pretty sure Gloria Steinem [a leader in the feminist movement] would have a problem with that."

As it was everywhere Sean appeared, his brilliant mind threw open doors for him in the Christian polygamist movement. Almost as soon as he started studying the subject, Sean became an expert on it, to the point that many who had been involved with it for years began coming to him for wisdom and advice. That pattern that had established itself when Sean was a twenty-one-year-old pastor, where older and more experienced people sought him out for spiritual guidance and leadership, had continued at the Cerullo ministry— and now, finally, into his latest venture: polygamy.

Because polygamy is illegal, paranoia permeates the ranks of "the movement," as Sean called it, even though Christian polygamists do not actually break anti-polygamy laws, since they don't actually marry their plural wives in the eyes of the law. As far as the law was concerned, Sean had one wife and Joy was his live-in girlfriend, with whom he had two children. But Sean considered them both wives in the eyes of God and that's where the paranoia about being caught as a polygamist stemmed from.

Christian polygamists are intensely secretive and suspicious of outsiders. In their minds, the government is just looking for reasons to swoop in and start arresting people for daring to marry more than one person. Fear of discovery leads many to take extreme measures to hide their involvement; Sean was no exception. As he dug his way into the community, mostly online, he took on two aliases: Sulimon and Barclay. The first, he told me, was an Arabic translation of Solomon, the biblical king infamous for having eight hundred wives and concubines; the second is Sean's middle name.

Adopting those aliases, Sean took on the persona of wise sage, doling out practical and spiritual advice—two things that had always been his strengths—to those struggling with "the lifestyle," which called itself by several names, the most prominent of which were Christian Polygamy and Patriarchal Christianity. Sean favored the latter. His advice was almost always insightful and practical. Sean had a knack for knowing how to solve complex problems with what seemed to be minimal effort and maximum efficiency.

Patriarchals were adamant about the structure of their belief about what they considered to be an inaccurate and borderline distasteful term for their lifestyle: polygamy, which means "often married." That word, to them, was a huge umbrella that covered what they believed but not accurately enough to define it. The term "polygamy" was offensive to some Patriarchals, because the umbrella was too large.

"I'm not a polygamist," Sean once announced to me. "I'm a polygynist."

Polygyny is a marriage between one man and multiple women, an arrangement the Patriarchals believe is created and approved by the Bible. *Polyandry*, however (marriage between one woman and multiple men) is believed to be an abomination, because there is no precedent for it recorded in the Bible. Patriarchals speak vehemently against such practice as usurpation of God's plan for man at the very least and open rebellion against God at the worst. *Men* were the spiritual leaders, not women. It was an abomination to suggest that a woman could marry multiple men.

Sean related a story he had read about a woman in India who had several husbands.

"It's disgusting," he said. Lost on him was the irony of criticizing anyone's marital arrangements in the face of his own, which were anything but mainstream. Polyandry found itself derided by almost all of the Patriarchals, though, none of whom seemed to see the hypocrisy in opposing one kind of plural marriage over another based on interpretation of a religious text.

Sean's nature would not let him commit halfway. He threw himself into polygamy the way he did with evangelism, India and working for televangelists. He became a leader in the far-flung and secretive community, molding his belief system to fit the strictures of the lifestyle he had adopted as his own.

Sean said that he had believed in polygamy since he was eight years old, though no one who knew him could remember him talking about it until he met and "married" Joy.

After Sean and I began to grow closer again, he talked me into becoming an impartial moderator on a polygamist message board. As a non-polygamist, he said, I could be counted on to administer the board fairly and make sure it stayed sane and civil—two things that were becoming increasingly rare in online discussion forums of all stripes.

On the board, because I had to read every post, I started noticing a forbidden possibility generating a lot of debate: what if a man's wives form a sexual relationship with each other?

Sean's position on the question was that it was perfectly fine, though he stressed that it wasn't something that happened—or would *ever* happen—in his family. That said, he added, the Bible's strictures against homosexuality apply only to men; women are free to have sex with each other as long as they don't stop having sex with their husbands. It was a view that initially generated controversy but ultimately gathered a following. Sean professed to be not that interested in the debate but he spoke about it almost daily.

The posters on the board, about 70 percent male, showed they mostly enjoyed the idea that their wives could get together sexually without drawing the ire of God. Many of the men were religious polygynists such as Sean, but as with anything on the Internet, others joined in the fray and made their presence known by posting questionable comments about such female unions. Sean asked me to lock the discussion after it became clear that it would descend into fantasy. But it highlighted that most on the board favored the "many women, one man" model of polygamy, and that such a model was so heavily in favor of men over women that it was actually taken seriously that female homosexuality was acceptable in God's eyes (as long as they continued servicing their husbands, too), whereas male homosexuality was not.

The homophobia and misogyny inherent in such a belief escaped all of them.

The group also actively shunned polyandrists and those who practiced what they called polyamory—love between many, regardless of which gender was in the majority in the relationship—because there were no strictures on the make-up of the relationship. They also spoke against "free love" and wife-swapping or group sex, though some of the board's members didn't see the problem with such arrangements.

"This is a spiritual arrangement," Sean said as "Barclay" on the board. "Group sex is the same thing as adultery and it has no place in Patriarchy."

In the Patriarchal way of thinking, "poly" could only mean one thing in the eyes of God: one man, many women. In that structure, a family could truly be a microcosm of the church itself, they said: a man, who is the head or "priest" of the house, then the women and children, who were his congregation. The Patriarchals (and fundamentalist Pentecostals, too, for that matter) take the man's "priesthood" in his family seriously. The structure of religion goes like this, from top to bottom: God the Father, Jesus Christ, the Holy Spirit, pastor, man, wife, child. The Holy Spirit isn't ranked beneath Jesus or the Father, because they are all believed to be one. It is listed closer to the pastor and the man because Pentecostals believe the Holy Spirit is the manifestation of God in humans, meaning it is God's presence on earth.

Though they would either deny it or profess confusion at the concept, Patriarchals are dispensationalists, meaning they believe God had represented himself to man in three dispensations: Father in the Old Testament, Son in the New Testament and the Holy Spirit since then. The structure of the family hasn't changed, and to them it is the most important part of the foundation of the church itself, where "church" doesn't refer to the building in which they meet, but to the combination of all believers into one composite group. It is that group that Pentecostals and Patriarchals alike refer to when they say "the church." And that church does not stand a chance, in their minds, without the proper understanding and focus on the family, the smallest but most important component in the hierarchy.

In his personas as Sulimon and Barclay, Sean hammered away at the importance of getting a true understanding of the nature of the family, and "family" became almost a sacred word. Real men, he said, would all eventually end up being polygynists, because they owed it to the women who needed their leadership and guidance. Lots of men would never have multiple wives, he said, because they weren't "real men," and couldn't be trusted to lead their women properly. It was a profoundly and deeply misogynistic view, but Sean did not see it that way and would deny holding misogynistic views unequivocally. Women, he would say, need men, not because men were superior (though he *would* profess that in private), but because God had structured it that way just as he had structured nature that way. Dog packs needed a pack leader; that's just the way it was. He ignored the fact that some dog packs are led by females, not males.

In Sean's mind, a woman's weakness was caused by estrogen. Because the same chemical that makes women more curvy and feminine than men also can sometimes intensify emotions, Sean believed women were unable to think rationally enough to be leaders. Their emotions, he said, clouded their decision making, and he took great pains to describe how women argued using inductive, not deductive, logic. The superior deductive logic, Sean said, was based on a foundation of facts—one fact logically led to another, and a person could follow the bread crumbs of those facts to reach a logical conclusion. Inductive reasoning, he said, was based more on feelings and personal experiences; someone had noticed something in the past, and using that experience as a foundation, they would reach a conclusion that might not be true because their past experience was subjective and possibly non-repeatable.

Women, he maintained, were hopeless inductive reasoners. Though statistics suggest men and women use both types of logic equally, Sean didn't care. Ironically, it was his experiences with women that had convinced him his point of view was correct. As inductive reasoners who tended to let emotions cloud their judgment, women needed a dispassionate man as a leader, he said. And in Sean, they found the perfect dispassionate leader, because every decision was based on reasoning and meticulous planning. He refused to let emotions enter into anything he did or planned.

Most men, he said, succumbed to their weaker natures, allowing women to manipulate and control them, and those men did not deserve even one wife, he said, much less multiple wives. It was only the true man of God who had opened himself to the true nature of a man as handed down by God who deserved multiple wives, and the wives of such a man were incredibly blessed to be with a true "priesthood" man.

He understood that some women would find his theology offensive, and he played up that angle as best he could.

He started writing a book, tentatively titled "How to Be a Male Chauvinist—and Make Women Like It," in which he proclaimed: "I know I will be termed misogynistic for my views. If I had ever allowed myself to be moved by such feminist propaganda, I would have already lost myself. I am a man who can only be loved by women who love manhood."

"Oh, that book title," said Tara Walzel, a photographer at Morris Cerullo World Evangelism. "That title was so annoying. I think he did it just to irritate me."

Though Sean stressed that polygyny wasn't for everyone, secretly he confided that men could never reach their true potential until they fulfilled God's original plan for them—and the women they married couldn't either. He believed he had discovered a long-lost secret to raising better families and fulfilling God's plan for mankind, and he committed himself wholeheartedly to making sure the secret didn't stay lost any longer.

By that time, Sean was getting more and more comfortable with letting people know his "secret," too.

"We were not hiding the fact that we were engaged in plural marriage from anyone," he would later say. But, while he was becoming more relaxed, the idea that he wasn't hiding the structure of his marriage from anyone still wasn't entirely true.

"Hardly anyone knew his marriage arrangement," said Victoria Mack, a book editor at the tech publishing company that Sean worked for. "I think, 'God, might I have been the only one?' I might have been. He didn't tell a lot of people, so I have often wondered why he would tell me. I don't know. He said he couldn't think of anything more disgusting than for two men to be together, but two women seemed natural."

Sean had discussed his polygamy—and the debate over whether women could be with each other sexually—with Victoria on a long trip they took together to Florida for a business conference.

"The way he approached this multiple wives thing was a total crock of shit," she said. "I asked him whether he was a Mormon and he said his religion didn't follow any known philosophy."

That was definitely a big change for a man who had long preached vehemently that everyone needs to submit to a higher authority in religion so that no one runs off the deep end.

"Pride in self-sufficiency is a demon," he had preached early on. "It makes you feel like you can stand on your own. It will tear you down, it will destroy your vision, and the word of God says where there is no vision, the people perish. We have got to get some perish prevention. When someone begins to think they're self-sufficient and they don't need someone teaching them, they're close to the edge. There is nothing that can replace a church, that can replace a group of people getting together. The Bible says we need a church."

Eight years later that conviction had left him, at least in practice, and Sean was on his own, submitted spiritually to a man he rarely ever saw in person, twisting his formerly relatively orthodox fundamentalist religion to fit his new lifestyle and as if fulfilling his own prophecy, Sean's morality began to float adrift.

Victoria had a rare opportunity to interact with both wives at a Christmas party, where changes in Sean's first wife had become apparent, too. Gone was the happy girl he had married when she was still a teenager, replaced by a dour, dutiful housewife.

"Everybody there was Joy's friend," she said. "I tried to be friendly with Sean's first wife, but she just wouldn't warm up to me. She was an automaton. She was walking around, picking up empty glasses, filling up bowls of nuts, acting like a hired servant. She wasn't chatting with anybody. But Joy was all friendly and bubbly and happy to finally meet me. She came bouncing out the door when I first arrived; I hadn't even gotten into the house. Boing, boing, boing, bouncy as can be, bounding out the door. She was so cute."

Even as Sean grew more comfortable being known by a select few as a polygamist, Sulimon/Barclay continually earned more and more respect in the polygamist community for his incisive understanding of the Bible, his everyman way of explaining complex concepts and the unassailable moral conviction that had made him such a powerful and in-demand preacher when he was barely into his twenties. Divorce, he said, was the sign of a weak man who didn't know how to lead his women. It was for men who didn't deserve to have even the wife they had, and ultimately, it proved they were unworthy of receiving the fullness of the blessings of plural marriage.

So it was a quandary when Joy started making intimations that she wasn't happy and that at some point in the future, it wasn't impossible to imagine walking away from the marriage. Sulimon, the wise and respected leader of so many polygamists, couldn't afford to have his junior wife leaving him and exposing any weakness in his God-given leadership skills.

"On our way home after the conference, he confided, 'This isn't working out. She needs to leave, because she's not doing what she's supposed to be doing.' It was September of 2003," Victoria remembered. She also related his dissatisfaction. "It was a long trip, like eight hours of us sitting next to each other talking. He was saying then that things weren't going well and something was going to have to change when he got back."

But because Sean was so known for being Sulimon/Barclay, the spiritual leader who preached that divorce was serial monogamy for which polygamy was the cure, Joy couldn't simply be kicked to the curb; she had to come to some other end.

On that trip he shared more with Victoria. "We talked about a lot of things. Everything, really," she said. "That's when he talked to me about watching crime shows and how hard it must be to try to get away with something. It struck me as weird, but nothing I could put my finger on. We had tons of time to talk about a lot of things, so it never really stuck out until later, but it was weird. Something felt off about it."

Chapter 12

THE PERFECT MURDER

"We need to write a book together," Sean said to me over the phone. It was the spring of 2003 and our friendship, which had been strained by his polygamy and my reaction to it, had just begun to heal.

Since my apology, Sean, Joy and I had been bantering back and forth on a blog I hosted; even his first wife got in a word or two but not nearly as many as Joy, who was much more outgoing and opinionated. She seemed too worldly for her age, completely self-assured and comfortable with who she was.

That said, Joy could still act like a little girl at times.

"I love hip-hop but not gangster rap or anything that degrades women," she wrote on "Joy's New Millennium Page," an extension of Sean's website, in 2002. "And as much as I hate to admit it, I love some dirty pop! OutKast, Missy Elliot, Nikka Costa are some of the names that pop out in my head, but these days I am all about some *NSYNC. What has happened in this world where five little men hopping around the stage can cause such a ruckus? I love them boys! I like Justin but JC has that certain something that makes me go hmmmm. He makes me want to put my son in dance lessons. But I'm getting ahead of myself."

We talked back and forth on my blog about which black star was prettier: Joy thought Tyra Banks was, Sean thought Naomi Campbell. I voted for Halle Berry. We talked about smoking marijuana; Sean was new at it. Joy and I were old hands and teased Sean about his lack of experience, though he proudly recounted his first contact high at a Bob Dylan concert, saying he couldn't have avoided it if he had wanted to. Was it a sin to smoke pot? We all agreed it wasn't. We talked about movies and music and, of course, their polygamy. But polygamy didn't really take up much space in our discussions—at least on my blog. Our conversations were wide-ranging and frequent, with Joy and Sean visiting my blog daily and cracking jokes on posts, offering advice for other commenters and floating ideas for new posts on subjects that interested them.

Joy complained about her inability to find a career path that kept her attention after she had left her job in San Francisco.

"This isn't a dress rehearsal folks," she wrote. "This is your life (who said that?) so I owe it to myself to find something I really am hip to. I went to weirdjobs.com to see if I could find any ideas but I didn't. So I'm back to the drawing board."

But that was as serious as Joy would let herself get. After that, it was back to the playful woman people described as always smiling: "I wonder if there is such a thing as a personal leg shaver. Not that I'd be one (that's actually a really nasty thought) but I just wonder if that profession is out there."

Joy posted on Sean's polygamy discussion board as well, throwing herself into discussions and debates while displaying a surprisingly deep knowledge of the Bible and of the mechanics of polygamous relationships.

I had gained a lot of weight after I got married, but six years later, I had lost it all and started working out twice a day at a gym. I had gotten positively buff by the time I reconnected with Sean, who saw a picture of me on my personal website and in disbelief had shared it with Joy.

"I call bullshit," Joy, who had only ever seen me fat, had told Sean, laughingly. "I won't believe it until I see him in person."

When I was out of town, I tended to eat at the only restaurant chain I knew that offered the vegetarian hamburgers I had taken to eating. Sean and I had agreed to meet at one in San Diego during one of my trips to work with Morris Cerullo, so when he showed up to the meeting, I was glad to see the surprised look on his face when he saw that I had indeed lost all the weight and buffed up in the years we hadn't talked. Unbeknownst to me, Joy was in the car, staring in disbelief as well, because she thought I had Photoshopped the picture Sean had shown her of me. When I later found out about her spy mission to confirm my weight loss and subsequent muscle build-up, we all had a laugh about it and I teased her for being a peeping Tom at the restaurant.

After dinner, Sean accompanied me to the hotel across the street from Morris Cerullo's ministry headquarters, and we talked a long time about what had gone wrong in our friendship and how we could move forward without having the same problem re-present itself. He had a family to take care of now, he said, including two children with Joy, so he couldn't have me messing up his life again.

It was a point that reminded me of how meddling I had been and I assured him that there was no chance of that happening again. Our friendship fired back up almost immediately and we were back to our old habit: collaborating on moneymaking ideas, one of which turned out to be a book or movie that we would write together.

We were both dissatisfied with the quality of what was available.

"What would we write about?" I asked. Sean was always better at coming up with the ideas, and I was good at implementing them. We worked well as a team and I was glad for the opportunity to collaborate with him again.

"How about a murder?" he said. I groaned. It was a tired subject. He, however, was adamant. "We could make it different. The *perfect* murder. We could make our guy know exactly how to keep the cops from figuring out that he did it and the cops, even though they think he did it, can't catch him because he's planned ahead."

Now *there* was an idea. A detective trying to catch a killer who had anticipated the detective's moves ahead of time. Maybe not the most unique idea, but at least one we could lend some new angles to. He and I had just recently talked about how odd it was that TV shows were giving away all the police's secrets on catching criminals. The O.J. Simpson murder trial had been watched by more than half of all Americans, and had lived up to its billing as "the trial of the century." The trial had also brought into the American consciousness the work of forensic examiners, who were featured prominently in O.J. Simpson's trial for the murders of his estranged wife, Nicole Brown Simpson, and her friend, Ronald Goldman.

The show *Forensic Files*, then on the TLC cable network and now on truTV, had quickly picked up on the interest in such investigative techniques and had become a cultural phenomenon. The series was so popular that NBC began airing it in prime time in 2002, and that's when it came to Sean's attention.

"Have you seen *Forensic Files*?" Sean asked. "It's crazy. They show everything, like even how leaving hairs behind can get people caught."

"Hmm," I said. "What about a killer who watches *Forensic Files* to get ideas on how to avoid leaving evidence? Like, he takes notes and learns from the shows so he can keep himself from leaving evidence."

Sean loved the idea.

"It would work," he said. "We can have the guy watching the shows and taking down notes, like 'don't leave hairs, don't get your own blood on the scene, don't brush up against any unusual plants. Only, he can't write the notes down, I guess, because that could be used as evidence, too."

I laughed. It was a chilling idea, but most killers were caught by the evidence they either left behind or allowed to become attached to them, such as gunpowder residue on their hands. Our book could focus on a criminal who educated himself before he killed so there was absolutely no evidence left behind to convict him. As he progressed, we decided, the killer would get better with each kill as he watched and discovered new techniques the police might use to catch people like him. He would always be one step ahead of the police because he was turning their own techniques against them.

"Would the killer dispose of the bodies or just leave them behind because he's so confident he hasn't left any evidence?" I asked.

"No, he's smarter than that," Sean said. "He's not cocky. He doesn't taunt the cops; he makes sure the only trace of his kills is that the victim suddenly doesn't show up at work anymore."

"Then that leaves a big problem," I said. "Disposing of a human body has got to be a lot tougher than it seems. Especially if you're not going to leave any evidence. I can't think of a good way to do it. Maybe dumping them in the ocean, but you'd have to be sneaky and really weigh them down, because people tend to float."

Sean paused. He hadn't thought of how to dispose of the bodies, but it was an important part of getting away with murder. If there was no body, it would be difficult to even determine if a crime had occurred. People disappeared every day, and not all of them were killed. In America, it was perfectly within someone's rights to disappear without leaving a trace behind. Without a body, it would be tough to say that wasn't exactly what had happened. Even if authorities could somehow otherwise determine that a murder had been committed, they would have trouble figuring out who did it and how if they didn't have a body. Hiding or disposing of the body would have to be a key plank of our killer's repertoire if we were going to write a compelling and believable book, we decided. But how?

"I heard somewhere that there are hundreds of bodies in the desert outside Las Vegas," Sean said finally. "Like every time the mobsters out there killed somebody, they just drove outside town, drove off the road for a while and buried them. I bet now that the city has gotten so big, there are tons of people living on top of dead mobsters they just built their houses on top of."

The idea was starting to take shape: The plotline centered on a killer who kept getting away with murder because he covered his tracks so well and never left bodies behind for police to investigate. The killer could be a suspect in multiple disappearances, but he would just keep killing because police could never find enough evidence to actually prosecute him. It was a story that I hadn't seen and one I thought Sean and I could tell well enough to get a book—or even a movie script—sold.

Sean liked that idea—the smart killer always being one step ahead of the authorities. He also liked the idea of a movie script rather than a book.

"Movies are the way to go," he said. "There's just a lot more money in it. We should hash out our story as if we're writing a book and then just write it as a movie script. Or both, but the script should come before the book, sort of like the way they do those Star Trek books after the movie has come out."

I wasn't as comfortable writing scripts, since the few I had done had been video or radio scripts for TV preachers, which I assumed would be significantly different from movie scripts.

"I like it," I said anyway. "But we need to have him dispose of the bodies in different ways. We can't just have him always burying them in the desert or dumping them in the ocean."

Sean thought about it for a second. There had to be more ways to effectively dispose of a body than burying someone in a desert.

"I heard a story about an old widow who died like forty years after her husband disappeared and when they were dealing with her estate, they found a deep freeze in a storage room," he said. "When her family opened the storage room after she died, her husband's body was in the freezer —she had put him in there and then just kept paying the rent for 40 years so they never caught her."

I laughed, imagining the family of a little old lady dis-covering that Mee Maw was a hardened criminal who had kept the most extreme secret for over forty years. It was a compelling story angle.

Sean went on.

"Our killer can't leave any evidence. That's the hook, right?" he said. I nodded, as if he could see me do so over the phone. "He gets everything he needs to know from TV; they spill all the beans about how they catch killers on there. All he has to do is watch TV to plan perfect murders."

The idea was starting to shape up into something we could use.

I could almost feel the wheels turning in Sean's mind. I just didn't realize they might have been turning as he devised the script of an actual murder instead of working on our book/movie concept.

But as we fleshed out our story, he was clearly soaking up ideas. I thought that was to move the story along. The killer would have to have all the right tools in advance. He couldn't kill on a whim; he would have to plan each one out so he didn't leave any evidence behind. That was a key to the story. A passionate killer would leave too much evidence. This guy would have to have a plan with each and every one—a plan with each kill, a way to make sure he never slipped, never made a mistake. He would have to be meticulous and never let himself diverge from his plan.

We both decided to do some draft work and then revisit the idea later. Drafting has never been a strength of mine, so I procrastinated on it. I prefer to have an idea in my head and just write and give the idea life, but Sean was more meticulous than that. Just like the character sketch document I had found on his computer four years before, he would methodically work out the details of each book before he wrote the book. It was probably a more efficient way to work, but I had never been able to make it happen that way. My style was more chaotic: just dive in and let the story tell itself. But Sean never could work that way. He used outlines, sketches and plans to write his books and I admired that about him.

When I started writing novels later, I tried his approach but it still wouldn't work for me. I just couldn't do it and perhaps that's why we worked so well together: each of us brought different strengths to the task. Sean's strengths in writing translated well into the real world. I would buy a car and change the oil when I heard the engine knock or when the "change oil" light got too annoying to ignore. Sean, however, never missed a scheduled oil change. That's just how he was; he was a planner and I was not.

Chapter 13

SEPARATION

Joy had a serious flirtation with another man early in her marriage to Sean, and the betrayal—even though he had all but forced it on her—haunted Sean as long as Joy was still alive.

Simon Greene, who is now a television production professional, was Joy's boyfriend when she worked at Morris Cerullo's ministry with him and was trying to cover up her relationship with Sean.

"She was definitely cheating on him," Simon told me while saying that at the time he didn't know Joy was married to Sean. "We didn't have intercourse, but it was...clearly cheating."

One day, after making out and perhaps a little more, Joy told him, "I really want to run away with you and be with you forever, but you just don't understand all the things that are going on in my life right now."

Those things, of course, were really just one thing: she was secretly married to her roommate, who was already married, and even then, her young and carefree spirit was struggling against the idea of a lifelong marriage that had begun before she even had a chance to figure out who she was and who she wanted to become.

When Simon found out about the secret marriage, the straightforward guy in him wouldn't let him do anything but confront Sean, who apparently had let Joy's fling with Simon go on in order to cover for his secret marriage.

"I confronted him to his face," Simon said. "I told him, 'If you're married to her, your wife has been cheating with me.' It probably wasn't the smartest thing I've ever done; he kind of lost it."

It was impossible for Sean's ego to accept the idea that his wife might find another man more desirable than him. Before that point, he had frequently praised Simon, who at the time was attempting to become a Christian hip-hop artist. But after Simon revealed the extent of his relationship with Joy, Sean could say nothing good about him anymore; he was dumb, lazy, entitled and shady, the kind of guy who would gladly sneak in and steal someone's wife.

The fact that Simon had no idea that Joy was secretly married did nothing to assuage Sean's vitriol toward him. In fact, the story Sean told about the boyfriend's relationship with Joy was completely different than the one Simon himself told.

In Sean's story, Simon wanted Joy but Joy continually rejected him, finally resorting to demanding that he leave her alone. Tara Walzel, Joy's friend, confirmed that Sean's account was false.

"Joy was in love with Simon," Tara said. "I remember thinking that they were really cute together and Joy was so into him."

Sean's story didn't ring true to me at the time but it didn't seem important, because Sean was in the middle of a litany of names of people who "wanted" Joy and were jealous that he had her, so Simon's was just another item on that list.

According to her friends, Joy's mind was again wandering away from Sean, but this time, not for another man—just toward freedom from the constraints of a religion that treated women as the property of men. The relationship, she told friends, wasn't "fulfilling." Plus, she wasn't sure she wanted to be married under any circumstances, much less the one she was in. She was young and aching to be free and explore her options, to improve the future for her sons. But she couldn't do that while her husband was directing her life, leading her where he believed God intended her to go.

But it was complicated. She had two children and a husband who would not willingly suffer the loss of both his wife and the children she had borne him. And there was no way Joy was going to leave them behind. So she couldn't just pack up and move out, even though that was her instinct. She was trapped, and with no obvious way out making itself apparent, she decided to settle in and get what freedom she could inside the marriage. She wanted to go to school to become a makeup artist and to learn American Sign Language, she told Sean, who at least verbally acquiesced to her demands while delaying their fulfillment to an undisclosed later date.

The family just couldn't afford for Joy to become a full-time student, so while she was perfectly welcome to pursue her dreams, she would have to wait a little while to see them come to fruition. In the meantime, Joy had reconnected with her friends.

"She eventually got back in contact with us," Rino said. "She came right out and told us (about the polygamy). She just kind of laid it out. She was pretty open about it."

That first reconnecting happened at a party and that's when Joy's old high school friends met Sean, who had come along with Joy.

"Wow. Polygamy," Rino said. "For me, and I think most of our group, we already thought something was off, because the Joy we knew was a really strong-willed young lady. For us to think that she would be submissive to that situation was kind of strange, but when we met him with Joy, it was, um, like we didn't skip a beat. There was no awkwardness, and she just kind of laid it out: don't judge me, you don't know the situation."

That was enough for Joy's friends, who had always accepted each other, even if they didn't always understand the decisions each had made. They weren't friends with Sean, after all; they were friends with Joy and if that's what made Joy happy, they certainly weren't going to shun her because of it. Plus, other than the obviously weird polygamy angle, Joy's husband was...sort of okay.

"He seemed like an all right guy," Rino continued. "Real respectful, and since most of Joy's friends were guys, who were a good chunk of her life growing up, he met like ten or fifteen of us that day, which can be intimidating to anyone. I thought he handled it real well, and I didn't get any kind of weird vibe from him at all."

However, signs began to show that the woman who had personified the name "Joy" was starting to have troubles, either with her lifestyle or with the husband who had led her into it. It was hard to tell which, because she wasn't really talking about the issues—which was also a new thing for Joy. Usually, she could be depended on to just blurt out whatever she was thinking, but now she seemed less bubbly than usual, less carefree, more dour than she had ever been, and she wasn't talking much about whatever was obviously bothering her.

"Something just seemed a little bit off," Rino said. "I remember that. I can't remember exact words of what she was saying, but she kind of intimated that she was wanting to go to school. She made it appear that she was making her exit plan to get out of that situation, although she didn't just come right out and say that."

Joy made the same kind of intimations to all the guys in the group. Whether she was feeling them out for reactions or whether it was just something bubbling up and over inside her, no one will ever know, but the group came to the same consensus: Joy was well down the road toward being done with the polygamous marriage, and now she was trying to think of graceful ways to call an end to the whole thing and take her kids in some new direction where their mother wasn't married to a man who was also married to someone else.

"We all talked later, and we thought, 'she's going to leave this guy.' We started talking to see if there was anything we could think of to do to help her."

Joy's friends' conspiracy to help her out never had time to gel into an actual plan; they really didn't realize that there wasn't going to be time to put anything into action to help Joy get away from Sean. The last time Rino saw Joy was at his wedding.

"I have this one picture of her from the wedding," Rino said, his voice changing, getting sadder. "I carried it around in my wallet for the longest time until it just disintegrated. It was Joy how I remember her best: dancing by herself. That's the Joy I remember. I remember her smile, her laugh, the genuine way she spoke and listened, and even though she seemed a little down at the wedding, she still loved to dance in that graceful way that was so unique about her. She seemed full of hope that when she got out of the situation, she could be happier."

She was going to go to school and get a good job so she could take care of her children, she said. She would move on with her life after the weird experiment with polygamy.

"I'm back to the drawing board," she wrote on her web page about her job search and plans for the future. "But that's all good. I'm still young. I have time."

But time was one thing Joy didn't have. Sean had already been planning meticulously how to make sure that Joy could never carry through with her plans.

On September 19, 2003, I got a phone call from Joy. I had flown to San Diego from my home in Oklahoma to attend a creative meeting with Morris Cerullo, for whom I was then chief writer.

"Leif," Joy said in a hushed voice. "You *have* to come to San Diego on the second. We're having a surprise birthday party for Sean."

Sean's birthday is October 2, and though I knew that, we had never really celebrated either of our birthdays; in fact, I don't remember ever getting him a present or him getting me a present for our birthdays. Neither of us considered our birthdays a big deal, so I guess it just never came up. But Joy was young. She loved a good party and I could hear it in her voice as she begged me to come help celebrate what would be Sean's thirty-sixth birthday. The idea was attractive; I thought San Diego was probably the most beautiful city in America and I loved being there.

"If you're going to be homeless," Sean said one day when we both lived there, "you should be homeless here. The weather is perfect; you can just sleep on the beach."

I hemmed and hawed when Joy invited me to the party, not because I didn't want to go, but because I was trying to stay within my budget. My meeting with Cerullo wasn't until later in the month, so if I went to Sean's party, it would be two trips across the country in one month, not to mention I'd have to take extra time off from my day job as an editor at my town's newspaper. And I'd have to book a hotel room. The flights from Tulsa to San Diego were expensive and they already took a significant bite out of my profits from the writing gig with Cerullo. Plus, I wasn't too keen on spending twice the normal amount of time in cramped airplane seats. The flight from Tulsa to connections in Dallas or sometimes Atlanta was almost always on a commuter jet or worse, a prop plane.

Plus, it was only a few weeks away, and just two years after 9/11. Sometimes rush tickets like that—besides being expensive—raised suspicions and I had no desire to sit in the office of the newly organized Department of Homeland Security answering questions about why I suddenly had to fly to San Diego twice in one month instead of my regular once-a-month visit.

"Couldn't you have given me a little more notice?" I asked.

Joy laughed. It was a throaty, magnetic guffaw that you couldn't help but join with your own. Whatever Joy was doing, you wanted to do that, too, including laughing—especially laughing. Everything Joy did was executed without a net; when she was in, she was all in. There was no halfway with her. No middle ground. It was part her youth, part just Joy. With her, there was a sense of being outside time: she had been born thirty years too late, missing her appointment with the Aquarius generation's carefree, flowing existence.

"You know I don't plan, fool!" She laughed again. I smiled. "Come on! *Everybody* is going to be here! Don't let me down. You *have* to come!"

I said I'd see what I could do. I had no intention of going but you just didn't tell Joy no. She had a way of being relentless about getting people to go along with her, so I thought I'd just defer the decision on whether to go until it was too late and then pretend like I had forgotten. I would still have to endure a good-natured ribbing about it but at least I wouldn't be stuck on a commuter jet twice in one month. Plus, there would always be another opportunity to see both Sean and her. It just wasn't worth the extra money and the extra time traveling.

Joy, appeased by my saying I'd think about it, gave a bouncy "Yay!" and hung up the phone.

That night, Sean's first wife took a trip to Santa Barbara with all three kids. Sean had told her he was going to use the night as a chance to try to "rekindle" his relationship with Joy—and short of that, to give her an ultimatum: shape up or ship out.

With his first wife and the kids up north, Sean took Joy to his favorite place in San Diego: Coronado Island, a beautiful tourist trap more like the Hamptons than something you'd expect to find on the West Coast. There, they went to Sean's favorite place, an opulent hotel where they had an expensive dinner of Kobe beef. Sean liked his extra rare.

"I want to hear it moo," he used to tell me as he ate bloody steak and laughed at the horrified faces I would make. Even before I was a vegetarian, the thought of bloody meat disgusted me.

After the dinner, Sean and Joy went back to their house in Kensington, a hamlet inside the greater San Diego area. There, Joy somehow got sedatives into her system. Whatever had transpired between Sean and Joy leading up to that moment, after they arrived home the docile and helpful preacher turned savage.

The self-proclaimed man of God murdered his junior wife.

"We need to come to the place where we take on a war-fare mentality," he had preached early in his ministry. "We need to take an attitude of violence toward the enemy and have our eyes set on the war that is before us. Everybody has specific evil things that come against them. It's time to decide you're going to go into warfare—all by yourself, if necessary, and you're going to rise up in power and defeat the enemy."

Though he had preached about spiritual, not physical, violence, it seems Sean now viewed Joy as an enemy. Somehow, the only way he saw out of the situation was violence—brutal, bloody violence. With the sedatives promethazine and codeine coursing through her system, Sean easily could have smothered Joy with a pillow and the final result would have been the same: her life would have ended. But Sean didn't kill Joy with a pillow after he had sedated her with the drugs. Instead, he attacked her, stabbing her again and again, deeply enough to scar her bones, brutally enough to sever her sternum.

Sean Goff wasn't mercifully ending a problem that had cropped up. He was attacking an adversary with all his might. He was going into warfare against the "evil thing" that had "come against" him. Joy was an enemy who had to be dealt with. She wasn't just an inconvenient side note. She had to be decisively destroyed.

"There is an accuser of the brethren, accusing them night and day," he preached in the same sermon. "We've got to deal with the accuser of the brethren. We've got to deal with it in warfare, in power and determination."

And Sean did deal with the enemy he had identified, his favorite wife, the young, happy, footloose mother of two of his children. He dealt with her the same way he dealt with every other obstacle that found itself in his way: he methodically planned the best and most effective way to deal with the situation. In Sean's mind, spiritual victory and physical victory were one and the same if done in the name of advancing the work of God.

Did he believe God had led him to kill Joy?

"When Abraham was walking up onto the mountain, he wasn't worried about killing his son," Sean preached in 1992. "When God moves in your life, you can't deny it. When God moves in your life, you know it's God and you can't say it was coincidence. I'm reminded of Moses: when he was growing up in Egypt, he saw one of his brothers, an Israelite, being come against by an Egyptian and he said 'I'm going to do something about it,' so he took the Egyptian and killed him, and later, when he found out it was known, he fled. He thought he had dug himself a hole so deep that he could never come out. Listen to me tonight. He said 'I've made too many mistakes, I've done too many things wrong, and God can't use me anymore.' But through that experience and his time in the desert, he was humbled and he became a greater man of God."

In Sean's mind and preaching, there was literally no difference between the God revealed in the pages of the Bible and the God he served. He spoke many times about what people today would do if God told them to kill someone as he told several of his heroes in the Bible.

"People today would just think they were crazy and go see a shrink," he said to me in 1997, smiling between bites of a sandwich at a downtown San Diego deli. "People think they serve God, but when he asks them to do something difficult or even illegal, they don't really serve him. They just give him lip service."

If Sean *thought* God had asked him to kill, he believed he would not hesitate. To him, serving God meant you gladly went to prison, you gladly laid down your life if necessary to

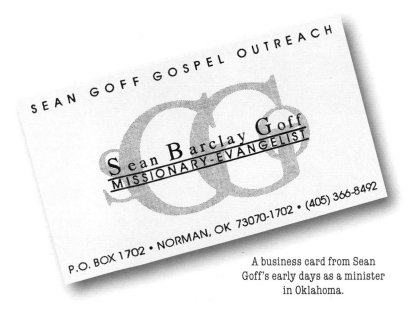

A business card from Sean
Goff's early days as a minister
in Oklahoma.

Sean Goff and Leif Wright both worked for
pentecostal televangelist Morris Cerullo, seen here
preaching to thousands of enthusiastic followers.

Photo © Tara L.B. Walzel.

Joy Risker, Sean's second wife, loved posing for art photos shot by her friend, Tara Walzell.

Joy being Joy.

Joy worked with Sean
at Morris Cerullo
World Evangelism.

The wedding kiss: Sean
and Joy were "married"
on the beach in 1997.

The cairn in the Arizona desert
where Joy's remains were found.

The jumble of bones was
painstakingly reassembled by
Dr. Laura Fulginiti,
a forensic anthropologist.

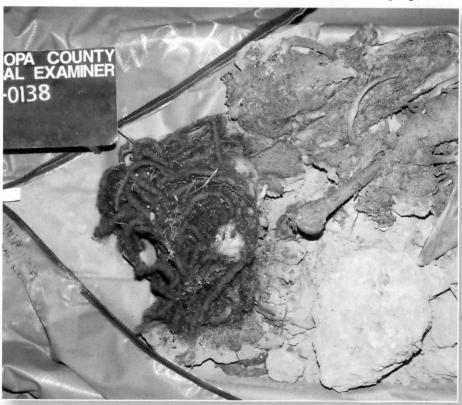

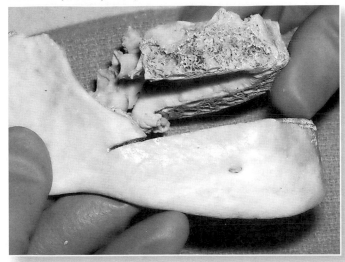

Joy's teeth had
been sawn off
and were missing
from the remains.

Joy Risker's skull was reconstructed
and a forensic artist created a sketch
based on her remains.

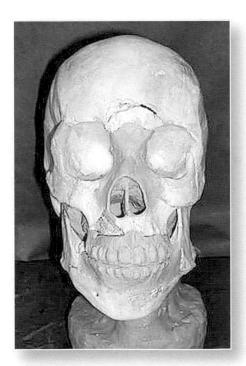

Welcome to www.ebarclay.com!

Arab
Bookstore
Guest Pages
India
Personality
Politics
News Analysis

Thank you for stopping by!

Barclay is here to inform you and help you with practically anything! If you need anything you don't find on this page, just click "e-mail" above and let Barclay know. If what you are asking is within the realm of possibility, Barclay will e-mail you back with the answer!

January 15, 2000 - Updated recently is the Politics and Indian areas and slighter additions to the Arab Resources page. Please check it out and e-mail me.

Sean Goff's polygamy Web site offered advice to both polygamists and monogamists.

Sean composed fake e-mails to Joy's friends to explain why she had disappeared. The messages, uncharacteristic of Joy's personality, led friends to contact police.

```
From:      Joy Risker [          @gmail.com]
Sent:      Monday, October 06, 2003 12:14 PM
To:        ████████████████
Subject:   Re: ██████
```

█████,

Listen, we've been friends a long time, but you're about to get on my last black nerve. I'll call you when I get things sorted out...when I choose and not when someone tries to force me to. I'm a big girl and can take care of myself, and I have the right to do what I want. This is the same crap Sean tried to do to me...know everywhere I am and make me call when he wanted me to. Did he ask you to do this? If the tables were turned, I'd understand your need for space, which I desperately need in order to figure everything out. I have too much to do right now to get all bogged down in emotional issues so I'm not going to play games right now and I don't have time to play email tag right now either.

I'll talk with you when I'm ready,
Joy

--- ████████████ <████████@yahoo.com> wrote:
> Joy:
>   Let me know something soon...by phone please
> lady.
> That's the only way I'm going to believe it for
> myself!
>
> Love You Girl!
> ████
>
>
> _ _ _ _ _ _ _ _ _ _ _ _ _ _ _ _ _
> Do you Yahoo!?
> The New Yahoo! Shopping - with improved product search
> http://shopping.yahoo.com

Sean Goff's defense attorney Albert Arena addresses the jurors.

Prosecutor Matthew Greco emphasizes a point during the trial.

During sentencing, Sean Goff (shown here with attorney Arena) continued to blame Joy for causing the crime.

fulfill the will he had revealed to you. Could such a belief system include killing the wife whose departure might destroy
your ministry to "patriarchal Christians?" Could it include
killing her if she threatened to take the sons God had given
you and raise them according to her will, not yours—the
man God had appointed to be spiritual head of the family?
Just how far would Sean take his belief in a God who had not
changed from the Old Testament stories to modern times?

Maybe lesser believers would say "God doesn't do that
anymore," but to Sean, that was part of their great weakness.
God was a violent God who demanded absolute service, no
matter what that entailed.

He once proudly told me the story of a young man in
Florida who had taken literally the Bible's admonition to "cut
off your hand if it offends you," and had cut off his own nose
because he could not stop himself from snorting cocaine.

"He's misguided," Sean said as we stood near my cubicle
at Morris Cerullo World Evangelism, "but you have to admire
his commitment."

To Sean, especially when it came to acts of faith, there
was a fine, almost indiscernible line between faith and insan-
ity. Did the man who once proclaimed that every action of his
life was a result of God's call on him believe that God wanted
him to kill Joy?

It's hard to say, and Sean certainly isn't telling.

Whatever actually happened after the dinner on
Coronado Island, only Sean knows. What *is* known is that,
likely using the contractor's sheeting he had purchased a
short time before and the duct tape he had bought at the
same time, Sean somehow managed to kill a full-grown
woman and only leave a few tiny drops of blood in the house.

He stabbed Joy at least a dozen times, according to
the autopsy report. He sliced her sternum off. He nearly

decapitated her. The lack of blood at the house in Kensington suggests that however Sean set up his "kill room," it was mostly effective in keeping Joy's bodily fluids contained as he stabbed her to death. Her stab wounds alone should have soaked every surface within several feet of her body, but Sean wasn't done with his messy work—it was about to get a lot messier.

When he was sure she was dead, Sean used a knife to sever her fingertips and then he methodically sawed her teeth out with a hacksaw. As a final measure to make sure she was unidentifiable, Sean bashed Joy's face in. He knew that many bodies were identified through dental records, so her teeth had to go. Fingerprints could also be used to identify her body, so he removed them—along with the tips of the fingers that held them. Both of those operations should have produced a flood of blood, but the Kensington house was almost completely bereft of it.

Then he systematically gathered up his tools and the contractor's sheeting, crammed Joy's body into a plastic container he had acquired at the same time, put her into the back of an SUV he had just rented and drove her two hundred and fifty miles away into the desert country of Arizona.

Where he disposed of her teeth and fingertips has never come to light.

Chapter 14

THE SCORCHING DESERT

I suspect these thoughts were running through Sean's mind as he made the long drive to his destination out in the Arizona desert, deep inside Gila Bend, just north of the Mexican border: The tomb had to be scavenger-proof, he had decided. He couldn't just trust that nature would take care of hiding everything; he had to make sure himself. His life depended on it.

She had forced his hand. He hadn't wanted this, but she had left him no choice. Jezebel. If he buried her body in the ground, chances were some hungry scavenger would dig her up—the desert was full of animals scraping by to eke out a living, and a rotting corpse would be just too much temptation, too much ready and easy-to-digest protein, he knew. And if something dug her up, the chances she'd be found—and identified—rose exponentially. He couldn't have that.

If his story was going to work, it was absolutely essential that she never be found. He knew there would be no way to hide the brutality of her death if investigators had her body, so his plan had two layers. First, make sure it was as unlikely as possible that anyone could stumble across her remains. Second, he knew that even the best-laid plans sometimes didn't play out as the planner intended, so he had to have a fail-safe to go into action if someone did manage to find her—to make sure it would take an act of God for them to figure out who she was.

An act of God. Ironic choice of phrase? In another circumstance, another time, he would have smiled, but he wasn't feeling very humorous at the moment. She had taken even his mirth. The anger welled up inside him again, but he slowly fought it back. It was done. She had gotten what she deserved. He focused back on the task at hand.

A lone palo verde tree poking up defiantly against the desert, with its roots deeply ensconced in the floor of the barren wilderness, seemed like the perfect place, he decided. It was far enough away from everything else that you would almost have to come out this way on purpose to find it. And the tree's very presence meant the elements he needed to fall into place were all most likely present. The roots would keep the sand from eroding with an unexpected downpour—like the kind that the Arizona desert's flash floods had become famous for—and exposing the body. If he put her near the roots, they should make sure the ground stayed relatively solid. Plus, they'd discourage digging coyotes from trying to scrape up an easy meal.

The tree also meant water was to be found in this place—at least enough to support this tree—and water also meant bacteria, which would speed her decomposition. He knew that process had started almost the second she had died but he needed her to decompose as quickly as possible, and since he knew that the desert was infamous for mummifying bodies, he had to make sure there was moisture near so she would rot instead of being preserved by the dry heat and moisture-leeching sand. He knew that in the best circumstances, it could take a year or so for natural decomposition to get rid of most of the flesh, so he needed a place that wasn't frequented by people who might get curious and start digging around and find her before he could be sure she would no longer be identifiable.

He didn't have to worry about her fingerprints; he had taken care of that by removing the tips of her fingers and discarding them. If someone actually did manage to find her, they wouldn't be able to just look at her face and tell who she was, either. He had thwarted facial recognition by...obscuring her features. He still gritted his teeth when he thought about that. And speaking of teeth, no one was going to identify her through dental records, either—though it had been a grisly and tougher-than-expected job—he had taken care of that, too. Other than DNA, there would be no way to identify her after nature had taken its toll, and he couldn't imagine any reason DNA would be able to do the job either.

She had no entries in any DNA databases, as far as he knew, but he wasn't taking any chances that she'd be found and her body identified by the fledgling science. With her body decomposed and other identifying marks removed, it would become nearly impossible to tie these remains to the beautiful and vibrant woman who had borne him two sons. Underneath the happy-go-lucky exterior there had been a woman who steadfastly refused to submit to her husband's authority. She had relentlessly and selfishly sought to advance her own agenda, go to college, find the right career and not just an unfulfilling job, no matter how that strained the rest of the family.

It wasn't like he didn't want her to have a career, but women who focused on their careers usually did so to the detriment of their children. That she would be willing to let her children suffer so she could gain her financial independence from the family was unthinkable to him. Her career had been decided anyway: at least for now, she was supposed to be a mom, not a sign language interpreter—a foolish vocation if ever he had heard of one—and certainly not a Hollywood makeup artist. Pie in the sky, that's what that was. But she had been willing to cast caution to the wind, no matter how it burdened the family financially, no matter how much pressure it put on his other wife to take care of the kids while she was off pursuing her selfish agenda.

No, he couldn't have it. It had been enough. She would not be allowed to tear the family apart by leaving, and she would not be allowed to continue making the family miserable by complaining about it every day. This had been the only way out. After all, if she divorced him, he stood to lose more than she could imagine: he would become just another failed husband who hadn't had the spirituality necessary to hold multiple wives and thus those who now sought him regularly for advice would turn their backs on him the same way traditional Christianity—and even his own mother—had done when they found out he was a polygamist. Joy had no right to force him to face that kind of rejection again. She was selfish, impetuous, petulant. No, this had been the only way things could pan out. At least this way, he could maintain she had simply allowed her fleshly desires to overcome her. No one needed to know he had killed her. It had to be done.

Slowly, methodically, he unloaded her body from the back of the SUV he had rented for the trip, careful not to leave any evidence in the vehicle, the plastic construction sheeting doing its job as he had planned, keeping her fluids from seeping into the plastic container he had shoved her body into. She was a lot heavier now than he remembered her being. Now he understood where the saying "dead weight" had originated. He had lifted her before, when she was alive, and her thin body had never been a strain. But now it was a struggle every step of the way. She was unwieldy. Every bit of her seemed to flop out at the most inconvenient times, and it was nearly impossible to get a good grip without her body starting to slip somewhere else.

TV shows and movies that portrayed people easily disposing of bodies were lies, plain and simple, he decided. This was hard work and he hadn't even gotten to the step he had assumed would be the hard part. He realized he was panting and sweat was pouring off of him. He heard himself grunt and groan as he tried to move her body bit-by-bit into position so he could build a tomb around her.

After he had laboriously placed her under the tree, he removed the plastic sheeting so the elements would have full access to her. He had mentally debated that part for quite some time on the drive out here. Would the plastic help or hinder her decomposition? He didn't know, and he didn't like that he didn't know. It was a hole in his research for this work. The plastic could work like a greenhouse, trapping in moisture and heat, speeding the work of the bacteria and parasites that were surely already gathering in and on her to turn her back into the dust from which she came. On the other hand, the plastic could work like a plastic bag, keeping out the essential microorganisms. It frustrated him that he hadn't figured this out before coming out here. It was unlike him to leave questions unanswered.

Finally, he had decided: without plastic sheeting, he might not get the "greenhouse" effect that would amplify her decomposition, but he could be certain he would get bacteria and parasites, so he would go with what he knew for sure: bodies decomposed when exposed to air. So he had removed the sheeting, storing it in the plastic tub for later disposal, plastic sheeting and tubs being far easier to get rid of than corpses.

Now, with her body laying exposed to the elements, he began searching the nearby desert for suitable stones. He had to make the tomb porous so the weather could get through and speed the decomposition, but solid enough to prevent animals from tearing it down. And the tomb couldn't look haphazard, either. It had to be purposeful. If someone did stumble across this place, he wanted the tomb to look uniform, careful—maybe even some ancient Indian burial site. If he could successfully make it look like that, people would tend to avoid such a structure, he knew, superstition commanding them to leave it be lest they incur the wrath of the venerable Indian spirits or ghosts or whatever it was people feared about Indian graveyards. The public's susceptibility to such silly superstition worked to his advantage and he would do his best to make sure this place evoked those fears.

Every plan had multiple layers. This one started with the hope that no one would ever find this place, but if they did, maybe they would avoid it out of laughable, superstitious fright. And of course, if neither of those plans worked out, he hoped that the place would remain hidden long enough that even when they found a body and identified it as human, they wouldn't be able to tell who that human had been or where she had come from. As long as she was anonymous, he could say Joy had just run off. People could have all the suspicions they wanted to have, but if no one ever found her here or identified her, he would never be forced to face trial for her death—a death she had brought on herself, though he was under no illusions that any jury would see it that way.

His body began to protest against the exertion as he stacked stones first around the perimeter of her body and then on top of each other and her, forming a geometric pile of stones over her. There were dozens of the stones—maybe hundreds—and they were getting heavier by the minute. It didn't help that he was having to walk some distance with each one, back and forth, fetching the stones, then dragging, carrying or driving them to her body.

As the tomb began to take shape, I believe Sean started to worry about how conspicuous it would appear to any pass-ers-by. This was clearly no accidental rock formation. Anyone who got close enough would immediately know this struc-ture was manmade. It was a dilemma he had thought out in advance. It was entirely possible that there was no place in the desert where such a thing would forever go unnoticed, so he had decided that if anyone got close enough, the tomb must appear to be conspicuous, not hidden, so that anyone finding it would assume it was legitimate, possibly even ancient—and thus not to be disturbed.

It was part of an entire "hiding in plain sight" idea he had seen on a forensics show on TV. Sometimes the best cam-ouflage was none at all. If you couldn't keep a thing hidden, make it look like your idea had been to display it all along. So he had made sure all the stones matched. This couldn't look like a rush job, like someone was trying to hide a body. No, it had to look like it had been constructed out of ritual, out of superstition. If anyone found it, they had to believe it had been a community effort.

He paused and looked all around. Not a road in sight. Nothing but desert sand and brush as far as the eye could see. Even the tire tracks from the SUV were starting to fade. He had planned to be out here until the sun began to descend down the west side of the sky, and he would use it to navi-gate back to the road. Way out here, it was unlikely anyone would just stumble upon the grave, he thought. Maybe it was wasted effort to make it look purposeful. But it was too late to turn back now. Besides, he couldn't load her back up into the SUV. He was running out of time and energy. It had to be here. He would just have to suck it up and make this place perfect. There could be no mistakes.

As he gathered and stacked stone upon stone, I believe Sean's mind began to wander as his hands seemed to perform their complicated task on their own. There would be questions. He knew he would have to give plausible explanations at the very least. I believe it was another thing he had been thinking about for weeks. How could he explain the disappearance of someone who had been so important and prominent in his life?

The long drive back to San Diego would give him plenty of time to work out the details of his cover story. For now, the tomb was complete.

He stood up, hands on his back, stretching as he inspected the nearly finished structure, squinting as the sun pounded down on him. This hadn't been his first plan. Initially, he had wanted to rent a boat and take her out past the Bay of San Diego, down toward Tijuana—where sewage in the water kept most people from swimming and fishing—and bundle her up with a set of weights, dropping her to the bottom of the ocean to become food for fish, her body literally disintegrating with each bite, until it was no longer identifiable.

But 9/11 had been just two years ago and that meant Homeland Security had the borders locked down tight— even the rarely-traversed border on the Western Seaboard. Security officials certainly would notice a thin guy in a rented boat with a suspicious-looking bundle beside him. He would almost certainly have gotten caught if he had tried it. So the desert, plan B despite all its downsides—specifically, the greatly increased chances of her body being found—had to do. He had also thought about trying to buy hydrochloric acid to dissolve the body, but that would be both suspicious and messy, and he wasn't sure he could even contain the acid, nor was he certain he could adequately clean up the mess it would leave behind. Luminol—the chemical police used to reveal where blood had been cleaned from a crime scene— would still have been able to detect the previous presence of blood, even after the acid had done its job.

So here he was, executing plan B in the desert, placing the last few stones on the tomb. It would work. His mind was starting to follow tangents now because of exhaustion. He had known that would happen, which is why he had planned in advance so meticulously. He had known beforehand that he would begin questioning his plan, finding phantom holes in it, doubting whether it would really keep the police at bay, which is why he had been so careful to lay everything out before he killed her. Now, he would just have to trust that his plan would keep her hidden until it was too late to identify her. The plan *had* to work.

Sighing, he packed up and got ready to start the long drive back to San Diego. He briefly considered praying over the tomb, but he wasn't feeling very spiritual at the moment. Out here in the desert, the engaging and sometimes flamboyant preacher was nothing more than a dirty, sweaty guy who was extremely tired. There were no crowds to shout "amen" as he delivered a clever take on a scripture with a flair and a smile. No women to fawn over his piercing blue eyes and biting sense of humor. No spiritual acolytes to fall in line behind his deep Bible knowledge and incisive delivery.

Out here, there was just him, the dirt, the exhaustion and what was left of Joy, the woman he had loved so much he had forced his wife to let him marry her too.

Unceremoniously, Sean climbed back into the rented SUV.

Chapter 15

CALCULATED COVER-UP

efore the murder, when Sean assembled his "murder kit," the similarities between his plan and our conversation were striking: gear to keep blood evidence to a minimum; something to eliminate fingerprint and dental identification; somewhere to dispose of the body where no one would find it. Sean knew forensic evidence was often found in cars, so he rented a vehicle. He knew blood could never be left behind, just like our fictional killer did. Though Sean left blood at the murder scene, it was precious little.

When his first wife arrived home the night after Sean killed Joy, he explained to her that he and Joy had argued and ultimately broken up, he had driven around for hours to deal with his grief and, oh, by the way, Joy had cut herself during the argument. He asked his first wife to clean up the blood, because he was too tired.

The thing was, when she went to clean up the blood out of the bathroom and Joy's bedroom, there wasn't very much, certainly not enough to set off any alarm bells in her mind. Sean had been careful when he was brutally stabbing

Joy more than a dozen times. This was no crime of passion, no argument gone wrong. He had planned it out, set up the bathroom and bedroom as his "kill rooms"—just as we had plotted for our fictional killer to do—and executed Joy Risker in cold blood. The lack of blood was later confirmed by police using Luminol; there was so very little. It looked more like a shaving accident than a homicide.

The control Sean had over his first wife was absolute. If people didn't understand that fact by the very nature of the way their relationship had ended up—with Sean taking on another spouse seemingly at will, to ever-decreasing objections by his first wife —then they certainly would when they learned that she didn't question anything when Sean told her that Joy had cut herself and asked his first wife to clean up the mess.

She went to the bathroom, found the tiny specks of blood and removed them.

And that was the end of that.

But it wasn't the end of anything for Sean. His work was just beginning. Almost immediately, Joy's friends started asking questions. But they weren't asking Joy, because she wasn't answering her phone. And she wasn't answering her e-mails—at least not yet.

As of September 19, all the online banter, the jokes, the debates, the posts, the…Joy…ceased, like a spigot had been shut off. End of conversation. Sean still posted once or twice on my blog and a few times on the discussion board, but Joy stopped cold. At the time, I thought nothing of it. We all had busy lives and though Sean had confided to me that he would probably be forced to divorce Joy sooner or later, it didn't even enter my mind that something might be amiss; I was busy too, so I never thought something was wrong when they went silent.

Joy had been a more frequent commenter than Sean, who had a full-time job at the book company. When Sean didn't comment regularly, it seemed par for the course; when Joy stopped posting, it wasn't strange enough to raise red flags but it certainly became more noticeable the longer her silence persisted.

In fact, though I had noticed that the two weren't commenting anymore, I only asked about it off-handedly when I called Sean on October 2 to wish him a happy thirty-sixth birthday.

He sounded tired.

"What's up with Joy?" I asked some time into the conversation. "She quit posting on the blog."

There was a long pause, then a sigh and then Sean Goff rendered me speechless with a completely unexpected announcement.

"Joy's gone, man," he said in a pained voice. "I didn't tell you before, because I was embarrassed."

"*What*?" I was incredulous. "When did this happen?"

"A couple of weeks ago," he said, his voice raspy and cracking. "Apparently, she's been talking with an old boyfriend and they met up and she ran off with him to drive around the East Coast or around Europe or something. I'm not really sure where they went."

There was a moment or two of silence as I soaked in what he had said. At first it didn't process. I hadn't expected Joy to leave Sean. She had sounded so happy when she was inviting me to his birthday party. I knew *he* might have been planning to leave *her*, but I had no inkling that the opposite might be true. I guessed that I hadn't known Joy as well as I thought I had, since it seemed completely out of character for her to hide something like that so well. When planning Sean's birthday party, she seemed sincerely dedicated to making sure it all came off perfectly, but then she had just left Sean? Clearly, if that was the case, she had already been thinking about leaving him the last time I had talked to her, which meant she had to have been faking her enthusiasm for his party.

Also, she never had struck me as the kind of person to pull up roots and leave on a whim. It was jarring to hear and it took me awhile to get my head around what he had just said.

"Dude, I'm sorry," I said, finally. "Are you okay?"

I also asked him how his first wife was handling it.

Despite his more recent protestations, I believe that Sean loved Joy—maybe even more than he loved his first wife. Joy had been his public wife, the one he went out on the town with while his first wife stayed home and cared for the trio's three boys. It was Joy who Sean talked about almost constantly, Joy who showed up in happy-couple pictures, Joy who people had begun to think of when they thought of Sean's wife. Those who didn't know about his polygamy simply assumed Sean and Joy were a normal married couple. They often knew nothing about his first wife.

Ever the faithful and obedient spouse, Sean's first wife withdrew more and more from the public face of the marriage while Sean doted on the younger Joy. So it had struck me as odd weeks earlier when Sean had told me he was going to have to "get rid" of Joy.

"Why?" I had asked at the time. "What's wrong?"

"She's lazy, Leif," he had said. Sean always made a point to use your name when he was talking to you, an old psychological trick, he had told me, that makes the listener feel indebted to the speaker, increasing their openness to whatever the speaker is saying. "She leaves dishes in the sink, she won't help around the house, she's not a good mother, and I think she might have hit (our youngest son)."

All of this was news to me. By all indications, Joy was a doting mother who loved her children more than anything else. She had told me numerous times how happy she was that her mother, Gwen, had gotten to see her first son shortly before Gwen had passed away unexpectedly the next day.

"I'm so happy God let her see [my first son]," Joy had said to me. "I miss her, but I know that she was happy when she died."

That feeling of Joy's great love for her sons clashed with Sean's description of her poor mothering but I figured Sean was in a much better position than me to observe her parenting. Maybe Joy had been a negligent mother who hid her apathy toward her children under a façade of lies, I thought, as I listened to Sean talk about how she just wasn't working out as a wife and mother.

Now that Joy had gone, the question in my mind remained unasked as Sean told me a divorce was likely imminent: how would Joy leaving affect Sean's standing in Patriarchal Christianity? One of the movement's key tenets was that monogamy led to divorce, which the patriarchals called "serial monogamy." Sean, a well-respected member of the movement who was often sought for advice, would be putting to lie the notion that polygamous marriage was the solution for the divorce epidemic that had swept America over the preceding decades.

Would he be ostracized for having divorced one of his wives? Would the loss of Joy deflate the exalted standing he had enjoyed among the polygamist community? Would he even tell them she was gone? The idea that he might not was a distinct possibility.

But those questions remained in my head. I had rebuilt our fractured friendship by accepting his polygamous life-style and the questions seemed too contemptuous to ask politely, especially as he was clearly grieving the departure of his favorite wife.

His first wife, he said, was overwhelmed by caring for all three boys full-time. She missed Joy almost as much as he did. I had seen Sean's first wife and Joy adjust to the strange marriage slowly. At first, though they all claimed everything was peachy keen, there had been jealousy and tension. One friend told me Sean had even been forced to break up a physical fight between the two women early on, with one choking the other. But as time had passed, they seemed to have ironed out most of the kinks and there were times when it seemed like Sean's first wife and Joy enjoyed each other's company more than either enjoyed being around Sean.

"He's okay," Joy had said in 2002. "But I have to get onto him when he messes with her."

Now, however, Sean's first wife was left alone to mother three children while Joy galavanted around the country with some old flame. And Sean had become stressed and exhausted by trying to play full-time daddy and full-time breadwinner for a family that had lost an integral part of the machinery.

"Wait," I said. "Joy left without her kids?"

"She's so irresponsible," Sean responded. "She only cares about running off with that guy; no one else matters."

It was difficult to believe but I had no reason to suspect my best friend, with whom I had spent the majority of the preceding fifteen years, of foul play. Hindsight, as they say, has twenty/twenty vision and the story seemed too pat, even though by the time he told it to me, Sean had already adjusted his narrative to account for Joy's lack of a passport to include

Europe "or something" among her possible destinations with the alleged boyfriend.

It turned out that "or something" was a pile of rocks in the Arizona desert just a short trip north of Mexico, where Joy's body was already disintegrating under the onslaught of the elements as time was ticking on the plan Sean had made to get away with her murder.

Joy's friends had also started asking Sean what was going on, because Sean was always the guy with the answers; he was in complete control of his family and he certainly would know what was happening with Joy.

Only this time, his answers didn't seem to make sense. Joy, he said, had never been able to get over Simon Greene, the guy she had messed around with at Morris Cerullo World Evangelism when she was still lying and telling everyone that she and Sean and his first wife were just roommates. Apparently, he had contacted her again, Sean said, and Joy, who was tired of living the domestic life, had run off with Simon, who was now "rich," to backpack across Europe, something she had always wanted to do.

But she hadn't mentioned any such thing to her friends and even though Sean had been hinting around for a while that Joy seemed like she might just pack up and leave without warning, none of them had known her to be that kind of woman. They kept asking questions, because it seemed like Sean knew more than he was telling.

And that's when, five days after she was killed, "Joy" e-mailed one of her friends.

"Hi Sugarsmacks," the message began. Joy often used nicknames with her friends instead of their real names. It was one of the endearing qualities everyone loved about her. "I'm sorry I didn't give you the complete details, but I've been so rushed and there are a hundred people wanting to know who, what, when, where, etc., and my family is madder than I ever thought they could be and making me feel so guilty about everything. I know you'll understand, but I just need some time away without any demands, calls or anything."

That didn't sound like the Joy her friends knew. She was the kind of woman who told her friends everything, and when she needed advice, she leaned on them to help her out.

"I really can't talk to [another friend] right now either because I know she'll be against my decisions, and I really can't deal with that for a while," the e-mail continued. But it was strange, too, because her friends would be all for any "decision" Joy made to leave Sean. They thought the arrangement was weird and creepy but they supported Joy, so they didn't pressure her to leave. If she had left on her own, they certainly weren't going to give her grief about it. And Joy, who had confided to a friend that she wanted a way out, would have known that. If it really had been Joy sending the message, that is. "I've picked up the phone a few times to call you, but I keep putting it back down. Please just give me some time, okay?"

The red flags were flying up all over the place but they were about to get even redder:

"I love you, but I've got to get all my emotional baggage in check concerning Sean, my Dad and my boys before I can focus on my friendships," the e-mail continued. Her friends weren't buying it. They were the sounding boards she had used already to get any "emotional baggage" about Sean or her dad or her children straightened out. Why would she now cut them off without so much as an explanation? It didn't make sense. "I'm going to put off school and go to Europe with Simon. Remember, he's the guy Sean caught me e-mailing a few months back. I kept in touch with him, and when I found out on my dad's recent visit that he was too much of a pussy to help me get out on my own, Simon made me an offer I've been mulling over since to come out here, go to Europe and then decide what I wanted to do with my life."

Mulling? Joy? It wasn't a word they were even sure she knew, much less would use. And putting off school to traipse around Europe? Without her kids? One of Joy's big reasons for wanting to get out of the marriage was to go to school so she could take care of her kids. Now, all of a sudden she was ditching both school and kids so she could run off on a fling? It was making less sense by the minute.

"No matter how much Sean's loved me, I've never been able to get Simon out of my head, and I just need to find out what it's all about," the message continued.

"I never talked to her after she left MCWE," Simon told me. "I hadn't talked to her in years."

But Sean couldn't get Simon out of his mind, and he seemed a convenient scapegoat. Maybe Joy had been caught e-mailing Simon, but Simon didn't seem to remember it if it had happened.

The message to her friend was just the beginning of Joy's postmortem communications.

On October 6, "Joy" e-mailed two more friends. "I'm safe and sound and there's nothing for you to worry about," it read. "I have been super busy getting things arranged for my trip to Europe...hopefully you'll get this e-mail before I leave to England to start my trip...I was bored to death living with this family as a wife and mother and doing the things a mother and wife has to do. I got so sick of it that I could not stand it anymore, and I couldn't stand the thought of an office job either."

The office job part was true, at least. Everyone knew Joy hated the mindless work in offices. But being sick of being a mother? Or a wife? Well, Joy had told her friends she was sick of being *Sean's* wife, but never that she was sick of being a mother. Her boys were everything to her, and her friends started really wondering what was up when "Joy" started mentioning in the e-mails how her children were tying her down.

"You know it's not like I left the boys in a crack house," the message said. "They are going to be fine until I can see them again."

Really? That didn't sound like Joy, the doting mother, the woman whose pride and joy were those two boys, who reminded Joy every day that her mother was looking down from heaven, proud of her and the children she was raising.

"I'm sorry I haven't called," the e-mail continued. "I have just not been able to deal with hearing everyone's voices and the emotions that it brings back to me."

While Joy's friends were receiving fake e-mails from Joy, Sean was too. He even misspelled words that a writer as gifted as himself would never have misspelled. It was intended to be a magnum opus of deception, but Sean seemed uncharacteristically off his game. As an author who had been paid handsomely to impersonate televangelists in print, Sean was adept at assuming the voice of someone else and writing like them. But the e-mails from Joy didn't sound like Joy at all. They were dour, choppy and juvenile, all three things unlike Joy.

"Sean, I know you are sad and that the kids are missing me," "Joy" wrote just a week after Sean killed her. "I have to get out of the house and experience the world around me...I know you've heard all this a thousand times and it's a lot of regamaro (Sean intentionally misspelled rigamarole) to you, but it's really how I feel."

That a doting mother could abandon her beloved children so callously for such a flimsy reason strained credulity, but likely, expanding the cover story was never part of Sean's original plan. He had hoped people would just accept the story of Joy running away, shake their heads and move on with their lives.

But as her friends remained persistent and the police got involved, Sean had to make rapid adjustments to his story—adjustments that didn't receive the benefit of his usual careful planning process, so they felt rough, rushed and half-baked. The police were asking pointed questions and in response, Sean wrote something bizarre while still posing as Joy. He mentioned an apparent deal that had been made before she "left," where she would be allowed to call Sean after a year to discuss visitation with the children she had left behind so heartlessly. In the same e-mail, she went out of her way to tell Sean that, of all people, her father, with whom she had only recently been communicating, would probably attempt to talk Sean into trying to track her down, but that he shouldn't, because she just needed to have some time to herself.

It all sounded to police a lot like someone trying to close holes in a story rather than the happy-go-lucky woman who was planning a big future and who had told friends she would stay in a marriage she no longer wanted to be in because she didn't want to leave her sons.

And the year-long period for having no contact with him? Seemed kind of convenient.

Sean responded.

"I am so sorry I could not make you happy," he wrote, again uncharacteristic for Sean. Admitting that it was his fault Joy had wanted to leave? Unthinkable for a man whose own unpublished book had preached the virtue of the godly man who had too much to give for one woman to receive it all. "As long as you want to see [the children], you'll e-mail me at least every three months and let me know how things are."

It just seemed like the kind of conversation someone in a children's book would have, not one between two people who had recently gone through the polygamist equivalent of divorce, and an acrimonious one at that. Every three months? It didn't make sense. Why not every week to check up on the children? An agreement to check in every three months sounded more like a convenient reason to not have to fabricate more e-mails than a legitimate visitation plan. After three months of expected silence, most people would have moved on with their lives and probably would have lost interest in where Joy had run off to. At least, that's what Sean was likely hoping.

Sean, an excellent writer, was not putting his best work into this exchange, which may signal that the pressure was starting to get to him. He was frantically looking for ways to cover up what he had done, and his mind was traveling down too many avenues to give his full concentration to any one.

"Joy" replied that she would try to e-mail every three months, but she might not be able to when she was back-packing across Europe—again, more like a convenient excuse for Sean than a legitimate statement from a mother who would have already been missing her two young sons and desiring ways to contact them as quickly and often as pos-sible. Besides, Joy didn't even have a passport.

In early October, Sean e-mailed "Joy" again, perhaps because police had contacted him and wanted to know what was up with her.

"Hi, Joy," he wrote. "I sold the bed like you asked. BTW, there's about $4800 in your saving account including some that you drew from your credit card. Please do something with this money...so you can take care of the bills you have.

Also, please write me back because [a friend] even called the police to write a missing person's report on you and they came in the middle of the night to ask questions. This kind of stuff really has to stop. I'm not trying to be mean, but I'm trying to provide a stable environment for the kids. Please take care of your friends, okay?"

With all his might, Sean was trying to build a case that he was the jilted husband, the forlorn lover whose wife had left him for a past paramour.

"Joy" responded that she had e-mailed her friends and mentioned Sean selling her car later so she could buy a new one "when I get back to the states." And then, in a chilling touch, Sean signed Joy's message with a nickname she had used with her children: "Kiss the boys and tell them Dhavi loves them." Dhavi is a Sanskrit word shortened to mean "daughter of David." David was a king in the Bible, and the father of Solomon, whose moniker Sean had assumed when he began posting in polygamy forums online. As Solomon's wife, she would be considered the daughter of David, a title she no longer would have borne if she had been divorced, as Sean was telling people.

After that e-mail exchange didn't produce the desired results of turning down the heat from Joy's friends, Sean began to plead with Joy in the messages: "Come home for a little while. I know [a friend] will let you stay with her. I'm trying to work and pay the bills, but it's so hard. Please do something for us. You don't have to be here for me. Just for them."

But the e-mails weren't working. Joy's friends weren't buying it and neither were police, who had started to investigate Joy's disappearance and were on the precipice of calling in homicide detectives.

Chapter 16

"PRAY FOR ME"

On October 20, 2003, I got a call from Sean. I was working in my home office at my house in Muskogee, Oklahoma, banging out lessons about Bible prophecy for insertion into a televangelist's upcoming video. The televangelist was widely touted to be an expert on Bible prophecy, so when I had written the script, I had left a hole in the middle for him to riff on the subject. When time came to film the video, however, he had balked, asking where his lines were, so I had to feverishly crank some out for him.

I always found it jarring that so many people around the world were listening to the things I was writing, even though I certainly wouldn't have considered myself an expert on any of the subjects I was writing about. Somehow, I had been pigeonholed by certain ministers as a Bible prophecy expert, but nothing could have been further from the truth. I had very little interest in Bible prophecy, but it paid the bills, so I wrote it when they asked me to.

I was quickly throwing together everything I knew about the subject of the televangelist's video: the war that most fundamentalist Christians were expecting to erupt in Israel between the Jewish state and its hostile neighbors. The war in Iraq had just begun (and supposedly ended) but tensions were still at an all-time high, so everyone was atwitter about the possibility that the war would boil over the border and engulf Israel, one of the Bible prophecies that many were clinging to as a sign that the "end times" had truly arrived. My personal beliefs were more metaphorical concerning such prophecies, but metaphor and even-headed reasonableness didn't pay the bills, so I wrote what they wanted to hear, even when that writing was incendiary toward the people of the Middle East. I was engrossed in that when the phone rang.

When I answered it, Sean's voice sounded more haggard and tired than I had ever heard it.

"I need you to pray for me," he started, his voice cracking and wavering. "I'm at a crossroads and I don't know what to do. I can't tell you the details of the situation, but just pray and see if God says anything. I'm not hearing him very well lately."

The request was reminiscent of a Bible story where the king of Egypt had suffered through a disturbing dream but had forgotten the details, so he had demanded from his court magicians that they tell him both the dream and its interpretation, throwing them into prison as frauds when they could not comply.

Sean's request, while not quite as extreme, was a good window into a fundamental Pentecostal belief: God speaks to people today just as he did in the Bible, giving them direction and advice for their daily lives. It's a natural outgrowth of the belief that God still works miracles. He is still personally active in believers' lives, and if they'll just listen for his "still, small voice," he speaks to them every day about matters both weighty and mundane.

I was on my way to disbelieving such a notion and although I had made no secret of my doubts—especially to Sean—he sounded like he really needed the help, so I agreed to try.

My personal religious beliefs had been going through a significant upheaval—I no longer considered myself a fundamentalist and, although I didn't put anything outside the realm of possibility, I was leaning toward the idea that most of what Pentecostals were viewing as miracles and signs of God's active participation in their church services were more likely psychosomatic phenomena—and possibly even unintentional mass hypnosis. It wasn't that I didn't believe in miracles or that God could visit people on earth if he wanted to, I just didn't believe such things were as common and pedestrian as they were being portrayed.

I had trouble denying some of the things I had experienced on my Pentecostal journey. I had been overwhelmed by what I considered to be God's presence at Sean's grandmother's church. I had personally seen a woman healed of a very obvious physical ailment. I had personally prayed for a deaf girl who left the service with her hearing restored. I had witnessed a friend dying of AIDS recover and live another twenty years without taking another pill or shot to mitigate his disease. All those things, I knew, could be explained by other phenomena, but I leaned toward believing at least some of them possibly could have been manifestations of God's power. So I hadn't transitioned into full heathen mode or anything but I was leaning toward the idea that if such things actually were physical evidence of God, they weren't the norm, or even very common.

My belief in God talking to people was taking a similar path. Many of the great men recorded in the Bible had heard God once or twice their *entire lives*, yet many Christians claimed God spoke to them multiple times daily about things as unimportant as which way to turn at an intersection—like a holy GPS system. I wasn't buying it. In one of my meetings with a televangelist, I had presented an idea for a ministry campaign. The idea had been approved, and weeks later, I had seen the televangelist on television saying God had told him to embark on the campaign, which God had revealed to him in prayer.

"God didn't tell you that, I did!" I had barked at the television screen. Of course, when I confronted the televangelist about it, he said it had been God working through me, which I found too convenient. If *I* was synonymous with the voice of God, how could anyone discern what was God and what was not? I hadn't felt particularly inspired when I came up with the idea; in fact it had struck me as kind of jaded. Yet here was a man who was listened to by millions of people saying my jaded idea was revealed to him divinely.

So I was no longer very keen on the idea of believers "hearing from God" daily and Sean knew that, which made his request all the more poignant.

For his part, Sean had both long believed and long preached that hearing from God was a function of having a relationship with him.

"Let me tell you the reason we're in fear many times," he had thundered from the MetroChurch pulpit in Norman, Oklahoma, eight years earlier during a revival he preached there. "We're in fear because we have forgotten what God has already said. We're going through this life and doing things we feel we're supposed to do, and God has spoken prophetic words over our lives...and we become afraid because we don't meditate and dwell on what God has said. We go crying to Jesus and we feel he is asleep and he is not hearing what we're saying and we try to rouse him and say 'master, don't you care that we are going to die?'...[Christians] today are forgetting what Jesus has said. Are you meditating on what he has said about you? Or are you meditating on your situation and what the devil is saying to you?"

Whatever the situation that he didn't want to tell me about, the preacher who had so intensely focused on hearing from God as a result of having a relationship with God was desperate for advice. I suspected it had to do with helping him deal with his grief about Joy leaving him, which shows that God clearly wasn't revealing any secrets to me. But Sean seemed like he was reaching out for a life vest.

So I prayed. And waited.

Nothing.

I prayed again, this time saying, "It's for Sean, not me."

Nothing. It wasn't that I believed God *never* talked to people. I just believed it wasn't all that common. And whatever had made Sean desperate enough to ask for help struck me as a need worthy of an uncommon event—and thus maybe an exception from God.

So I prayed a third time.

Nothing.

Sighing, I called Sean back.

"I'm sorry," I said. "I didn't hear anything."

Sean sounded disappointed.

"Thank you anyway," he said. "I just don't know what to do."

On the spur of the moment, I was hit by inspiration: "Just do the right thing, Sean. You can never go wrong with that."

Was it God or just dumb luck? I don't know. Either way, it turned out to be the best thing to say, though it had seemed kind of hollow to me at the time.

"Okay," he said. "That actually helps."

"Really?" I was surprised. The advice had struck me as borderline platitude. "Well then, I'm glad. You know I'm here for you."

Sean had long preached that hearing from God was a direct byproduct of having a relationship with God, of having Jesus in your life to lead and guide you along life's winding roads.

"If you are hearing the voice of God," he preached in 1995, "and I am hearing the voice of God, then we will hear the same thing. If God tells me to do something and then tells you to do something else, then somebody did not hear God."

God was the end-all of answers to every question, he preached many times, and if you're worrying about something or if you find yourself unable to come up with an answer to one of life's problems, it's not because you're confused, it's because you've lost your connection with God. If he had lost his connection to God, whatever was bothering him had to be of magnitudes greater than anything I had ever witnessed him go through, because the one person you could always count on to have inroads with God was Sean Goff. He was the rock upon whom other people leaned. He was the one who always had advice and inspired wisdom because he was always the one everyone knew was praying and reading the Bible for a deeper relationship with God, a stronger and more bulletproof hotline directly to heaven.

He had been impressed once by an old black preacher who had died by the time we heard his sermon on tape. The sermon, however, contained a simple yet powerful message. There was a small boy riding a train by himself, the preacher had said. His parents had put him on the train to visit his grandparents in a different city, charging the conductor with making sure the little boy made it to his destination safely. The conductor, however, came looking for tickets, and it seemed the boy didn't have one, so he kicked the boy off the train. A few feet later, the train refused to move forward any more. The conductor and engineer tried everything they could but the train stubbornly refused to budge, though nothing appeared to be obviously wrong.

Finally, a little old lady stood up and said, "Conductor, you better back up and let that little boy back on this train!"

The conductor, out of ideas, backed the train up and helped the boy back onto the train, at which point it lurched forward and began moving down the tracks toward its destination.

The preacher likened the story to having a life without God: If you find yourself unable to move forward, you should "back up—and let Jesus back onto your train!"

Sean loved that sermon and often would quote it and imitate the preacher, who would yell "Baaaaack up!" at the top of his lungs.

He copped parts of the message for his own preaching and applied it to the Bible story of Mary and Joseph, Jesus' parents, visiting the temple in Jerusalem. "When their child was twelve years old, they went to Jerusalem," he preached. "Why? Because it was a religious journey they took every year. They went to a religious city and went to a religious place called the temple and hung out with a lot of religious people doing the same thing. And they talked about what? Religion. And when they had had all the religion they could stand, they'd go back home. But on this one trip, they began to walk, and after a day, they looked around and said, 'where's Jesus?'

"Now, Jesus is the son of God, right? Jesus *is* God, right? How is it that these people were all wrapped up in doing this religious stuff, and when they left town, they forgot God?"

At that point, the congregation laughed, and Sean continued.

"That's what religion will do for you," he preached. "When they got to the place where God wasn't with them any longer, they said, 'where did we see him last?' If you think God is not with you any longer, if you can't feel his spirit anymore, you better back up and go to the last place where you knew God was."

But by 2003, he seemed to have forgotten his own admonition to "baaaaack up" and let Jesus back onto the train. Instead of looking for answers to why he felt he wasn't hearing from God clearly as he had always thought he had, Sean reached out to me to see if maybe I could hear from God for him.

Sean long preached that if you were putting your trust in God, you would have no worries in your life, even when circumstances might otherwise dictate that maybe you *should* be worried. During one sermon in 1995, he said as much:

"There was one thing about Moses that not everybody in Israel had, and that was that one day, God put him in the cleft of the rock and walked by so Moses could look upon him. And God spoke to Moses face-to-face, and what that tells me is his ability to rest in the omnipotence of God was a direct result of the increased relationship he had with God. It is not enough to know that God can move on your behalf, it is not enough to know that he has the power to move on your behalf, but once you know him very well, you'll find that he's more than *willing* to move on your behalf, and that's when you begin to rest in God. That's when you begin to put aside your worries and your distractions and begin to walk in the Spirit instead of the flesh, because he will use his power for you."

Whatever the situation, Sean had been fond of preaching that a true Christian finds that relaxing and trusting in God is the solution, even when it seems like all hope is otherwise gone. In that same sermon eight years earlier, he had reiterated the point:

"If he is your friend, you can be at rest. You won't worry. You won't be afraid of what the day will bring, will you? The world will look upon you and see a peace that passes all understanding because Jesus is in your heart. If we know the God we are serving, we will have rest. If we don't know him, then we will have fear, doubt and unbelief."

It seemed when Sean called me that he had anything but the "peace that passes all understanding." He was uncharacteristically confused and just as uncharacteristically reaching out for help. It was completely unlike the Sean I knew. He *never* asked for help with anything. If Sean had problems, you never knew about them, because Sean preached that problems stemmed from lack of intimacy with God. And if there was one thing Sean prided himself on, it was that kind of close relationship with God.

"I led my entire family to Jesus," he told me once. "I got saved when I was six years old, and I was the first one. All of them followed me later."

In that spiritual strength, he had finally found a situation in which his brothers—and even his seemingly always-in-control mother—were at last less adept than he was. He reveled in the biblical story of Joseph, whose older brothers had sold him into slavery, only later being forced to bow down to him once he had been promoted by the king of Egypt to the position of prime minister. That filial subservience always attracted Sean, who was physically weaker than his brothers, and if he was smarter than them it was just barely so. Only in spiritual matters was he truly their superior, and he never allowed an opportunity for that situation to reverse itself.

So to see him admitting spiritual weakness was a watershed in the religious evolution of Sean. It was then that I knew something serious was weighing on him, but I still thought Sean was struggling with the departure of his favorite wife— for another man, no less. That was the ultimate insult for a guy who had written a draft of a book proclaiming that most men didn't deserve even *one* wife because they didn't know how to take care of them. Those whom God had "anointed" to marry multiple wives were chosen to do so because God saw them as worthy spiritual leaders who could be trusted to lead the women faithfully in God's plan. Being left for another man flew in the face of that belief, and I knew it had to be killing him.

"A true man will attract a woman who loves manhood," he wrote in the draft of his book. "If I can be successful living with two women at one time, surely I can help other men live successfully with one."

But with Joy leaving, the foundation for such moral high ground had all but eroded away, and that meant the entire premise for his last several years of preaching was undermined.

It had to have affected him more deeply than I had first understood, I suspected, for him to be having trouble hearing from God—and admitting that openly to another person. I felt sad for him, because I knew he loved Joy possibly even more than he loved his first wife: I obviously didn't have a clue about the extent of his attachment to her, especially in light of the fact that he was thinking of divorcing her anyway—at least I thought.

I told him I was there for him and if he needed me to do anything, just let me know. We said our pleasantries and hung up.

I had no idea that Sean's sudden spiritual crisis was caused by anything like a murder, nor that San Diego Police investigative aide Linda Koozin, who was assigned to the case, was turning up the heat on Sean, asking questions that made him nervous, such as requesting cell phone records, bank statements and rehashes of conversations Koozin and Sean had already had.

Koozin was the police department's advance guard; the case wasn't even serious enough in their minds yet to warrant putting a detective on it. But she was like a pit bull and Sean started sweating, believing, according to prosecutor Matthew Greco, that the police were a lot closer than they actually were to catching him. In fact, it was Koozin's surprise visit to Sean's first wife at her job that was the final reason Sean turned himself in. Sean's first wife had no idea the police were involved or that Joy's disappearance was anything other than how Sean had described it.

But when Koozin started asking questions, Sean's first wife freaked. As soon as Koozin left, Sean's first wife called him and asked why the police were interested in Joy's whereabouts. She immediately went home, and Sean told her something that had her in tears. She told Sean he needed to call his mother, and then he needed to turn himself in.

The next day, Sean drove himself to the San Diego Police Department, only to find it closed. He got back into his car and drove to the San Diego County Jail, where he calmly told the officer at the front desk, "I killed Joy Risker."

Chapter 17

STRANGE CONFESSION

T he San Diego Police Department proudly traces its past to the wild west of California's frontier days in the early 1800s. After an outbreak of fights, duels, murders and battles between soldiers and drifters, a twenty-six-year-old lawman rounded up eight vigilantes and formed a small police force to keep the tiny desert town under order.

About a decade later, the town was formally incorporated and an official police force created, setting the stage for the decorated and professional force the city now enjoys. And the force is doing its job. The city, now the nation's eighth largest with 1.3 million people, sits just a short drive south of the nation's second largest, Los Angeles. But if the crime rate is to be believed, they might as well be on different planets.

Los Angeles has almost three times the murders per capita as San Diego, almost three times the robberies per capita and more crime overall per capita, despite a police force ten times larger than San Diego's. The police in Tijuana's northern neighbor are proud of their success in keeping crime to a minimum and they play it by the book.

So when San Diego detectives took Sean Goff to an interrogation room on October 21, 2003, they started off directly as they're taught to do.

"We've never met you before, and I just don't know much about you," Detective John Tefft said as he sat down adjacent to Sean in one of the police department's interview rooms. And Tefft certainly didn't know much about Sean if he thought for a second that the police would be in charge of the interview they were about to have with him. "It's my understanding, Sean, that you came down to the Sheriff's Department..."

Sean, managing to sound remorseful and contrite, interrupted nonetheless, wanting to make sure the record was exactly straight.

"Well, I came *here* first," he said. "But I couldn't get in the door, so I went down there."

"Okay," Tefft said. "You came here first, then went to the Sheriff's Department. You had some conversations with them there and then San Diego Police came and brought you over here."

It seemed Tefft knew this wouldn't be an ordinary interview, and he should be sure to get everything by the book.

"We would like to talk to you, and it's our understanding that you'd like to talk to us," he continued. "There's some things you want to explain to us, and some things you'd like us to do, and we're good with all that. But we have certain rules we have to follow, and you understand all that; you've seen it on TV."

Sean nodded. He had, indeed, seen it on TV—along with a great many other things.

"Before the police can speak with you in any formalized setting, we have to read you your Miranda rights, so I'm just gonna read them to you and we can move on and talk about what you need to talk about," Tefft continued. "You have the right to remain silent. Do you understand?"

Sean didn't reply, but he did shake his head from side-to-side, indicating that the man with the genius-level IQ did not understand that he had the right to remain silent.

"I'm not sure," Sean said. "Just going back to the TV programs, you're going to ask me if I give up that right. Does that mean I have to answer any question at that time, or can I..."

"You can pick and choose," Tefft interrupted.

"Okay."

Already, Sean was setting boundaries, finding the limits of what the police could force him to say. Already, he was planning to say only what he had intended to say, and if the police wanted him to say anything beyond that, he wasn't going to play ball.

He may have looked contrite, remorseful—even repentant. But it was an act, they'd soon find out. This man had no remorse and no contrition had driven him here. Sean Goff had no intention of letting the interview with San Diego detectives slip out of his control for even one second.

Tefft read Sean the rest of his Miranda rights and then the interview began.

"Okay. Now, you can pick and choose, you can stop this interview at any time," Tefft said. "You can do whatever you want to do here. Would you like to talk to us? We're very interested in what you have to say."

"There's a few things I'd like to say," Sean began, his long experience preaching in front of expectant crowds coming into play as he made his rehearsed speech sound extemporaneous. "I came down here to turn myself in because I killed Joy Risker. And...she was a missing person, and I was being very misleading to the investigator and everyone else who was concerned about her, and I wanted to confess that."

Police had no way of knowing it at the time, but that's *all* Sean wanted to confess and ultimately, that's all he *would* confess. The very next question, in fact, slammed the brakes on the seeming cooperation with which the interview had begun:

"All right," Tefft said, writing notes. "Okay. All right. And there's a location, evidently, where her body is?"

The wheels had clearly turned in Sean's head long before he stepped inside police headquarters.

"I'm not sure I want to answer that at this time," he said, even though a "yes" would have been enough to answer the question without giving Joy's body away. But Sean didn't even want to go that far. No explanation. He didn't mind admitting he had killed Joy, but already, Sean was forming the basis of his criminal defense in his mind, knowing that once he told investigators where Joy's body was, he could never take that information back. He couldn't yield control to the police as a truly contrite man would have. He had to, as he had during her life, remain in control of Joy, even after her tragic death.

Tefft, not wanting to end the interview so quickly, rapidly acquiesced.

"Okay," he said, not missing a beat. "We'll go back to that. We'll get it all squared away."

In Sean's mind, however, it was already "squared away." And "squared away" meant he wasn't about to relinquish control of his most prized piece of information.

"That may be something I want an attorney to discuss it with."

Tefft, realizing he was on the brink of clamming Sean up, changed the subject.

"What is your relationship with Joy?" he asked. "I don't know who she is to you and what's going on with that."

Sean's expression changed to a combination of smile and grimace, the same expression his face would assume when he was about to simplify a difficult point of theology as he was preaching.

"This will get very complicated," he replied. "I am married to a woman who I have a son with, um, but Joy was also...it wasn't like she was my wife legally, but she also lived with us, basically as my wife. Like, you know, like a girlfriend type thing."

Tefft, either dumbstruck or relying on his training to keep his mouth shut when a suspect said something outrageous, kept his silence, so Sean continued.

"My wife obviously didn't like that," he said. "But she was willing to put up with that for me."

It was the first time Sean had ever admitted to anyone that his first wife had been less than ecstatic with his polygamy. In his usual way of portraying things, she had not only been hunky dory with the arrangement, but had actually been actively involved in selecting Sean's second spouse. But as he confessed Joy's death to police, Sean saw no harm in letting the cat out of the bag: his first wife wasn't a willing participant; she had merely tolerated the polygamy because it was what he wanted.

She would later testify to the same fact. Sean had conveniently left out one piece of information: she had let him take another wife because he had threatened to take her son away from her otherwise.

Tefft, a seasoned veteran of the police force, had heard a few strange stories in his day. If he was shocked at Sean's arrangement, he wasn't letting it show. Again, Tefft changed the subject.

"What do you do for work?"

Sean replied that he was a marketing director for a high-tech publishing company—the same company where he had met Victoria Mack, the book editor he had traveled cross-country with discussing many subjects, including how

Joy was the kind of woman to just get up and leave, and how television crime shows were giving away all the information criminals needed to get away with murder.

"Did Joy have an occupation?"

Sean's impatience with Joy, still hot even after he had killed her, snuck into his voice despite his best efforts to control it.

"No, she kind of...um, she was actually taking college courses," he said, trying to compose the frustration out of his voice, but it crept in anyway. "She had dropped out of school two or three times, and she was taking some courses, thinking about going to makeup school and things like that. But she wasn't working."

Though his knowledge of what Joy was doing—or more specifically *wasn't* doing—seemed to be comprehensive, Sean was caught flat-footed when the police asked him what his first wife did for a living.

"Um," he started, pausing. "She is, um...I believe a customer service representative."

The police weren't really that interested in Sean's first wife's occupation. It was their way of redirecting the conversation to safer, ostensibly more familiar and comfortable ground, so they could later re-ask the question they really wanted to have answered. But Sean was no typical criminal. He carefully thought out his answers to each question, even the trivial ones.

"Okay," Tefft said. "And you have a child with your first wife."

"Yes."

"Girl or boy?"

At that point, Sean's subtle pride came out as he gave an answer he had clearly given proudly before.

"Boy," he said. "All my children are boys."

Boys, in Sean's eyes, were more valuable than girls, because they could become leaders in their own right if they were raised correctly by a spiritual, godly leader who was following the Spirit and living in the "anointing" of God.

Sensing that he had with that question pulled at least part of Sean's guard down, Tefft shifted directly to one of the questions he really wanted answered.

"Sean, you seem like a nice guy, pretty easygoing here," he said. "You seem sad and remorseful, and that says a lot for you. How did this all go bad? What happened in all this?"

It was walking pretty close to the line he didn't want to cross, but being respected by the officer put Sean at ease, and he answered.

"I don't know," he said, dipping his head. "I honestly don't know. Joy and I were...incompatible and, you know, we had been talking about splitting up. Her mother died three years ago, and since then, she had been very unhappy, you know, being in a family, having kids, that sort of thing. So our relationship...I mean, we were friends, but our relationship wasn't...um, you know...We were going to split up. Eventually."

But the detective didn't want to know why the two were incompatible. He wanted to know why one of the two people they were talking about was dead and why the other one refused to tell him where the body was.

So he tried the same tactic again, flattering Sean with respect:

"You don't seem like a bad guy; I don't think you're a bad guy," he said. "How did this happen? How did you end up hurting her? How did that happen?"

Sean, however, sensing that control was teetering toward the police, invoked his Fifth Amendment right against self-incrimination.

"That's also probably things I'd probably rather talk about with an attorney," he said. Then he feigned ignorance of the legal system to explain. "I just...I...I don't know, I mean, I don't know. Honestly, in my situation, I came in here voluntarily to tell you what I did but I don't know what is wise for me to say or wise for me to be silent about. I have no legal knowledge whatsoever. I'm sorry. I'm not trying to be disrespectful."

Tefft, realizing that his opportunity was slipping away, sought to reorient the conversation to be more favorable to himself.

"No disrespect taken," he said. "Now when you say, I asked you that one question, you say you want to talk to an attorney about that. That's just regarding that one question. If I ask you other questions, you can pick and choose. Is that...am I understanding you correctly?"

Sean, however, was done.

"I understand that to be what you are saying," he said. Working for televangelists had given him plenty of experience sticking to the letter of the word, meaning he refused to say he agreed with what the detective said, in case it would later be used against him. Instead, he acknowledged that he understood what the detective was saying, not that he agreed with it.

Tefft, desperate, tried again.

"Because sometimes when people say 'I want an attorney,' we're supposed to stop the interview," he said. "But you say you want an attorney just regarding that one question, am I understanding that correctly?"

Sean, not willing to become trapped in any statements he had made, or tricked into making any more that he didn't want to make, dug his heels in.

"Well, I don't know," he answered, still in the same soft, measured tone he had used throughout the interview. "I mean honestly? I don't know what's wise to do at this point. I don't know if it's more wise to talk to an attorney before going on at all. When you asked me the question about how did things go wrong, I thought you were talking about our relationship, I didn't know you were talking about anything happening."

Sean's mind works at blinding speed. While in the midst of a conversation with police detectives about him killing his wife, he had already analyzed the conversation that had transpired and had maintained enough composure to clarify a point that he believed could have been borderline outside his control, making sure detectives—and certainly later a jury—understood that he had not willfully made any comment about what had led to him killing Joy Risker. All of that he reserved as a key plank of his defense, which had already formed in his mind.

"But about what happened, just like I know, I know...I know it's going to be in the newspapers et cetera, et cetera, but there's certain things I'd rather...certain people I'd rather...I don't want to hurt any more people, obviously," he said. "So I want to be respectful to them, but I also don't want to get myself into...I don't know."

Trying to let Sean know he was on Sean's side, the detective tried again to stand on common ground.

"Well, let me put it to you this way, Sean," he said. "You've come down and turned yourself in for murder."

Sean interrupted.

"For killing someone."

It was a key point. Sean knew that murder was homicide with malice. He didn't want to confess to that. He wanted to confess that he killed "someone," even avoiding recapping that the "someone" was his beloved wife. Killing "someone" could lead to jail time, but certainly not a significant stay such as would be imposed for a murder.

"It was my understanding when they called me from home and asked me to come down here, it was my understanding that you wanted to lead us to where we could locate Joy," Tefft said.

Sean shook his head immediately.

"I never said that to anyone," he said. "I'm sorry, I never meant to mislead anyone in any way."

Strangely, it seemed Sean was already adamant that Joy's body wasn't on the table, so to speak. Her location was not going to be divulged. Why? It was the burning question in the minds of police, so Tefft began to push a little harder, shedding a bit of the "good cop" image in order to see if Sean might be susceptible to a little psychological pressure.

"You've already made the big step here," he said. "Clearly, I mean, you have a couple of children that were with Joy, and you've obviously cared for her. Obviously things didn't go all that...you've had some problems, but you did have a caring relationship with her, and I think it's been my experience most of the time, I don't know where she is at or what's going on, but usually it's probably best that we take care of the matter, don't you think?"

Sean didn't. In fact, nothing could be farther from his perception of the way things would be best.

"Well, like I said," he said, "I just think I'd rather talk to an attorney about that."

Tefft pressed the "bad cop" image just a little farther, seeing if maybe guilt could work its way past the stolid defense Sean had so cunningly erected around his flow of information.

"So you wanna leave her out there?" Tefft asked to absolutely no reaction from Sean. "That's fine. Whatever you want to do. I mean, you know, you know. I don't."

"I know," Sean said.

"It's up to you."

"I know."

"If that's the way you want to do it."

Sean put the coup de gras on the conversation by reiterating what he had said from the very beginning, back when Tefft thought that maybe some of the standard interviewing techniques might lend some results. Tefft hadn't, however, counted on encountering someone who had so meticulously pre-planned what he would and would not answer, and who was mentally disciplined enough to make sure no one could budge him from that position.

"I think that would be wise," Sean said, and the interview, which had started so promisingly for the police, came to an abrupt and dissatisfying end.

Police found that at the conclusion of the interview, they knew nothing of substance they hadn't already known before they started when Sean had walked in and admitted he had killed Joy Risker. Not why, not how and certainly not what he had done with the body.

Sean had pulled a fast one on them—he had used what was intended as an interrogation to form a platform for a criminal defense he had already decided on in his mind: self-defense.

All he had done by turning himself in was end the need for him to tell more lies and possibly jeopardize his ability to later claim that he was acting out of shock and panicked self-preservation when he had lied to police and all Joy's friends.

So, even in his confession, Sean was the masterful controller, using the police as pawns in a defense he had already solidified.

Chapter 18

"GODDAMN CSI"

S ean Goff had certainly done his best to disguise Joy's body, to make sure if it was ever found, no one would be able to tell who it was. But even the best plans sometimes encounter a kink. The desert can play tricks on you. The site wasn't as remote as he might have thought. In fact, it was just a football field's distance from the closest road.

Four months after Sean buried the body under a pile of rocks in the Arizona desert, a man hiking around the wilderness near his campsite happened upon it.

Ruben Conde was a former hunting guide and he was familiar with the area. There is really nothing in the vicinity except scrubby desert, but Conde loved the place and spent a lot of his time there. However, on this day he saw a very unusual rock formation underneath a palo verde tree around three hundred feet north of the nearby dirt road.

The odor was strange and noxious. He had smelled dead animals before but this was different.

Later, Conde would say, "You could smell...different smell from an animal." He added that the tomb was "too big to have an animal like a dog buried there."

Conde's son, also named Ruben, was a federal ranger with the Bureau of Land Management. The next day, he went out to the area his father had described to him and began gently moving the stones to see what lay underneath.

"I found a partial portion of a head and a torso," the ranger said. "It just became apparent it wasn't an animal."

When investigators found the decayed remains, the bones told a story that was violent, graphic and desperately depraved. Almost completely decomposed except for the bones, the female body still had a bit of flesh on the legs and ten-inch dreadlocks clinging to the skull. It lay on its side in a loosely fetal position beneath the rocks that had entombed it. The body seemed to be curled up as if the woman wanted to get back into the womb which had once protected her. However, the truth was that the murderer had positioned her body that way after brutalizing her and trying to disguise who or what she had been.

Dr. Laura Fulginiti, the forensic anthropologist, laid out the body parts, putting each piece as close to its proper anatomical position as possible. Fulginiti soon ascertained that some pieces were missing and the condition of the skull and ribs indicated that something terrible had happened to this poor woman.

Her hip bones showed that she had given birth at least once. Through the shape of the skull and other factors, Dr. Fulginiti tentatively identified the remains as those of a young black woman who had been in relatively good shape when she died.

Much of the body above the sternum had been severed. The aorta, the largest artery in the body ascending from the heart, lies directly beneath that bone. The end result of such a wound would be massive and fatal bleeding. The left side of that same bone, which is where most people assume the heart sits, had deep cuts, as if someone had jammed a knife between the woman's first and second ribs, beneath which her vital organs sat vulnerable to the blade.

Many of the ribs recovered from the woman's left side were rife with signs of being stabbed through, including two that had been completely severed by the knife. The murderer had obviously wanted to be very sure she was dead. The hyoid bone, just below the chin, had been damaged by what appeared to be a saw blade as if someone had tried to cut the young woman's head off.

"The most stunning thing is the back of the sternum is sliced off," Fulginiti said. "That's the most startling thing. The sternum is thick, but not so heavy. When the knife went in, it must have caught, and [the killer] pulled down on it so hard that he literally sliced the back half of the sternum off of the front half."

That wound, Fulginiti said, is the most striking aspect of what happened.

"I have never seen that before," she said. "And I never expect to see it again."

The skull to which the long dreadlocks had been attached, even after an extended period of decomposition, was missing something important: a face. The familiar smiling skull with which anyone who has been spooked on Halloween is familiar wasn't all there. Between the orbs that once housed eyes, there should be a bone called the maxilla, which forms the nasal cavity and at its bottom houses the top row of teeth. That bone was mostly missing, though the part that should have contained teeth was still there. The woman's cheek-bones had been smashed, and lay in pieces near the skull to which they had once been joined.

The bone that should have held her top row of teeth had been sawn clean on the bottom where the teeth would have been attached. The teeth hadn't just been sawn out; the bone that held the teeth had been sawn away, and the sawing had been done so violently that the blade had ended up cutting into a wisdom tooth at the back of the bone that the killer probably hadn't known was there.

"It had to be a pretty bloody, gory business," Fulginiti said. "[The killer] would have had to cut the skin away on her face several inches, sort of like the Joker. I bet he couldn't see the wisdom teeth because of all the blood and gore."

That lone wisdom tooth had a twin on the jaw, where the killer had also sawn away the bone so violently that the blade had become buried in the actual bone that attaches the jaw to the skull. On the other side, part of the wisdom tooth that was hiding there had also been sawn into. On both the top and the bottom, the roots of this woman's teeth were visible, where they had been exposed by the killer's saw.

The front of the woman's jaw showed cuts that indicated what might have been false starts with the saw blade that had cut her teeth out. But finally, the killer had gotten an angle he or she liked, and had made one clean cut all the way across her entire jaw, hacking and hacking away at it until there were no more teeth—and no more gums—left in her mouth.

Her killer hadn't been satisfied with brutally stabbing the woman and trying to cut her head off. When that had failed, the killer had instead violently and repeatedly bashed her face in with what looked to be a hammer, from the marks it left, and then had sawn her mouth completely off.

But that wasn't all the killer had done.

As she examined the bones that were laid out in front of her, some were missing, but that was to be expected with the condition the body was in. What wasn't expected was that each hand was too short. By one bone on each finger.

Human fingers are composed of three bones each, with the smallest bone lying between the fingernail and the fingerprint. On this woman's hands, that bone had been cut off of each finger, likely by the same blade that had so violated her mouth.

"Goddamn CSI," Fulginiti said. Her anger was triggered by the condition in which they found Joy's body, as if someone had planned to prevent investigators from identifying her. "Somebody had watched too much TV and they knew exactly what to get rid of to try to thwart us."

Sean had hacked Joy's teeth out, cut her fingertips off and bashed her face in just a few months after he and I had invented a fictional killer who watched TV forensics shows to help him get away with murder. Now Phoenix forensics investigators were left to literally try to pick up the pieces to do their best at identifying the young mother someone had hidden underneath a pile of rocks in the desert out by the Mexican border.

All they knew was that it had been a violent death.

"This was calculated," Fulginiti said. "I don't even know if you would use the word 'crazy.' It's crazy to normal people, but it looks to me to be far more calculated than crazy."

Laura Fulginiti is proud of her work as a forensic anthropologist. She's on the cutting edge of her profession. If Joy could have looked beyond her own death, she couldn't have picked a better person to handle the case of the unidentified black female in the Arizona desert.

If Fulginiti is prone to the occasional outburst of profanity, it can be excused by her expertise—and her determination to see the victims of violent crimes get justice.

"When they found the gravesite, they weren't sure what was in there," she told me. "It was this weird cairn that someone went to a lot of trouble to make. All the stones matched, and he had to have traveled quite some distance to find them all. There were hundreds of them. The guy walking out there had a dog, and the dog is what sparked to it. He just knew there was something there with that cairn built up there."

When investigators painstakingly pulled the cairn apart, stone by stone, they realized the remains were human when they saw a partial, skeletal hand sticking up from inside it. But they didn't know yet what they had. No one at the scene even noticed that the fingers were missing the ends, the parts where fingerprints would have been. That wasn't noticed until detectives had a look.

"Bill McVey [an investigator at the Maricopa County Sheriff's Department] came to the autopsy," Fulginiti told me. "It's kind of standard practice, and they ask questions through the intercom as we're doing the autopsy. On this one, he said, 'Doc, are her fingertips cut off?' That's exactly what was there."

Fulginiti then examined the maxilla and mandible—the upper and lower jaw—of the remains, and when it became obvious that the victim's teeth had been sawn off after the victim had died, she said she knew then this wouldn't be an average case. The front of the skull had been viciously bashed in to the point that it was completely unrecognizable.

"Someone had done a tremendous amount of damage to her face," she said. "There was a lot of trauma. Immediately, we were all on the same page, and we all knew whoever had done this to her knew this person."

Generally killings with extreme violence are crimes of passion during which the violence is sparked by love—or hate. But there's a huge gulf between being able to tell someone has been through a lot of trauma and finding out who did it to her—or even who she was. And in this case, the violence actually wasn't done out of passion, they later discovered, but out of a calculated desire to disguise the identity of the victim.

"Looking at her, I told the detective, 'this is going to be a weird case.' And it was. It was even weirder than I imagined."

Throughout the course of the autopsy, one thought continued to strike Fulginiti: Someone had gone to a great deal of trouble to obscure the identity of the woman she was reassembling, piece by piece, on her examination table, and that effort on the killer's part begged an equal effort on her part to try to find out who had done this to such a vibrant young woman. From the autopsy, it was clear the woman was probably middle class, since she seemed well nourished.

But finding out who she was—and who she had left without a mother—would be akin to finding the proverbial needle in a haystack. There just wasn't much to go on and investigators didn't even know if they could get DNA from the remains. They weren't sure the existing DNA databases would be anywhere near comprehensive enough to have this poor woman in them even if they could. The various DNA databases were far less interconnected than TV shows made it appear, which meant the effort might not pay off anyway.

"Getting DNA from bones was still in its infancy then," Fulginiti said. It was also prohibitively expensive. "We weren't sure what we would get, so in the beginning we didn't even try."

Frustrated, Fulginiti told the team investigating the case that they should focus on the unique aspects of the remains: "Follow the dreadlocks."

The style of the woman's hair indicated that she was probably from an urban area with a straight line to Arizona on Interstate 8, which was just six miles south of where the body was found, about 2,500 feet off of Agua Caliente Road, out in the middle of nowhere. This woman was from either Texas or California, Fulginiti told investigators. But she didn't stop there. She got together with Detective Bob Powers, who was a forensic artist, and decided they had to do more to identify this body. After all, she had given birth at least once; she was someone's *mother*.

Powers was relentless in his quest to find out who this young woman was.

"Bob is the real hero of this story," Fulginiti told me. "He and I spent a couple of days piecing together the parts of her skull. At the time, he was experimenting with casting skulls, trying to piece them back together after a lot of trauma. He had reassembled the face of a guy who had gone off a parking garage, so he had some experience, but it still was tough. We barely had any of this woman's face; we weren't convinced we could get a drawing done, but we had to try. So with me holding the bones where they should have been and Bob sculpting it with clay, we finally got somewhere and he could do a drawing."

Powers put the drawing, which bore some resemblance to what Joy looked like in life, out everywhere he could but initially there were no hits on it. It seemed like no one knew who this missing woman was. It was frustrating for the investigators, who had put so much time, effort and emotion into trying to make sure their unidentified woman could get some kind of justice for what had been done to her.

Fulginiti and Powers were both busy investigators, so circumstances forced them to move on to other cases, though the unidentified mother with the missing teeth and fingers never traveled too far out of their minds. The brutal manner of her death and the dismemberment of her body afterward left too deep a scar in their minds to just forget about her after their efforts had been thwarted.

Months later, Powers came across a "have you seen me" flyer from Nevada that fit the description of the woman he and Fulginiti had reconstructed—and who neither of them could get out of their heads. He was elated and called Fulginiti to let her know he had a possible lead on the unidentified woman.

The drawing was a close enough match that the department thought it might be worth the expense of trying to get a DNA sample from the remains to see if it was her.

"We submitted the DNA from our lady," Fulginiti said. "It turned out not to be her, but when they ran the DNA, they discovered 'guess what, it's someone else.'

"I'm getting chills as I tell you this story," she continued. "They said, 'We have identified this girl.'"

The DNA, which Maricopa County's team had initially been pessimistic would yield anything useful, had put the puzzle back together quite accidentally—almost as if God *wanted* the killer to be caught. Joy Risker's DNA, it appeared, had been entered into the FBI's Combined DNA Index System database by San Diego police when Joy was still considered a missing person, before Sean had turned himself in.

The database had only been launched five years before, so police weren't yet accustomed to its use on a regular basis. In the beginning, in fact, only nine states had participated in the database. California was one. And Joy was in there, the detectives discovered.

"[The detective] said, 'this is weird. This girl was in a bigamous relationship and then she disappeared,'" Fulginiti said. "I was in my truck at the time and I stopped right then and yelled, 'I *told* you this was going to be weird!'"

Putting a face to the unidentified body, Fulginiti said, was the key to finding out who she was, even if that face had just been the first stumble on an accidental trip that quite chaotically put the pieces of the puzzle together. The long, tireless work of Powers, she said, gave Joy Risker the only hope she could possibly have had to not end up just another Jane Doe found decomposing in the desert, forever unidentified. Now, thanks to Fulginiti and Powers—and the new FBI DNA database—Joy could tell her story from beyond the veil of death.

In a sense, she was resurrected just long enough to tell police that Sean's story wasn't true. It wasn't the final resurrection her religion had taught her to hope for, the one her friends and family were now hoping she had already entered into, but this metaphorical resurrection was at least enough to give Joy the final say in the disagreement that had left her dead.

With Joy identified eight months after she was killed, a key plank in Sean's plan had fallen out of place. Without a body, it would have been nearly impossible to convict him of murder, because his story that it was self-defense—that Joy had attacked him and he had merely defended himself against her attack—depended on no one seeing the damage he had done to Joy, and on no one being able to find out that Joy's body had no defensive wounds, as might be expected if she had participated in a fight over a knife. But with a body, and with the brutality of the killing—and the heinous mutilation of her body after she was dead—it would be a lot more difficult for Sean to say he had acted merely in self-defense. Suddenly, because Fulginiti and her team had worked tirelessly to find an identity for the nameless woman they had discovered in the desert, not only did the remains have a name—Joy Risker—but the person whose remains they were stood a much better chance of seeing her killer come to justice.

When I heard that Sean had killed Joy but wouldn't reveal what he had done with the body, I immediately recalled our conversation.

I was on the phone with Sean's first wife's younger sister, who had broken the news to me about Sean turning himself in and confessing, when I blurted out, "Holy shit, Sean and I had just had a conversation about committing the perfect murder."

She was silent for a moment, then she screamed, "You helped him plan this? Oh my God!"

And then she hung up the phone. It took several calls for her to finally answer the phone again.

"I didn't help Sean plan anything," I explained. "We were talking about writing a book about the perfect murder. How the hell could I know he was actually planning to kill someone?"

It didn't make sense initially that he wouldn't tell any-one where Joy's body was after confessing that he had killed her. I, along with everyone else who knew about the case, wondered what he might have done with Joy's body, and why he wouldn't tell police where she was. It was only after the body was found and identified that the true reasons behind Sean's silence became obvious.

He had kept Joy's location to himself because her body told a story that no claim of self-defense could support. The tale Joy's remains told was brutal, but more importantly, they told another tale: that whoever killed her had done so with a plan.

For Sean and his defense, the finding of Joy's body was incredibly bad news. He had to come up with a revised narrative that now accounted for a stabbing that was shockingly violent—and a dismembering of the corpse that sounded more like something out of a horror movie than the actions of a loving husband who acted merely out of self-defense.

Sean had to come up with reasons for how he treated Joy and her remains; anything he said would be a tough sell, though. He had mutilated her body so violently out of fear of being caught while acting in self-defense? Anyone who knew Sean knew he was smarter than that. If Joy had attacked him and he had killed her while trying to stay alive, the genius mind that had helped him become so successful at everything he tried would have known his best bet would be to call the police and tell them what had happened; sure, he might initially have faced arrest, but the facts would have come out and borne out his side of the story if that's really what had happened.

Sean wasn't the kind of guy to crumble when a situation spiraled out of control. If he had really killed Joy out of self-defense, the in-control-at-all-times guy would have done the most logical thing and contacted the authorities. But he hadn't done that. Instead, he had hacked up her body and disposed of it as far away as he could reasonably get it— and then had spent weeks telling people she had run off with another man.

So with her body found, Sean and his attorney had to tell a story that made it plausible that he was a reasonable guy who had momentarily lost his cool and panicked, doing everything he could to disguise Joy's body and keep it from discovery. They would also have to explain the litany of lies

Sean had told, the fabricated e-mails, the lack of blood and the carefully-assembled "murder kit."

Suddenly, by finding and identifying the body, the Maricopa County forensic investigators had put Sean in a whole new level of, as Fulginiti said, "deep shit."

Chapter 19

GRECO V. ARENA

B y the time his trial neared, I hadn't spoken to Sean since he had called me the day before he turned himself in and asked me to pray for him. A friend, however, asked him about me.

"That guy," Sean told Trevor Whitken, the piano player who had traveled with him, rolling his eyes after Trevor had mentioned me. "He hasn't called, he hasn't visited. Nothing."

It appeared that Sean was as upset at me as I was at him. And that was okay with me.

At the time of Joy's death and Sean's arrest, polygamy was not a subject of primetime TV. There was no *Sister Wives* TV show on TLC, nor was HBO's *Big Love* airing yet when Sean killed Joy—it started just before Sean's case went to trial. So the topic of polygamy was still very taboo and the idea that a non-Mormon polygamist had murdered one of his wives after he had composed the Bible study materials for one of the world's biggest evangelists seemed too juicy to pass up.

But apparently, the news outlets weren't paying attention. And I certainly wasn't going to tip them off about the case, so it slid under the radar for three years until it was about to go to trial.

In 2004, one of Sean's lawyers called me and asked what kind of information I had about the case. I told them about the phone call, about the book idea and everything else, and that was the last I heard from them. Later, Sean unceremoniously fired them and hired Albert Arena, who would eventually defend him in court.

Matthew Greco, the rookie assistant district attorney who was picked to prosecute the case, had his hands full with Sean, who began claiming he had killed Joy in self-defense. But Greco, who was prosecuting his first murder case, didn't even flinch when he stared down a defendant he would later call a "super genius" and a "master manipulator."

Greco pounced like a tiger right from the starting gate: "The secret [was in] the tomb of Joy Risker, waiting to be found...so that the story of her murder by the defendant could be told; the story of nine, ten, eleven stab wounds to her chest by the defendant, who then cut off her fingers with a saw, her fingertips, gone. And then turned the saw to her teeth, sawing out the teeth. And then turned the saw to her face to cut it off from the top and from the bottom, and finally with something hard, strong, heavy like a sledgehammer, pulverized the face so that it wouldn't be recognized," he said in his opening statement. "This case was a calculated plan to preserve his reputation, a crime of pride."

It seemed like Greco had a bead on Sean, the motivation behind his despicable acts and the underlying fears of being exposed as the weakling emotionally that he always had been physically.

Greco keyed in on Sean's controlling nature and his belief that women needed someone to lead and take care of them.

"He was controlling of the finances," Greco said. "In fact, he bragged…that he had to control all of the money for both of his wives because they couldn't do it themselves; the household would fall apart without him controlling their accounts. And literally what he said about his wives is…'I give them an allowance.'"

Sean watched dispassionately as Greco tore into his character, insinuating in so many words that Sean was so full of himself he had to murder his second wife rather than suffer the embarrassment of her leaving him.

"On his computer…was a book that he began. It was entitled 'If I can keep two women happy, why can't you please one?'" Greco continued. "In it, he writes, 'I have dealt with some of the greatest challenges in relationships a man will ever face and feel compelled to write about what I have learned so other men can benefit from my own successes and failures. If I can be successful living with two women at one time, surely I can help other men live successfully with one. Some people out there writing books and holding seminars on marriage…have lived through several failed marriages. Their knowledge is suspect, at best, and their success is based on a marketing machine. Don't trust them. Trust someone who is successful in relationships.'"

The irony hanging thickly in the air, Greco went on to accuse Sean of being a doppelgänger of sorts, assuming Joy's life as he simultaneously sought to squelch the fire in her that attracted so many to her.

"Not only was the defendant attracted to Joy's life, but he ended up not really having any of his own friends and only associating with her friends."

And then Greco dramatically described Sean's shopping trip a week before Joy's death to assemble what Greco would later refer to as a "murder kit."

"He goes to [a hardware store] and he buys a hacksaw, a shovel, a pickaxe, an axe, a chisel, a sledgehammer, fifty feet of chain, two padlocks and seventy-five yards of rope," Greco said. "Thirty-one minutes later, he goes to [another store], same day, same credit card, [and buys] a butcher knife, a butcher block, two rolls of duct tape, 500 square feet of plastic drop cloth, five five-gallon buckets, gloves, a stepladder and a very large cooler."

Then, Greco said, immediately after the murder, Sean didn't seem at all upset or like someone who was shocked at the horrific things he had just done to his wife.

"[A friend] calls him on that Saturday morning..." about a party she had invited them to, Greco said. "The defendant didn't seem upset. He talked about this great dinner that he and Joy had had, and he said, 'no, the romantic weekend is continuing, we will not be able to make it to the party.'"

Joy was already dead and loaded into the SUV that Sean had rented when that phone call took place. The cover-up, however, had begun the night before, Greco said, because when Sean's first wife returned later to the house with instructions to clean up the blood that Joy had shed after cutting herself during the argument, she found only tiny spots of blood, not the pools that would be expected during a stabbing death brought on by a struggle for a knife.

In fact, what little blood was left told a sobering story, Greco said: a story of someone being executed, not of a blood struggle.

"There is one DNA profile on those walls and on those floors," he said. "And that's Joy."

One DNA profile. One person bleeding, not two. Joy was the only one with wounds. Sean had none. And Joy's wounds, which should have coated the house in blood, didn't. When she died, she died in a "kill room" coated with plastic sheeting to keep her blood from getting everywhere.

"There were little spots up on the wall, on the shower curtain," he said. "The house was incredibly stuffy, all of the blinds were down, everything was closed up."

And when Sean had arrived back at the house on Monday in the filthy SUV with 1,200 more miles on it than when he had rented it, soil and little rocks all over the interior, there were two "big" gas cans in the back, Greco said.

"Those were new," he said. "What were those needed for?" A contingency plan, he would say later during the trial. It was Sean's way of planning ahead. If one method of disposal didn't work, he would have a backup plan: torching the body.

But Greco wasn't the only attorney in the room. Sean had hired one of San Diego's best lawyers to sit at his table, a resilient defense attorney named Albert Arena. Arena actually bore a passing resemblance to Morris Cerullo, Sean's former employer.

He began by admitting that most of what Greco had said was true.

"Those things did happen," Arena said in his opening. "And a most difficult situation I have to get over in this particular case is the horrific nature of the postmortem actions by Mr. Goff."

But Sean, Arena said, wasn't a cold, calculating killer. No, he was a man in a situation involving three consenting adults who had entered the arrangement with "eyes wide open."

Joy, he said, wasn't a team player. She didn't want to pool resources; she selfishly wanted to use the family's money for her own ends, to go to college and have a career of her own. Joy was taking full advantage of all the benefits of polygamy, but she wasn't contributing her full share to that situation. She had, he said, a "secret agenda" to promote her own self-interest. She was, he said, "draining" to the family, always taking and never contributing.

The fancy dinner Sean took Joy to the night she was killed was an attempt by the longsuffering Sean to "reintroduce her to the life that she had committed to," Arena said, "to the life of a loving husband, to what they all had; to try and explain to her that either you accept this lifestyle that we have all agreed upon or you will have to go."

Joy's expensive last dinner, he said, had been discussed earlier by Sean and his first wife as a "shape up or ship out" dinner. Life is full of people who get angry and say things like "I could just kill you," Arena said, but that doesn't make them murderers.

"He gets to bat first," Arena said, referring to Greco. "I am in the outfield shagging flies. I am asking you to wait and hear the evidence that the defense will present, and then in closing, murder, manslaughter or self-defense. That is your promise—and your decision."

The stage set, Greco then hurled himself into building the case of a sensational crime that had to be told utilizing evidence from forensics experts who would testify about the information they could cull from Joy's corpse and from the house in Kensington where she had been slain. He introduced receipts showing Sean buying a "murder kit" days before the killing. And through it all, Sean sat silently, watching the case unfold and awaiting his chance to get on the stand.

Arena's strategy was to allow Sean to admit that most of the forensic evidence was true. Admit that he had killed Joy.

Admit that he had cut her fingers off, sawn her teeth out, removed her jaw and bashed her face in. Admit that he had left her in the Arizona desert. Admit that he had lied to her friends and family—and eventually to police as well. Admit all that. But then Arena introduced a new claim: that Joy had attacked Sean and he had been given no choice other than stabbing her to death to protect himself from her.

Greco subpoenaed me to testify as part of his section of the trial, but met with me only briefly before he put me on the stand. The district attorney's office paid to fly me out to San Diego and put me up in a hotel room.

When I got on the stand, I felt Greco's questions were not at all what I had expected. Had Sean ever asked me to use my middle name on an Internet forum instead of my first name? Yes. Did I reveal that to the people on the forum? Yes.

It struck me as strange. I had been Sean Goff's best friend for sixteen years. Joy had called me shortly before she died. Sean had called me shortly thereafter. I had posted on my personal blog about the conversation we had about the perfect murder just days after the revelation that Sean had turned himself in. Greco had not spoken with me before putting me on the stand or he would have discovered that Sean and I had talked at great length about how to get away with murder during our discussions of writing that book together. He thus was unaware that Sean had told me a very short time before he killed Joy that he felt that he had to "get rid" of her.

I called the district attorney's office from the airport and left a message saying I felt strongly that the office seemed to be missing a lot of evidence and questioning. And then I got on the plane to Oklahoma.

As soon as I touched down in Dallas and turned my cell phone on, it beeped. The DA's office had called while my flight was in the air. They asked if I had I known Sean for a long time.

I explained to them that Sean and I had met in college, and suggested they should do more research on things he was saying and doing before he killed Joy. Of course, I had no way of knowing that they had already been trying just this and that my testimony would simply be icing on the cake they were already baking.

The DA's office thanked me and hung up. The next day, while I was at work, they called me again, asking if I would come back to San Diego and testify again about the things I had heard Sean say. I sighed. My newspaper job wasn't going to be very understanding, I explained.

"We could subpoena you," they offered. I told them that would probably be preferable, so I could show my boss that I *had* to go. I didn't really want to go back; I just wanted to be sure justice was done for Joy. However, they seemed adamant that I come back and testify about the things I had mentioned to them in the voicemail I had left.

But first, after Greco had finished his presentation, Arena signaled the desperation of his own case by calling the defendant to the stand—a move always seen as a last resort.

"My family has always been a Christian family," Sean started. "No matter where we lived, we always attended a local church and we were very involved in worship."

"As you developed, would it be correct to say that religion was a part of your life experiences, Mr. Goff?" Arena asked.

"Yeah," Sean replied. "I gave my life to Jesus when I was six and continued going to church basically throughout the rest of my life."

Arena moved on quickly. "Were you ever tested for your IQ at any time?"

"Back in the ninth grade, I think. It was a long time ago."

"Try to be a little humble," Arena said, "but could you tell us what the score was?"

"145 or 150," Sean replied. "I don't remember exactly."

An intelligence quotient above 140 is generally considered profoundly gifted.

"The activity in the church, how much depth did that entail?" Arena asked.

"We would go on Sunday morning, Sunday night, Wednesday night," Sean answered. "Any kind of special services we would attend. My grandmother was a minister, as are some of my uncles, so that was a big focus of our lives. I would say that was *the* focus of our life."

That focus led to him meeting both his wives, Sean testified. The first was back in 1988, Joy in 1995 or 1996.

"She was attending church with her mother," he said. "My first wife and I would show up at the services occasionally and talk to her. She hung out with us a little bit; she became friends with my wife's younger sister, who lived with us at the time."

Joy, he said, was "the life of the party. She demanded attention when she came into the room."

But her commitment to church wasn't as great as Sean's, he testified.

"She was kind of a raver, so she was a little torn between her commitment to church and doing those things."

That "raver" lifestyle was because Joy was being raised by a woman without a man around to guide her.

"Her mother was very traditional," he said. "But Joy was an only child and her father wasn't in the home, so she had a lot of time on her hands."

And it wasn't Sean who pursued Joy, he said. It was the other way around.

"She was about...I guess she was sixteen and I was driving her home from the church," he said. "She looked over at me and she told me she was in love with me."

Sean said he laughed.

"I said 'well, it happens sometimes,'" he said. "'I'm just an older guy and next year you won't even feel that way. Don't worry about it. It is one of those big brother crushes or whatever.'"

A year later, he said, he started studying polygamy as an academic exercise.

"Being able to debate and prove that it wasn't something that people ought to be doing," he said. "But the deeper I got into that debate, the more I realized it was something I couldn't win on a biblical basis...Someone posed a question to me and I wanted to answer it. And digging into it, I couldn't really find a biblical basis for saying, 'Hey, that is a sin.'"

Sean's research eventually branched out onto the Internet, he said, where he found a few sites hosted by people who were actually practicing polygamists. He reached out to them, though at the time, he said, he still wasn't considering becoming a polygamist. He saw the issue the same way he saw alcohol, he said. Growing up, everyone in churches said alcohol was a sin but the Bible contained no such restriction.

Then, he said, he asked his first wife about it, and she said she couldn't find fault with polygamy either. Later in the trial he and his first wife both would contradict that story but he continued:

"Then we kind of accepted the idea that it was okay."

After that revelation, there was a "gradual change in" Joy's feelings, he said.

"She was growing up and she didn't want to be treated like a kid anymore," he said. "It began to progress."

Then, he said, he casually asked his first wife if polygamy was something they should engage in.

"She said yes," he stated, as if it was that simple. "And I said, 'Do you think that Joy should be asked to join our family?' And she said yes, so we did it."

After the marriage, he said, the family gradually got to a place where they believed they needed some concrete rules about finances. Sean had already filed for bankruptcy once, and having three adults and a child in one household was stressful.

"My first wife made a suggestion that all the adults in the family get some type of monthly stipend that they could spend," he said. "We decided each of us will get $300 a month."

In 1998, after I had "outed" him to Morris Cerullo, Sean and his family left San Diego and moved to the San Francisco area. In 2000, Joy gave birth to her first son, but the day after that her mother had died, leaving her depressed, Sean said. It was Joy, he said, who pushed the family to move back to the San Diego area after the death of her mother. Sean agreed a move back south would be a good idea.

They leased the house in Kensington where Joy would eventually take her last breath. All three of them signed the lease—a signal that the polygamy was out in the open.

In 2003, Sean said, "Joy was becoming increasingly unhappy with her life situation. She felt that she wanted more freedom, that she wanted to have more fun. She wanted to go to Hollywood."

Her unhappiness had a profound effect on him, Sean testified.

"Unless we were out doing something, she seemed unhappy," he said. "So it was an every day issue."

Then Arena asked Sean a question that would become a point of contention later on: "What was the money situation like in the house?"

"My wife and I were both working," Sean reported. "We didn't have money to burn at the time. Basically, we were living paycheck to paycheck. It was difficult to save at that time."

Sean and his first wife would take money they had earned, he testified, and transfer $300 a month into Joy's bank account, and then $600 so she could buy groceries for the family.

Joy, it seemed, was living off the hard work of the rest of the family. The $300 stipend wasn't enough for her, he said. Each month, she would put $200 more on her credit card, straining the family's finances when she wasn't even working.

Greco would later hone in on this to impugn the truth-fulness of the rest of Sean's testimony.

Joy became increasingly unhappy, he testified, until it reached a boiling point when she wanted to go to Los Angeles to attend beauty school—which would cost around $10,000—and live in an apartment there while she attended, which would cost more money.

But he hadn't assembled a "murder kit," he maintained. Instead, he had good reasons to buy all the things he had acquired a week before he killed Joy.

It seemed that the house at Kensington had California Pepper trees, which made the soil acidic in the backyard, so Sean had determined that, even though he had hired some-one to mow the lawn each week, he would take it upon him-self to uproot a tangled mess of trees and clear the yard of their stumps.

The backyard was "jungle-like," he testified.

"I was going to remove the soil from six to twelve inches down, get rid of all the roots, replace the soil," he said. "I was also going to trim a lot of the trees. There were a couple of trees I was going to cut down."

He bought the shovel to dig the dirt, he testified. The pickaxe, as well, was for digging up the soil to get rid of its acidity so grass would grow. The rope was for tying trees to two points so when he cut them down, they wouldn't fall in unpredictable locations. The logging chain was to pull stumps out of the ground. The padlocks were to put on the logging chains, because "it is easier sometimes to just padlock them."

"Because you didn't trust them to hold?" Arena asked.

"Yeah," Sean replied. "I mean, the hooks generally hold, but I have seen occasions when they don't."

The chisel and sledgehammer, he said, were for splitting logs. The axe was for the same purpose. The hacksaw was for cutting a pipe that was sticking up in the front yard. The contractor's sheeting? It was to put down over the house's wood floors so paint wouldn't get on them when the family was repainting the interior of the rental. The duct tape was to hold the sheeting in place. The buckets would be used to hold dirt and paint. The stepladder was to reach the ceiling during painting. The gloves were purchased for all that hard work.

"To spare myself some blisters during the digging."

The cooler, he testified, was to hold snacks for his first wife's trip to Santa Barbara with the children.

But the biggest claim Sean made was about the knife. It wasn't even him who picked it out, he testified. That was Joy. She wanted the knife and a good cutting board to use with it. Joy, he said, was with him throughout the shopping trip, both to the hardware store and the big box store.

Then, a week later, Sean planned to take Joy out to the most expensive restaurant he could think of, on Coronado Island, to rekindle their romance—or to tell her to ship out, depending on how the night went—and then go out dancing afterward. His first wife would be in Santa Barbara with the kids so Sean and Joy could have time together alone.

The truck, he testified, was rented to impress Joy.

"Joy really liked SUVs and she was always talking about Escalades," he said. "But I didn't think I could rent one, so I got this other truck for the weekend. What I intended to do was to do everything I could to show her that it was possible to have a good life in this situation, if we so chose to work things out, that we could do fun things like that on occasion and still take care of our family and do the right things that were necessary. If we couldn't work things out, I was going to ask her to leave."

It was Joy's last chance, a chance given because Sean was such a good person, he testified.

"I felt for the kids' sake that I needed to do everything that was possible in order to try and make the relationship work, by my own conscience," he said. "That's how I felt about it."

On Coronado Island, Sean and Joy actually arrived before the restaurant opened, so they sat in the bar where Sean ordered a scotch and Joy had some other kind of drink that he couldn't recall, he testified. When the restaurant opened, Joy ordered Kobe beef, while Sean ordered the rib-eye. They stayed at the restaurant for "a couple of hours," talking and having a good time.

"We just talked about, you know, the restaurant," he said. "It was great. It was a nice experience. We didn't really get into much of a personal nature until probably the end of the dinner."

But that personal conversation quickly became contentious, he said.

"Joy was planning on going to a makeup school in Burbank," he said. "We were talking about how much that would cost and when she wanted to do it and how our finances were in relation to that, and also what impact it might have on her sign language pursuit. I told her...it would be better to stick with her studies at the college until she got her degree and perhaps then pursue the makeup school."

After the discussion, the couple went on a walk on the beach and then headed back to the Kensington home to change into less dressy clothes to go out dancing. Sean was wearing a black suit and Joy was wearing a black mini dress, and they wanted to be wearing something more comfortable for dancing.

On the trip home, however, the makeup school issue wouldn't go away, he testified. Joy wanted to stay in Burbank while attending school.

"She wanted me to do a corporate rental, maybe get her a condo in the area; maybe Burbank, L.A., somewhere in that area that she could commute to the school from," he said. "It was only going to be like a month or three months or something. My position was that a corporate rental wasn't a good idea because it was going to be very expensive and the makeup school itself was very expensive."

After they arrived home, the discussion continued, he said.

"She was pretty adamant about the corporate rental," he said. "I was explaining to her, 'Do you realize that renting a condo for three months in that area may cost us $6,000? And you are talking about a school that will be between $3,000 and $10,000.' I told her that wasn't feasible. She was adamant that that was her plan and that's what she wanted to do."

Sean went to his first wife's bedroom, which was at one end of the house and had two closets, one of which held his clothing. There he changed into more comfortable clothes while Joy went to her bedroom, which was on the other end of the house. When she came out of her bedroom, she was wearing shorts and a t-shirt, he testified, which meant to him that the plans to go out dancing had changed.

"'We need to discuss this whole thing,'" he said she told him. "'Let me make some margaritas and we'll talk.'"

At that point, he said, he told her his plans.

"I said, 'If you want to talk about it, I'm not really for you going to makeup school,'" he testified. The reasons were multiple: it would cost too much money, it would interrupt her studies for a sign language degree and it would force her to be away from her children for between one and three months. But he wasn't done.

"'Listen, if you want to go to the basic makeup school, perhaps we can pay for that,'" he said he told her. "'But I'm not paying for a corporate rental and I'm not going to pay $10,000 for extended school. I just can't.'"

Joy, Sean said, became very upset, so to avoid the argument getting more heated, he stated that he left the house for a walk down the street so things could cool off. He walked toward a coffee shop that he frequented. Between three and five blocks from the house, he said, his phone rang. It was Joy. Her cell phone records showed a call indeed happened, but they did not show where the respective phones were when the call was made.

"She said, 'Listen, it is all right,'" he said. "'Come back. We will talk. We just need to get through this. We need to figure it out so we need to settle our differences.'"

The call, he said, lasted less than a minute and he returned to the house to calmly discuss the issues. But he was, he said, 90 percent convinced he would ask her to leave by that point.

Sean said he went to Joy's bedroom to take his shoes off, a routine he followed each night, whether he was staying in Joy's bedroom or not. After he took his shoes off, he left the bedroom and walked into the kitchen.

Joy, who was pouring herself a margarita, began talking about makeup school again, he said.

"I was surprised," he said, "because I thought when she called that maybe we could make some concessions and, at least theoretically meet in the middle somewhere."

That's when he told Joy he didn't think the marriage was working out.

"'In fact, I didn't want to pay for makeup school,'" he said he told Joy. "So we started arguing back and forth at that point. It just seemed to me that she was making statements that were irrational. She was very upset."

Sean said he then reiterated that the marriage wasn't working and they would need to figure out how to proceed with that understanding.

"She mentioned the kids," he said. "She said, 'well, you are not going to take the kids away from me.'"

And that's when Sean said Joy wouldn't have to worry about custody, since he had a picture of bruises on her younger son.

"'That's all there is to it,'" he testified that he told Joy. "And I backed out of the room..." and slammed the door.

Afterward, he grabbed the photograph and went to Joy's bedroom to retrieve his shoes and leave.

"I go in there and I toss the picture down on the bed and I hear her coming up the hall," he said. "We have wood floors and it is a raised foundation and she walks heavy."

He said he turned around and there Joy was, standing in the doorway holding a knife. Joy yelled and swung the knife, he testified.

"She said...she said, 'you son of a bitch, I will kill you.'"

Sean said he punched Joy twice in an attempt to fend her off.

But Joy, according to the man who had now confessed to killing her, was determined. She shook off the punches and kept coming at him, and for the first time, he said, he was afraid of his young wife.

"I was frightened. I thought, 'she is serious.'"

Sean said he then grabbed Joy's hand, the one that was holding the knife, and a struggle for control of the blade ensued.

"I got it turned around toward her, and we were still fighting over the knife," he said. "And I pushed the knife into her. At some point, I took the knife away and I stabbed her again."

Arena asked Sean where he had stabbed Joy with that second blow. Sean indicated that it had been somewhere near Joy's left shoulder.

"What happened then?" Arena asked.

"She kind of, um, at that point, she kind of went limp."

The story was compelling. It was a brutal struggle for life, not a vicious, cold-blooded killing, he had testified. But as engrossing as the story might be, it was at odds with the evidence. Joy had been stabbed at least a dozen times, not the two that Sean testified he was guilty of inflicting. And the stab wounds had been so violent that they had severed her chest bone and broken several ribs. But Sean wasn't done with his performance yet.

After Joy "went limp," Sean said he was two completely opposite things: panicked and in shock. Realizing what had just happened, he said, he leaned over her prone body and tried to resuscitate her by performing CPR.

"I pulled out the knife," he testified. "A lot of blood came out with it. And I checked her breathing and her pulse, and she didn't have either at that time."

And that's when Sean started crying on the stand, leaning his head down, wiping his eyes and even grabbing a tissue. It was wrenching. Except for one small detail. There were no tears. Not even one.

He hadn't called the police, he testified, sobbing tearlessly, because Joy was a woman, and Sean was a man, and the police would never have believed that he had killed her in self-defense, he thought. He didn't see the sense in his sons losing both of their parents in one night.

"I thought about, 'This is my sons' mother,' and they were going to have to live without her," he said. "I felt like that they were probably going to live without me too."

And that's when he decided, he said, that he had some terrible tasks in front of him if he was going to try to cover up the death of his sons' mother. It was fortuitous that he had taken that hardware shopping trip six days earlier, he realized. The gear he had bought was purchased so he could work on the house that weekend, not clean up a murder, but since he already had the stuff around...

"I thought about what to do next," he said. "I thought for a minute I had to take Joy somewhere. I thought about covering up her identity."

Using multiple towels from the bathroom, he covered the bloody corpse up, he said.

"I knew I had to remove her fingertips."

Using a small meat cleaver from the kitchen, he said, he placed her fingers between towels and cut them off.

"I felt horrified," he said through more dry tears. "I felt frightened. I felt sickened."

Arena wanted to know what he did after removing the fingertips.

"I thought for a few moments, wondering if there was anything else I should do," he said. "I decided in order to cover up her identity, I would have to remove her teeth as well."

Using an unidentified saw that never made its way into evidence—not the hacksaw from the "murder kit" shopping spree, he maintained—he started the gruesome work of removing the jaw and hacking the teeth from the skull of the woman he had loved so much that he had to marry her even though he was already married.

"I couldn't look at them," he said. "I arranged the towels where I wouldn't see anything except what I was cutting."

Sean said after her fingertips and teeth were gone, he calmly walked to the garage, emptied a large plastic container's contents into two other containers and returned to the bathroom, where he placed the container on its side beside Joy, shoving her body into it and then turning the container upright, because he couldn't lift the body without using that leverage.

He tried to lift the container to remove it, he said, but it was too heavy. Instead, he placed the edge of the container on an area rug and used the rug to drag the container out to the garage.

Then he returned to the bathroom to clean up the blood and put all the towels and other soiled materials into the trash receptacles outside the house.

"At that point, I was kind of just stunned about everything," he said. "And probably for awhile, I just sat and did nothing. I couldn't do anything. I couldn't function. I just sat there for a long time."

But eventually, he was able to get going again and backed the SUV into the garage, close to Joy's body, which had been crammed into a plastic container.

But the body was too heavy.

"I couldn't get it in there," he said. "There was some firewood in the garage. There was a rather large piece that I set up on end at the rear of the truck. I pushed one end of the container up on that and then I swiveled the rest of the container onto the bed of the SUV."

Stunned and disoriented, he said, he went back into the house and wandered around in a daze until morning, when he went out to the garage and drove the SUV into the desert.

Once he was in Arizona, a random exit sign caught his attention and he turned off onto the Agua Caliente Road.

"I was going to put the body somewhere," he said.

Several miles from the Interstate, he sat in the SUV, staring off into space.

"I decided to put the body underneath a tree," he said. "I saw that there were a lot of these rocks. From there, if you look the other direction, you can see some little rock formations that probably hikers or somebody made, and that gave me an idea to use those rocks."

Gathering the rocks from around the tree quickly turned into quite an effort, and he soon overheated, he said.

"It got so hot I couldn't continue," he said. "I got back into the car. I turned on the air conditioner and I waited until the sun started going down [and] I just continued, basically picking up rocks and carrying them, placing them there."

While her body was laying under the tree, surrounded by lava rocks, Sean decided his mutilation of her body wasn't thorough enough yet.

"I needed to do something to cover up who she was, including her facial features," he said. "I picked up one of those rocks and I hit her face with it."

Arena immediately brought up that earlier testimony had indicated the marks left on Joy's skull were consistent with the sledgehammer he had bought on the "murder kit" shopping spree, not with a lava rock.

"Did you use this sledgehammer?" Arena asked.

"No," Sean responded. He stated that he had used a rock, not the sledgehammer.

If the testimony was starting to sound a bit like the old board game Clue—lava rock in the desert, not sledgehammer in the kitchen—it was about to wrap up. Sean testified that Joy's body was in the fetal position when he started placing rocks on top of it to cover it.

"I made a little tower that was similar to what I had seen there," he testified. "After everything I had done, it was like the only way I could show some respect for her body."

In one fell swoop, Sean had touched on every bit of evidence the prosecution had raised in the first part of the trial. He hadn't bought a "murder kit;" he had simply assembled the implements for house projects that had long needed doing. He had hoped to keep Joy in the family but, ultimately, it was Joy who had made the decision to stick to her guns against the best interests of everyone else. After their argument, Sean had tried to walk away but Joy had called him back. And it was Joy, not Sean, who had gotten violent, who had pulled the knife, who had swung it in a threatening manner.

Sean, the angelic minister who could justify all his actions (including polygamy) using the Bible, had been the innocent victim only trying to look out for the best interests of his family. Joy hadn't been able to play along, so she had forced his hand. She had, essentially, killed herself. He had even turned himself in because that was the right thing to do. If he was guilty of anything, it was only that he had wrongfully covered up her death, and hadn't he already been in jail for three years? Certainly that was long enough to pay for that crime.

But there are two sides in court and Matthew Greco then stepped up to cross-examine Sean.

His first order of business: putting to rest the notion that Sean had turned himself in because he was such a good Christian.

Sean's co-worker, Victoria Mack, had testified that she had given Sean an ultimatum in October. Sean had been telling their boss that he had to work fewer hours because his wife had left and he was now a single father struggling to raise his children while still working. Mack, who knew that wasn't true, that Sean had another wife still at home, had told him that when she returned from vacation on October 20, he had better confess to their mutual boss that he still had a wife at home, or she would. But Sean denied that the conversation ever took place.

"She told you that you had to come clean with your employer, right?" Greco asked.

"No, she did not," Sean replied.

"She told you that you had been misleading [their boss] into believing you were a single father, correct?"

"That's not how the conversation went, no," Sean replied. Not a strict denial from the man who was an expert

at mincing words to tell the technical truth while still con-
veying a lie, a trick he had bragged to me about when we were
both working at the ministry together.

"She told you that you had to fix it with [your boss] or
she was going to tell your boss?" Greco asked.

"She never made an ultimatum," Sean said. "She said she
was very concerned."

Greco tried to introduce evidence from Sean's first
wife's testimony that she had come home from work on
October 21 after police had showed up there and started
questioning her. When she had gotten home, Sean told her
that he had killed Joy and his first wife, literally holding her
hands to her ears so that she couldn't hear Sean's attempts
at explanation, had screamed at him to turn himself in at
the police station.

Arena, however, objected that this was irrelevant.

"I am questioning him on his assertion that no one
forced him to go to the police," Greco said to the judge.

The judge, however, sustained Arena's objection, so the
prosecutor moved on.

"On October the 21st, 2003, you went to the police
department," Greco said. "And at this time, you want this
jury to believe that you did this because it was the right thing
to do?"

"I'm not thinking about what I want the jury to believe,"
Sean said. "I'm just telling the jury what happened."

Greco, however, wanted to know why, when Sean confessed to police, he didn't tell them that Joy had attacked him
with a knife, a statement that could have changed the way
detectives were handling his case.

"Mr. Goff, Detective Tefft asked you 'How did you end
up hurting her?'" Greco said. "At that time, you didn't tell
him that she attacked you with a knife?"

"No, I did not."

"You never told Detective Tefft anything about a photograph, correct?"

"Correct."

"Detective Tefft asked you—there is a location, evidently, where her body is. And your response was 'I'm not sure if I should answer that question at this time. When you said that at the police station, you knew Joy Risker was underneath a pile of stones in the middle of the desert, correct?"

"Yes."

"When you were speaking to the police, when you 'knew what the right thing to do was,' your response was..."I think I would rather talk to an attorney about this,' correct?"

"Yes."

"You made a choice to leave Joy Risker in the desert, under the rocks, correct?"

"No," Sean said. "I made a decision to speak to an attorney first."

"You made a decision, in your words, to do the right thing, correct?"

"That's true."

"And the right thing in your mind was leaving Joy Risker out there in the desert, correct?"

"The right thing in my mind was to speak to an attorney before I spoke about that."

After establishing that "the right thing to do," for Sean didn't include telling where Joy's body was, Greco brought up me.

"You met Leif Wright when?"

"I believe in 1987," Sean said.

"You were in college together?"

"Yes."

"You became close friends?"

"Yes, we did."

"In 2002, you had a conversation, or actually a series of conversations with him on how to commit a perfect murder, didn't you?"

"No," Sean replied. "I did not. I never said anything like that."

Greco then asked if Sean remembered a conversation with me about how Joy was lazy and he was going to have to get rid of her. No, he replied. He didn't recall that conversation. Then he asked if Sean recalled in September speaking to a friend of Joy's and saying, "Don't be surprised if Joy packs up and never comes back."

"No, I don't recall that," Sean said.

"She testified to that," Greco looked straight at Sean. "Was she wrong?"

"Yes."

"On September 6, 2003, you told Victoria Mack that Joy had two weeks from when you got home to shape up or ship out," Greco said. "You said that to her, correct?"

"I recall telling her the 'shape up or ship out' part, but I don't recall the two weeks."

Victoria Mack had also testified that Sean had told her from watching *Forensics Files* and other similar TV shows, that it was nearly impossible to get away with anything, but Sean denied that.

Greco then brought up a party where an argument between Sean and Joy had broken out in the presence of Joy's friend, where Sean had gotten into the car and demanded that Joy get in if she ever wanted to see her kids again.

"Joy's friend called the house shortly after her party," Greco said. "And you told her, 'If you ever call again, I will kill you?'"

"Unfortunately, I did say that," Sean said.

Greco then turned his focus to the plural marriage itself. Sean had testified that his first wife had been for it but her testimony had been that she wasn't in favor of the marriage.

"Your first wife did not approve of this arrangement, did she?" Greco asked.

"Over time, I learned she did it for me."

"She did not like this arrangement, correct?"

"At times."

Greco was on a roll. He turned his attention to the financial arrangement, where Sean had taken over the finances because the women weren't able to handle the family's money.

"After you took over the family finances, how many bankruptcies did you have?" Greco asked.

"Two."

Sean testified that he filed for bankruptcy in the early 1990s and again in 2000.

"In 2000, Joy's mother, Gwendolyn Risker, died, correct?" Greco asked.

"Yes, she did."

Joy, Sean testified, had inherited $75,000 from one of Gwen's insurance accounts, but there were two or three more policies, so much that Sean couldn't remember the total amount Joy inherited. So Joy, Greco asked, had her own money from 2000 on because of the inheritances? Sean said she did not.

"Why not?" Greco asked.

"Because when I stayed home to deal with some problems, Joy volunteered to use her inheritance in order to maintain the family."

"In fact," Greco said, "You didn't work, correct?"

"For about ten months," Sean answered. "It may have been less than that."

In 2002, Sean's lease for the Kensington house listed income as more than $105,000, the source being "inheritance," referring to Joy's inheritance from her mother's death.

Next, Greco asked about the fight that Sean had said led to Joy's death. Had he been cut during the fight, or was Joy the only one with wounds?

"I had some nicks on my hands and there was one cut up here on my arm."

Greco then showed Sean a video showing his hands after he turned himself in, less than a month after Joy died.

"Could you point to where the nicks are on your hands?"

"I can't tell."

"In these photographs, there are no wounds, no scars, there is nothing, correct?"

"No."

"That day, you did not bleed anywhere, did you?" Greco asked.

"There was a little of my blood that...not much."

None of Sean's blood had been found when the police investigated the house.

Greco then attacked Sean's account of the timing of the events the night Joy died. Specifically, he asked whether Joy had seen or heard about the photograph Sean had supposedly taken of her younger son's bruises, which he was intending to use to show Joy to be an unfit parent—and the reason he had said Joy grabbed the knife and threatened to kill him.

With Sean in the bedroom after leaving the kitchen and slamming the door, Greco asked what happened next.

"I heard footsteps coming up the hall."

"At this point, you have never talked about this photograph with Joy, correct?"

"Not the photograph."

"She has never seen this photograph at the time she has the knife, correct?"

"She has never seen the photograph."

Sean may not have realized it, but it was a major discrepancy within his account of what had happened. When he had testified under the friendly questioning of his own attorney, he had said he had threatened Joy with the photo, and that's when she grabbed the knife and started swinging it at him. But under Greco's questioning, he had changed the story. Joy, in this story, had the knife having never heard about or seen the photo.

Driving the point home, Greco continued: "At this point she says what?"

"She said, 'Son of a bitch, I will kill you.'"

"At this point of the evening, without having seen the picture, she has a knife and says, 'I'm going to kill you,' correct?"

"Yes."

Greco quickly moved on to the fight itself, but he would recall the discrepancy during his closing arguments.

After Sean left the stand, Greco subpoenaed me to fly back to San Diego as a rebuttal witness.

When I arrived in San Diego, Greco *still* didn't meet with me. He did, however, send word that I should get something to wear that was more appropriate for court. In my first session on the stand, I had dressed as I do in everyday life: T-shirt with a cartoon on it and jeans. For my second trip to the stand, however, he wanted me to look more professional.

My initial testimony had been unnerving. Not only had it been my first time in court as a witness, but Sean, knowing I was about to testify against him, had smiled at me and winked as I made my way to the stand.

This time, there was no smile from Sean, no wink as I approached the stand and swore to tell the truth, the whole truth and nothing but the truth.

"Where do you live?" Greco asked. Strange question, I thought, but okay.

"Muskogee, Oklahoma," I replied. Then he asked me how long I had known Sean. I said I had known him since we met in college in 1987. He asked me about the incident in the dorms where Sean had held the guy out the window, demanding that he apologize for using profanity in front of women.

I told him about Sean's temper. I told him about holding the kid out the window of the dorms at OU. I told him about the book or movie we had discussed. I told him about how Sean had told me he needed to "get rid" of Joy. I told him how Joy had seemed like leaving Sean was the last thing on her mind when she called me, just before she was killed, to invite me to his birthday party.

Greco touched on the fact that I was shocked that no one had asked me in court about the conversation Sean and I had had about a book or movie in which the killer learns how to get away with his crimes by watching TV forensics shows.

"Why hadn't you ever told anybody about this prior conversation?" he asked.

"I actually had mentioned it in a personal blog that I had, and that's why I figured, because I did see on my IP logs lots of San Diego County official hits reading those blogs," I answered. "So I assumed that was information gathered for the district attorney."

"So you just assumed that everybody knew about this conversation?"

"That's true."

And then Arena got up to cross-examine me. Wasn't it true, he asked, that I was only there to testify again because I wanted to get in front of the TV cameras that were behind me and at the back of the courtroom?

"I wasn't aware that those were cameras until you just pointed them out," I replied. I had had no idea that there were cameras in the courtroom.

"Have you ever smoked marijuana?" Arena asked. Either the question was relevant to something I wasn't aware of, or Greco didn't feel the need to object, because he didn't say anything.

"Oh, absolutely," I replied, probably a bit too vehemently, and the courtroom burst out in laughter, which was probably the worst thing that could have happened to me. I tend to rely on humor when I get nervous, and the last place to be funny is a courtroom where someone is on trial for murdering an innocent woman, the mother of his children. I hadn't intended my marijuana answer to be funny but it opened the floodgates and even the judge got in on the act.

"I assume your marijuana use has been far outside my jurisdiction," said the judge, Robert O'Neill, laughing.

"As far as you know," I replied.

It was getting out of hand but humor was always the safe place I could rely on and falling into it was only spurred on further by the laughter that was erupting in the courtroom.

"I knew you were testifying," Sean's first wife said later. As a future witness, she had been restricted from going into the courtroom but she was sitting just outside. "As soon as I heard everyone laughing, I knew it was Leif up there."

I, however, didn't want everyone laughing. I knew that it would look like I wasn't taking the case seriously, but either Sean had wisely informed Arena to get me into that spot, or Arena was just good at seizing the moment, because he did, pressing me further and further, until he got to the real point of his inquiry, which I knew had to have been fed to him directly by Sean.

"Mr. Wright," Arena said after the laughter had died down. "Did you ever use a weapon on anybody back then?"

I knew this line of questioning was trouble, because I knew Sean was claiming he had killed Joy in self-defense, that Joy had approached him with the knife and he had been forced to kill her with it. But I had taken an oath to tell the whole truth—an oath I took seriously, even if fulfilling it meant my testimony would be muted by it.

"Yes," I replied. Sean knew all about my knife fight, and I knew he had told Arena about it in an attempt to make his own claims seem more reasonable. "A guy pulled a knife on me and I told him I would stick it up his ass if he didn't put it away. He didn't, so I did."

"You didn't like people pulling knives on you?" Arena asked.

"I didn't take it very well, no," I answered.

Sean smiled. It was a brilliant move on Arena's part, probably prompted by Sean. The guy on the stand testifying that Sean had a temper, that Sean had planned to kill Joy and get away with it, was now the guy who had done the same thing Sean was claiming to have done when he had faced a similar situation. Of course, my knife fight had been in a crowded parking lot against a man, not in a secluded bedroom against a woman, but I couldn't say that; I could only answer the question and Greco hadn't spoken to me before I testified.

I hoped the jury had listened to the relevant parts of my testimony, not the comedy the defense attorney had masterfully prodded me into and not the other misdirection he had so deftly managed with the knife fight testimony. I had testified that Sean had been discussing ways to thwart police at identifying a body and solving a crime. I had testified that Sean had said he wanted to "get rid" of Joy shortly before he actually did. I had testified that Joy had called me, happy about throwing a surprise birthday party for Sean, and that she had not seemed in any sort of mood to be leaving Sean or attacking him with a knife. Hopefully, I thought, the jury was listening to that and not to the tangential stuff Sean's lawyer had steered me into.

If my testimony had been nullified by the fact that I had once been in a knife fight, so be it. I had sworn to tell the whole truth, I told myself, and with Sean's brilliant lawyer working against the state's rookie, it would just have to be up to the jury to figure out what was right and wrong. As I left the stand, I remember wishing they hadn't called me to testify the second time. I hoped I hadn't hurt the case against Sean by being funny but it seemed to me distinctly possible that I had, in the final misstep of a long line of them that I had made during my relationship with Sean.

But the evidence against Sean was stronger than the nervous comedy act of a witness who should have only been called to testify once. Sean's first wife was called to the stand after I left. And her testimony was only the second-most damning that Sean would face in the trial, next to his own, which would end up sealing his fate.

Greco's team had carefully made a case, using receipts, that Sean had assembled what Greco—who, despite his numerous rookie mistakes, seemed to be a pretty good lawyer—called a "murder kit" six days before he killed Joy. The "murder kit?" While Joy was away at a friend's wedding on September 13, Sean had bought a hand saw, a butcher knife, a butcher block, duct tape, plastic sheeting, a shovel, a big insulated cooler, a sledgehammer, a pickaxe, two padlocks, seventy-five yards of rope, fifty feet of chain and a chisel less than a week before he would find all those items useful in the most grisly of ways.

The hand saw, Greco contended, was used to saw out Joy's teeth. The knife was used to murder her and cut the tips off of her fingers. The duct tape was used to secure the plastic sheeting, which was employed to keep Joy's blood from staining the bathroom, leaking all over the place as Sean brutally stabbed and then mutilated her en route to dumping her body. The shovel was used to dig her in at the roots of the palo verde tree. The cooler, Greco contended, was used to keep her body hidden en route to its final destination. The sledgehammer was wielded to bash Joy's face in after she was dead and her teeth had been hacked out of her head. The chisel was probably intended for the teeth if the saw hadn't worked, and the pickaxe was probably used to help dig her shallow grave underneath the stones.

But Arena had posited what he deemed reasonable explanations for all those items. So when Sean's first wife got up on the stand, Greco wanted to know if there would be any kind of acceptable reasons for Sean to buy all those things. Was Sean planning some big home improvement project?

"Was Sean the kind of person that had...hobbies like woodwork?" Greco asked.

She smiled and simply answered "No."

Greco asked if Sean was into plumbing. She said no. Landscaping? No.

"What was his level of being a handyman?" Greco asked.

She laughed again. "None."

The tools he had assembled, the ones that seemed so well-suited to creating the "murder kit" Greco had spoken of, were completely out of character for Sean, a guy who— even though he was nearly obsessive about making sure maintenance was done on his car—couldn't change the oil by himself. A chisel? Would Sean even know what to do with one in a handyman setting? His first wife said he wouldn't—at least not that she knew of, and she had been married to him for a long time.

Greco also asked the question that was really on everyone's minds concerning his first wife: How could a woman who had married a man with the expectation of them being a couple—and *only* a couple—"til death do us part" then allow her husband to add another wife to the mix?

"I felt I didn't have a choice," she responded. "It was either that or lose my son and the relationship I had with Sean."

Greco raised his eyebrows. "Why did you believe you would lose your son?"

Sean's first wife was tired of the whole subject. My memory was that she had told me years earlier that Sean had threatened to leave her and keep their son if she didn't comply. However, when Greco asked why she thought she would lose her son if she left Sean, her answer was different from the one I remembered her giving me: "I don't know."

But Sean had made it clear to her—and as Joy's friends had testified earlier, to Joy as well—that leaving Sean meant you left the children with him, and if you didn't like that, you'd better dig yourself in for a long custody battle, because there was one thing that was not going to happen in Sean's world: you weren't going to take his children away from him if you left him. Joy knew that, her friends had testified to it and I felt that Sean's first wife had told me the same thing. Sean knew he had precious little real leverage in the relationships but he wasn't above using what he had and that meant threatening mothers with losing their children.

And it had worked. Sean's first wife testified that the fear of losing her son was the deciding factor in prompting her to allow Sean to add another wife to their marriage, even though she later told me she hated it. But she had gotten to know Joy and, despite the fact that Joy was technically the "other woman," his first wife had grown to love Joy, probably more than she loved Sean. The women were, in some ways, fellow prisoners of the Sean Goff regime. They both operated under the same strictures of his religious and secular control. They did what he said.

So they formed a bond, and that bond in many ways was stronger than the ones they individually shared with Sean.

The night Joy was killed, Friday, September 19, after Sean had spent over $200 on Kobe beef for the dinner on Coronado—the last food that Joy would ever eat—Joy had called Sean's first wife at 8:36 P.M. so she could say what would turn out to be the last words she would ever say to her sons: "Good night."

Joy, the first wife testified, sounded happy during the call; she certainly didn't sound like there had been any sort of argument. She wasn't angry, upset or distressed. Instead, she seemed to be her normal self, and there was nothing in Joy's voice to make Sean's first wife believe anything was amiss at all. The fact that she didn't hear from them on Saturday was further indication that things had probably gone well, she thought.

But then Sunday, as she was headed home to San Diego with the boys, she got a call from Sean. The indications she had gotten from Joy that things had gone well were wrong, Sean told her. They had had a big argument when they got home after the meal, and then they had broken up and Joy had left. Oh, and also, during the argument, Joy had cut herself, Sean had said. Nothing big, but there were a few spots of blood. Could she clean them up when she got home with the boys?

His first wife, conditioned by so many years of doing exactly what she was told when she was told to do it, didn't question Sean's version of the story for a second. Instead, when she arrived home to the empty house that had once been so full of Joy's personality and laughter, she went to the bathroom and cleaned up the tiny, almost imperceptible, spots of blood Sean had mentioned. She had been meaning to throw her shower curtain away anyway, so instead of spending too much effort cleaning it, she tossed it and decided to finally get a new one.

Sean didn't arrive home until Monday.

When he did, he pulled up in an SUV he had rented, his first wife testified. And it was filthy. He said he had rented the SUV and gone for a long drive so he could work out his emotions about the end of his and Joy's relationship. She testified that she never thought anything other than what Sean was telling her was the truth. So she went to the driveway with Sean and helped him clean up the SUV so he could return it to the rental company.

"I really didn't believe he would do something like that to our family," she testified when she was asked why she didn't suspect something might be amiss.

Greco, who described Sean's first wife as "easily led"—a description that might have been true at the time of the murder but I strongly felt was no longer true by the time she testified—didn't pursue charges against her for helping with the cover-up because he believed that she really didn't doubt what Sean was telling her. There was no reason to. Sean wouldn't kill someone, especially his favorite wife. And if he had, there would certainly be a lot more mess to clean up than a few tiny spots of blood.

It was all Joy's fault; that was Sean's story.

The jurors weren't buying it. The story was too convenient and it absolved Sean of all the things that would appear to make him less than angelic. But more than anything, it was the lack of tears that pushed the jury over the edge, jury members later told a television news program.

The way Sean had bald-facedly lied to the jury was "insulting," one of them said later.

"He was so full of himself," another told the news show. "It was his world and we were all living in it."

That same juror said Sean's crying was the ultimate deal-closer.

"Like, come on, just give us one tear. One tear."

When Sean had picked up a tissue and blotted his dry eyes, that had sealed the deal.

Chapter 20

CLOSING ARGUMENTS

The judge gave his instructions to the jury, then said soberly, "Now is the opportunity for counsel to argue their respective positions on the case. And Mr. Greco gets to go first. The burden is on him.

"Mr. Greco?"

San Diego County Assistant District Attorney Matthew Greco was positively in attack mode as he began his closing arguments.

"Thank you, your honor.

"This case remains about one thing," he said. "A calculated plan by a calculating man, a man consumed with control and preserving that control and his reputation at the same time, a man who believes he is smarter than the judge, myself and all thirteen of you. It is a simple case."

Sean, he said, was the kind of man who would do anything to preserve that view of himself as above others, as being an authority.

"A man who will thumb his nose at the world," he said. "Do it when you plan the crime, cover it up and then when you sit in this chair, turn over, cry those crocodile tears, those false, phony tears, lie to this jury, to their faces, thumb your nose at the world. That is his definition of being a man."

The choice, Greco said, was simple. Either Sean Goff had planned and executed a plot to kill Joy Risker and dispose of her body or he had merely been defending himself against the attacks of a woman who was nearly the same size as he was. If the jury believed Sean was attacked by Joy and simply defending himself, they couldn't find him guilty of manslaughter or second-degree murder, he said. They would in that instance have to find him innocent—period.

But if they believed he had planned to kill Joy and hide the evidence of his crime, they had to find him guilty of first-degree murder.

But this was no self-defense, he said. Joy "fell under the spell" of Sean Goff when she was just a teenager. She had barely graduated high school, he said, so Sean was attracted to her because of that as well.

"Why is he attracted not to the person with an IQ of 145 like himself, the super genius," he asked, "but instead, someone twelve years his junior? Because he was living vicariously through her. She was a real person, and he latched onto her."

The polygamy was all Sean's idea, he said, not the way Sean had portrayed it as a family decision that was entered into equally by him and his first wife.

"It wasn't a joint decision," he said. "It was all about him. It has always been all about him, about exerting control over [his first wife], keeping the pressure on his first wife, the one who is honest and decent and obedient. It is not something she wanted. She said, in her words, she had 'no other choice.'"

Joy, meanwhile, was the "life of the party," as the jury heard from multiple witnesses.

She was "the type of person who made you feel good about who you are, that you are special, that you are important," Greco said. "And the defendant is drinking that up. He can't get enough of that. An ego the size of Texas. He can't get enough of it."

Sean's entire reason for being tired of Joy, however, didn't ring true, Greco said.

"I will remind you again of the defense promises to you of what this case was going to be about," he said, "of somebody who was taking from the relationship and never giving. You have the tax returns and the testimony, and you suddenly find out she was making more money than he was. They are living off her inheritance but what was being portrayed to you was a calculated move to make a suggestion about Joy that just wasn't right. This isn't someone who was siphoning off or getting all of the benefits of a polygamous relationship and giving nothing in return. She was contributing, doing everything that she could, all the while the defendant is in control of all the money. He is a true control freak."

Joy wasn't a leech or the bad mother Sean portrayed her as being, Greco said. In trying to assassinate her character, Sean had revealed just how self-centered he was. Joy had told people over and over again that she would stay for her children's sakes.

"She stuck it out," he said. "As bad as things got, she was telling her friends she was not going to abandon them. She gave up a lot to support the family, all of her inheritance. She was a proud, hard-working, decent parent who was young and challenged."

In one fell swoop, Greco was tearing down the support beams of Sean's claims that he had been the poor victim of a rampaging woman who was draining the family finances and demanding to be supported as she abandoned her children and pursued a beauty education in Hollywood. Instead, Sean, a "man with murder on his mind," had planned to kill her for exactly the opposite reason: she was going to fight him for custody of the children, something the prideful polygamist leader in him could not suffer.

"He had that conversation with Leif Wright," he said. "Mr. Wright told you about it. He said 'we were talking, it was an academic discussion. I didn't think much of it at the time.' In fact, it didn't even really register until later on, when he assumed everybody must know. You might have that perception that police or the prosecutor are all-knowing. You heard the tape. He assumed that we knew. And now, knowing something about the facts, it does take on some significance. He talked to the defendant about how to commit the perfect murder, the way to do it, to hide the body, to obscure the identification of the person. An incredible coincidence, or is it the germ that tells you about something that is going on in the defendant's mind?"

And then he said the jury had to decide who was telling the truth: me or Sean.

"There aren't two right answers here," he said. "The defendant on the stand looked at all of you and said, 'I never had that conversation.' Leif Wright had already testified, and he was brought in ostensibly to say the defendant had told him to lie—a minor point, and from the defendant's perspective, he got off scot free: 'They don't know about the conversation.' And you know what? He was right. He could get up here and lie and tell you 'I didn't know anything about it.' Knowing Mr. Wright came from Oklahoma, we would have to fly him all the way back. Are they really going to do that just to prove a small little point that the defendant lied? Yes."

He apparently had decided at that point that he had to deal with how Albert Arena had tried to sully my testimony.

"You heard from Mr. Wright, a colorful character, to say the least," he said. "But he gains a certain amount of credibility when he comes up to this stand and we challenge him, 'Have you used drugs?' He said, 'Yeah, I have.' Have you ever fought? 'Yeah. I was a jerk. There was a time.' What do you think of the defendant? 'I still consider him a friend.' What is his axe to grind? It was suggested he is playing to the cameras. What did he do? You got to see him when that was pointed out, when Mr. Arena made this big gesture, his response was to look over and say, 'I didn't know what that was.'

"Two weeks before that day, the defendant and Leif Wright had a conversation. 'She is lazy and messy'—not 'she is a drug user,' not 'she is beating the kids' or anything else. 'She is lazy. I'm going to get rid of her.'"

Blogs, Greco said, that the defense had introduced corroborated my story, not Sean's. Sean, he said, had been insinuating throughout the trial that he was wanting Joy to leave because he was concerned that she might be doing drugs.

"There has been suggestion throughout this case that somehow she is this drug user and this made the defendant mad and upset him and as a father, as a parent, he was putting his foot down," Greco told the jury. "But if you read the blog, about marijuana and the use of it, [Sean's] response was 'I agree with Leif. You should hold onto it and use it for the next creative meeting.'"

That blog, from a couple of days before Sean killed Joy, showed him endorsing the use of marijuana, not condemning it or putting his foot down about drug use, Greco said.

"He is not saying that drug use is wrong," he said. "He is a chameleon. He's trying to blend in. That undermines his position that he is the president of DARE, that he is the man standing there against his immoral wife with drugs. Not at all true.

"Two weeks before she disappears, he tells Leif Wright, 'I'm going to get rid of her, she is lazy.' Again, two weeks, at the same time, he tells Victoria Mack, 'She has two weeks to shape up or ship out.' and he tells her he enjoys those forensics shows. I mean, it just doesn't get much better than that in terms of a man who is thinking about it. When you talk about premeditation and deliberation, it means if you are talking about getting away with something, that's a pretty good marker that you understand the consequences of what you are doing."

Greco's closing statements were shaping up to be a major attack. Kick by kick, he was tearing down every shred of Sean's credibility, every plank on which he had based his story of the killing being a spur-of-the-moment act of self-defense and the cover-up being a shock reaction to the death.

"Very close friends end up weaving their way into Joy's life and meet the defendant and he comments, 'She will never be allowed to leave with the children," he continued. "He is saying this as a man who is supremely confident that he is the man. The children are, in essence, the physical manifestations of his success as a polygamist. These are his trophies. 'She will never be allowed to leave with them.' This is a man who is all about control, all about power."

Sean, he said, had begun marketing the idea before the murder that Joy might just pick up her bags and leave, telling multiple friends just that.

"Again, a man who feels he is smarter than all of us," he said.

But the Rubicon was crossed, so to speak, when Sean made that fateful shopping trip on September 13. It was then that Joy's fate was sealed, that she was dead already, though she wouldn't actually be killed for six more days.

Pointing to the time stamps on the two receipts, Greco said that Sean, who checked out at the hardware store at 10:41 A.M., had to take the "murder kit" to his car, unload it all, leave the parking lot and drive through dense Saturday San Diego traffic to the big box store, three miles away. Assuming there was no traffic and he made it in four minutes, Greco said, Sean picked out seventeen items at that store in thirty-two minutes.

"He has got to be flying," he said. "What does this mean? He has a list. The guy knew what he was doing. He has a list. And let's make no mistake about it, there are no home-improvement projects. They are not painting; they are not going to make painting their Saturday project like he testified to. You heard from [his first wife], right? 'Why would we paint? It is a rental. Why would we paint on the inside?' What is he doing? The perfect murder. He had a gardener. This is a man who's so lazy that he would rather spend his time in front of a computer and pay someone else to mow his lawn because he doesn't want to do it himself. Yet he decides for the incredible task of pulling out a tree stump, that's something he wants to do himself?

"Please, please. That's absurd," Greco continued. "Joy wasn't with him. In the calculating cunning of someone who is a manipulative, super-intelligent liar, sitting on this stand, an act of genius, a really gutsy liar, to sit here and tell you it was Joy who picked out the weapon that ended up killing her. So the one item he had admitted to using in this whole cover-up never even occurred to him to purchase."

His first wife never saw the butcher knife or the cutting board, he said. Sean's testimony had made it sound like it was a spur-of-the-moment shopping decision, like they were cruising the aisles and Joy said, "Oh, let's get this."

"He had a list," Greco repeated. "It was a flat-out lie, a gutsy move by the defendant. Let's go and look at all of the items he purchased: a hacksaw, a shovel, a pickaxe, an ax, a chisel, a sledgehammer, the chain, locks and rope...then the knife, the butcher block, the duct tape. Duct tape again for painting? You would use masking tape. He has to come up with some explanation, but please. Drop cloth, five buckets, gloves, stepladder and cooler. He is a man of contingencies, ready for anything."

Then, he said, Sean rented the SUV and took Joy to Coronado Island, where he wined and dined her at that super-expensive restaurant.

"Why would anybody who's not earning much money, who has to rely on her inheritance and on his other wife working, who can't make ends meet, why spend this much money?...There is only one reason, and it is not so they can patch things up. It is to get her defenses down, to get her guard down. It is easy to spend two hundred and twenty-three dollars when you know you will not have to spend anything more. That's what this is. This is the last supper. It worked. It worked. She is happy. She knows there are problems, but you have to remember, this is the same person who is preparing his surprise birthday party. She is planning his surprise birthday party and trying to get his friend of twenty years to come out."

When his first wife phoned Joy after Sean and Joy had arrived back at the Kensington house after dinner, according to Sean, the argument was already in full swing. But, Greco said, Joy's conversation revealed nothing of the sort.

"How is she? 'I'm about to leave? We are having problems?' None of that. Why isn't she talking about it? Because it never happened. This is truly to get her defenses down. It's easy to spend that amount of money when you know that's it. I mean, he just spent $400 on tools; must be a pretty important project for a guy that doesn't want to mow his own lawn."

Sean, he said, also didn't get any scrapes or cuts during the purported struggle with Joy in the bedroom.

"This is a man with no defensive wounds, who struggled for a knife back and forth twelve times. Then we heard from Pinocchio on the stand, 'Well, if the jurors want to look at my hands now, I have scars.' Well, that's very helpful; you also have quite a story two and a half years later. We are not interested in what your scars are today. Where are your scabs [in the photos taken 30 days after Joy's death]? It didn't happen."

Sean didn't struggle with Joy for the knife, Greco said. Instead, he stabbed Joy at least twelve times—more, probably, but because Joy's body was decomposed by the time it was discovered, only the bones could speak, not soft tissue—and twelve stab wounds are not self-defense.

"What do we know about the stab wounds? Thank you, Dr. Fulginiti. Thank you, Maricopa Sheriff's Department. Thank you, Detectives McVey and Powers. Thank you for not giving up on Joy Risker. She wasn't just a bag of bones; she was a person. And they cared enough to take that case and make it their own and do the work and figure it out so we would have for you what happened.

"It was a knife plunged so hard into her chest that it went right through the bone," he said. "It severed it straight across. Let me tell you, you can't be playing beach blanket bingo, struggling back and forth, dancing. No. She is on the ground. That cluster on the chest, that's to finish her off. The first part, she wakes up, she is moving. He doesn't have complete control over her. That last cluster, she is down on the ground face-up and he has something to keep her up against. To get through the bone.

"We are talking about two huge stab wounds that are going all the way through bone. Look at where they are: right over the aorta. This is the kill zone.

"The reality is, this is an execution. He is finishing his job with these blows. These wounds are not something you could do on the bed on your knees. That's not how it happened."

Sean's entire claim of self-defense wasn't just put to rest by the evidence that he lied about how the stabbing occurred, Greco said. The cover-up also gave a good indication that he was lying.

"She didn't come at him with the knife," he said. "This is a man who is super-intelligent, by his own words. We all know if somebody's coming at you with a knife, you have the right to defend yourself. That's common sense. That is something that a third grader understands. It is universal. Despite what he says, that the death was instantaneous, we heard evidence that even with this number of blows, because of the bleeding, Joy had a horrible, horrible fifteen minutes, at least. None of us want to think about her bleeding out, fifteen minutes where she could have been taken to [a hospital] a mile and a half away. Why not? Because that wasn't the plan. There was one goal, that's it. And it was to kill her."

Seven of the stab wounds went through Joy's bones, Greco said, which isn't possible if there was the struggle that Sean had described. The knife was being repeatedly and violently plunged into her chest, not see-sawing back and forth during a struggle.

Sean, he said, got rid of all the implements he used to kill, dismember and hide Joy. The knife? Gone. The cutting board? Never found. The towels he said he used? His first wife never reported any missing. No pools of blood. Even luminol failed to show that a lot of blood had been shed in the house. The duct tape? Maricopa County officials discovered some underneath Joy's body. The sledgehammer? Contrary to Sean's testimony, Greco said, the indentations in Joy's face showed that he had pounded her face with the sledgehammer, not a lava rock.

"He used it like a barbarian against a piece of cement," Greco said. "All part of the plan."

Being prepared, Greco continued, meant that Sean was thinking about contingencies. "'What if I need to get rid of her in water? What if I'm going to cut her up and spread her all over? What if I'm going to bury her?' Get a shovel. Get a pickaxe. It doesn't mean he is going to use everything. He is Mr. Contingency."

And everything Sean did from that point forward, according to Greco, was a lie intended to preserve his reputation as the head of his family—a man who was the shepherd of his children and the one obedient wife who remained, not the irresponsible, spendthrift drug addict who had fled her responsibilities under God and her husband.

"This was a man willing to use his kids, play on family relationships, play on an image, a reputation as a God-fearing, loving man, to manipulate people," Greco continued.

Then Greco discussed the twenty-four pages of transcribed e-mails. "You can read all of the stuff back and forth to Joy. The important thing here is to realize that everything in here is a lie. He is sitting on the stand—'Yeah, I lied about that.' He goes to a family law attorney and tells him she has abandoned him and asks for child support. Why? Because it makes the lie more convincing."

"He conned everybody; the man is unbelievable. There is nobody he can't dupe, so it shouldn't be a surprise to any of you that he is the type of person who has the personality that believes he can get on the stand and he can fool you. He can sit here, sit in this chair, raise his hand, cry and come up with a story and [assume that] you will believe him because you are stupid, because you are not like him. You don't have a 145 IQ."

The pressure, Greco said, began to build on Sean after he killed Joy. First, Joy's friends kept asking questions, kept demanding answers, kept e-mailing "Joy" when her responses didn't satisfy their curiosity and concerns. Then the police kept digging even though they believed Sean's story, believed that the tears he cried when they interviewed him were real, believed that he was distraught over the sudden departure of his favorite wife. Then the pressure from Victoria Mack, who had told Sean he needed to come clean with his boss about having another wife at home or she would do it for him, and finally, Sean's first wife, who freaked out when the police visited her at her work and who, when she got home early that day, screamed at Sean to turn himself in.

"Right after that confrontation, he goes to the police," Greco said. "He didn't make this choice. It was forced on him by the moral compass of the family. And when he goes to the police, he is comfortable leaving Joy in the wilderness. Charles Risker and their family will have no one to bury. That's who Sean Goff is."

That was the lynchpin of Sean's scheme, Greco said. It was his trump card, his ace in the hole. He was under the mistaken impression that a prosecutor wouldn't prosecute if they couldn't find a body.

"He is under the misimpression that no body, no crime," Greco said. "That's not what happens. It took a long time to get the body, during which he never mentioned a knife or self-defense. No mention of drugs. No mention of anything. All of that is something he concocted for you on the stand."

Joy, he said, was nothing more than meat to Sean—meat to be butchered.

"Imagine this case without a body," he said. "I would be up here arguing to you that she is dead but in the back of your mind you would be thinking, 'What if she walks through that door?'"

Sean, he said, wanted to leave the case without a body, because without a body, no one would be able to show that he had stabbed her at least a dozen times, "...because even a genius, someone with a 145 IQ, can't explain twelve stab wounds."

Greco had called Sean "Pinocchio" several times during his closing statement, at one point saying his nose should be somewhere in the middle of the Pacific Ocean. Toward the end, he seemed to reconsider that characterization.

"Pinocchio is also cute and somewhat redeeming," he said. "Do not misunderstand me. I do not think there is anything redeeming about this man. He is a liar. He is a murderer. He has no compassion. Make no mistake. There is nothing funny about him."

Finally, Greco attacked what he foresaw as a desperate tactic by Sean's lawyer: an attempt to get the jury to convict him but reduce the charge to second-degree murder at worst, manslaughter at best. Albert Arena's idea, he said, was to try to get a lesser charge ultimately for a lesser sentence.

"This is a homicide. It is clear. You heard it from the judge, but I want to walk you through what murder is."

Manslaughter is when someone dies through the negligent or unintentional actions of another, he said. Second-degree murder is a spur-of-the-moment homicide with malice aforethought—even an instant beforehand. But first-degree murder, Greco said, is when someone plans a murder for a while and then executes that plan.

"You have a very easy task in front of you," he told the jury. "If she attacked him with a knife, he is not guilty of second-degree murder. He is not guilty of voluntary man-slaughter. If you believe him, he is not guilty. If you think he is a truth teller, if you believe that and disregard all the physical evidence, all the people who say he is lying, if you believe that to be true, then your verdict is clear. But if you find his testimony uncorroborated, unreasonable and in fact, the People's case proves it beyond a reasonable doubt, there is only one verdict and that is first-degree murder."

Sean, he said with a stern look on his face, clearly planned his crime for a long time beforehand.

"What is the evidence we have of premeditation?" he asked. "The conversation with Leif, a perfect murder. Two weeks before, 'I am going to get rid of Joy.' The conversation with Victoria Mack, 'she has to shape up or ship out.' And 'I love those *Forensics Files*, it's hard to get away with any-thing.' The murder kit. Getting the [SUV]. And his cover-up. He is thinking so far ahead, he is actually manipulating a lot of people on a lot of different levels. Fairly sophisticated. You have to give him credit."

For the coup de gras, Greco recalled Sean's inability to keep his story straight, whether he had shown Joy the photo or told her about it and then she had snapped, or whether she had snapped before she heard about it or saw it.

"He is a liar," Greco said. "This isn't somebody else calling him a liar; it is him. Nobody put those words in his mouth. Two days later, he can't remember his own story and he has told us why, because it wasn't rooted in truth. It's hard to remember lies. The purpose of having him tell everything all over again was because all of it was a lie."

Greco concluded that Sean "...has to look at you and conceive that you all believe what he tells you. 'Yes, I am a liar. Yes, I have lied to everybody. But now I'm telling you the truth.'"

Albert Arena, brilliant lawyer that he was, had just watched a fly ball cruise over the fence, just past his glove. Like a master illusionist, his only tactic, it seemed, was to misdirect the jury's attention away from the details of the case and to the overarching law that he hoped would get his client a lesser sentence—or perhaps even an acquittal.

"What the criminal defense attorney does is protect the constitution," Arena began in his closing statement. "He prohibits a government agency from walking into a room and saying 'my theory is this man murdered someone, and based on that theory, he should go to jail.'"

He bemoaned how, in his judgment, modern society was prejudiced against defense attorneys because of the overwhelming public perception that prosecutors were the upholders of justice and liberty.

"I wasn't there the night of September 19, 2003," he continued. "And guess what? Mr. Greco wasn't there either. Everything Mr. Greco has talked to you about is his theory of the case, what he thinks the evidence shows. And it is only that—a theory for your consideration."

Reasonable doubt, he said, was far more encompassing than most people assumed.

"If you are at a barbecue three or four months later and someone is talking to you about the case, you can't think to yourself, 'But what if? What if this was really what happened?'" he said. "Because if you are thinking that, you have reasonable doubt."

This case, he said, was more difficult because of the gruesome acts Sean had admitted to performing on Joy after he killed her.

"I'm equally as bothered by it as anyone," he said. "It was a poor decision by Mr. Goff, a decision he has to live with the rest of his life—a decision he has paid for with time."

But the trial, he said, wasn't about the horrific things Sean did to Joy's corpse, it was about whether Joy attacked Sean and he defended himself.

"You have to be convinced beyond reasonable doubt that it was not possible for Joy Risker to have introduced that knife into the bedroom."

The sensationalism of the case—the polygamy, the cover-up, the mutilation of Joy's body—was a mitigating factor that could sway a jury to ignore the actual evidence, he said, and convict a man simply because the jury didn't like him personally. The jury's responsibility was to make sure they weren't swayed in that way.

"Because if you are, I'm wasting my time talking to you," he said. "Mr. Greco put up quite a display in his statement; quite impressive. But I thought about what Solomon once said: 'any theory is good until it is cross-examined.'"

Solomon was never actually recorded as having said that, but Arena was on a roll. He had sat silently through the prosecution's case, because he wanted to wait for them to introduce their theory so he could pick it apart.

"The people's case relied, in part, on the 'murder kit,'" he said. "Okay, a shovel, the pickaxe, the cooler, the chains, the chisel, among other things. And I chose to wait. What did I learn through examination? That none of those things had anything to do with this case."

Greco, he said, had provided a compelling case that the 145-IQ genius had prepared for any contingency, with a rope and a chain for a possible plan to submerge Joy in water, or the two extra gas cans to possibly burn her body.

"Perhaps it is best that Mr. Goff didn't take the car and get the oil changed, because perhaps the prosecution would have said that he wanted the engine to be running smoothly so he could run Joy Risker over," he said. "Anyone can draft a manuscript for murder, and that's what Mr. Greco has provided for you—a manuscript. It is very, very strong and compelling. And if that's all you had to consider, there would be no reason for you not to come back with a murder conviction."

But the jury would have to consider Joy's part in this drama, he said. It was Joy, he said, who was selfishly draining on the family. Joy was the one who wouldn't compromise on beauty school. Joy was the one who had come at Sean with the knife. Joy was the problem here. She was dead as a result of her own actions, not as the result of some plan by Sean.

"Let's talk about the deceptions of Joy Risker," he said. "This isn't easy; she is the decedent in this case. She never told her uncle about the relationship she had with Mr. Goff. That is deception. She never told Mr. Goff about her relationship with her ex-boyfriend. That is deception. She never told her ex-boyfriend about her relationship with Mr. Goff. That was a deception. She never told him she had two children. That was a deception."

Such deceptions, he said, spoke to the character of Joy.

"If the prosecution wants you to look at the character of an individual and the propensity for deception as part of the overall proof that they are capable of attacking someone with a knife, I ask you to look at the deceptions of Joy Risker."

It was, possibly, the wrong tactic to take for a jury that was clearly enamored of the Joy they had heard the witnesses describe, but Arena was between a rock and a hard place. The prosecution's case was devastating and Sean's own testimony had made it worse. And Greco's closing argument had been a virtuoso performance. Arena was trying to dig out of a very deep hole.

"As Mr. Goff told you, she came in and swung the knife toward him," Arena continued. "Who is to say beyond a reasonable doubt that couldn't have happened?"

If there are two reasonable explanations for a piece of evidence, he told the jury, you must believe the interpretation that supports the defendant, according to the law.

Arena continued, "Then we have the controlling factor, that Mr. Goff somehow was this absolutely controlling individual. I listened to the testimony. Joy Risker didn't seem like she was chained to the kitchen sink. She didn't appear to be locked in the closet at night, only allowed out when Mr. Goff said she could go out. She was the one who had all of the friends. Mr. Goff didn't have any friends come over. Was that controlling?"

Arena then discussed the night of the stabbing. Sean had taken Joy out to dinner. "When you talk about what is reasonable and logical in support of this cold, calculated, alleged murder, you have to ask yourself why. Why would Mr. Goff take Joy to such an expensive restaurant if he had plans of killing her? Mr. Greco tells you it is a last supper. Isn't it more logical to conclude that, along with the SUV, it was an attempt to show Joy Risker that she could have a good life, to show her that it was important to keep the family together, that she didn't have to leave?

"And I have heard evidence from Joy's friends that she was unhappy, that she wanted a different life, that she got married too young, she had children too young, she really wanted to get this education so she could move on. The bottom line is, she wanted to backpack in Europe, she wanted to travel, she wanted to dance on the table tops. Does that make her a bad person? No, it doesn't. But those were her dreams. She was hoping to get that from Mr. Goff. It just wasn't happening."

Arena then set the scene in the bedroom that fatal night: "She came in and swung, she swung the knife toward him. I heard no evidence to the contrary.

"And then the struggle. The prosecution would have you believe that he was taking this knife and just plunging it inside her over and over again. Remember, it is just a theory. They weren't there.

"At some point, the knife turns during the struggling back and forth. Remember, she was five foot eight, about 140 pounds and robust, athletic. She was no lightweight. She was young and she had strength.

"And then what happens?" asked Arena. "Well, she is dead. This is where Mr. Goff's good judgment goes south. He later tells Officer McEwen, 'I wish I would have called right then.' Mr. Goff, I wish you would have called, but you made a different decision. You panicked.

"But the cover-up doesn't change the fact that she came at him. No evidence to the contrary. That's what we have.

"Mr. Goff then takes the body ultimately to Arizona, where he places her," he said. "Doesn't bury the body, but rather he places the body on the ground and builds the rocks around it, and builds...what do you call it?"

"Cairn," Sean chimed in.

"A cairn; builds a monument. Is that the act of a cold, calculated murderer? It just doesn't make sense that he would do it that way."

Arena then proceeded to attack Greco's contention that the stabbing was premeditated.

"I told you that anyone could write a manuscript for murder. If there was a death in someone's family, you could pick out how the sixteen-year-old said to her parents, because they wouldn't let her hang out at a tattoo parlor, 'I wish you were dead.'"

"Mr. Goff is entitled to his constitutional rights. When he did that interview with the police, he made it very clear that he was willing to talk about certain things and not about others. That is everyone's right. I'm sorry to say that Mr. Greco mocks that right when he puts before you that is indicative of his guilt. Let me tell you something—if we exercise our constitutional rights and by doing so it means we are guilty, then we are finished. Our American way of life is over."

Arena's voice rose meaningfully. "This is a difficult case. Homicide always is.

"Nobody wins in these kind of cases," he said. "It is tragic, the loss of that young woman, but equally as tragic is the loss of our form of justice. If you are merely swayed by what happened postmortem, if you are swayed by the fact he chose to live a polygamous lifestyle in a free nation, if you are swayed by that, then the tragedy continues."

Sean, he said, had the right to defend himself when Joy came at him with the knife.

"He had the right to stab her."

No matter what, he said, the burden of proof beyond a reasonable doubt for first-degree murder had not been satisfied.

"Mr. Greco will be attacking most of these statements that I have had to say to you," he said. "When you attack a defense attorney so much, you are somewhat worried about the state of the evidence you are presenting."

Arena took a step forward, paused and then slowly, clearly, lingered over his next words: "This is a manuscript for murder. It makes for a good book but this is real life and I'm asking you to consider that. Mr. Goff deserves that consideration from you. He deserves your review of all of the evidence."

Arena sat down and Greco had the opportunity to give his final rebuttal.

"At the very beginning, you were all asked, 'Can you spot someone blowing smoke? Are you a good judge of credibility?'" he began. "Ultimately, to find the defendant not guilty, it is all predicated on one thing and one thing alone: his word. Because all the physical evidence in this case points in another direction. The only evidence you have that he was entitled to self-defense is his word. That's it. Did the witness admit to being untruthful? What is the witness's character for truthfulness?

"If you decide that a witness deliberately lied about something significant, you should consider not believing anything that witness says. You don't need the law to tell you this; it makes a lot of sense because ultimately somebody who lies about something important is going to lie about a lot of things."

Sean, he said, was a calculating manipulator who had invented the self-defense story for the trial.

"Did he ever tell anybody about this self-defense?" he asked. "Not the police, his friends or family. The reason is, that's not the way it happened."

There was one piece of evidence that the defense hadn't tried to skirt, he said, and that was the alleged meat cleaver that Sean had said he used to remove Joy's fingertips.

"They didn't have a meat cleaver," he said. "It was a big, calculated lie that he made on the chance that [his first wife] wouldn't be brought back. He is playing the odds there. And second, what are the odds she would be as clear as she was: I never saw one, it wouldn't be kept in that left drawer. Again, calculated liar. There is a very good reason he is distancing himself from that knife—that he didn't use it to cut off the fingers—that he distances himself from the cutting board and the drop cloth and the duct tape."

Sean didn't want to be associated with those items because if he had used them in the cover-up, they would have supported the prosecution's contention that he had created a murder kit.

"Let me stay on the defendant's lies, because even during his testimony, initially we didn't hear anything about this photograph," he said about the alleged photo of the bruises Joy had inflicted on her son. "We sat through an hour of defense closing and we didn't hear about it. Why? Because the defendant changed his testimony in the span of two days. Why? Liar, liar."

Greco noted that, at first, Sean testified that he had told Joy about the photo and said, 'That is all there is to it," and that's why Joy had snapped. Two days later, Greco said, Sean changed the story to Joy having not seen nor heard about the photo when she attacked him.

"Lies are tricky," Greco said. "If you are patient and if you ask every question, very detailed, people slip up."

But the worst lies, he said, were the character assassinations about the victim in the case, Joy.

"There have been insinuations about drugs. There have been insinuations about child abuse," he said. "Which Sean Goff do we believe?"

The blood, also, was troublesome for Sean's case, because there was none of his blood.

"There isn't a struggle in the sense that he is bleeding and his blood is anywhere," Greco stated quietly but definitively. "They tested thirteen [blood samples]; all hers, none of his.

"When defense counsel says the bruises on Joy's face were consistent with a fist fight—you have pictures of what she looked like. There are no bruises. Her face was smashed in. That is consistent with somebody using a sledgehammer. This isn't a fist fight; this is a mauling."

The defense, Greco said, was loose with its definition of "reasonable doubt."

"You have to believe that it is not only reasonable, but it is credible," he said. "The law tells you you should consider consciousness of guilt if they make false statements. If the defendant made false or misleading statements regarding the charged crime, knowing the statement is false or tending to mislead, that conduct may show he was aware of his guilt.

"When counsel said 'Is it possible that what the defendant said is true?', that is not the standard you apply. The standard you apply is proof that leaves you with an abiding conviction that the charge is true. He did it. The evidence need not eliminate all possible doubt, because everything in life is open to some possible or imaginary doubt."

There was no evidence given that Joy was violent, Greco said. There was no evidence that she had a motive to attack Sean.

"The reasonable inference is she was a loving parent who would not leave without her kids," he continued. "The defendant had his contingency plans. She is either dead or they are going to have it out. She is leaving, she is keeping the kids and he is like, 'No that's not going to happen,' and he finishes her."

Greco had saved the most dramatic and compelling part of his closing argument for the end:

"Murder cases are different. Because we don't have our best witness, Joy Risker. We don't have Joy to come in and talk to you.

"If somehow someone could perform a miracle and we could have Joy walk through those doors and talk to you all for a couple of minutes and we could ask her, 'Joy, what happened to you?' she would say, 'I have already told you. I have told you with my blood in the house. I have told you with my sternum that has stab wounds on it. I have told you with my ribs. And I have told you that this crime is so unspeakable with my hands and my fingers missing and with my jaw cut out and with my skull that was bashed in.'

"Hear her. Hear her."

Less than two hours later, the jury returned.

The judge announced, "Good afternoon, ladies and gentlemen. We are back in session in the case of *People v. Sean Barclay Goff*. All parties are present. I'm advised the jury has reached a verdict in this case."

The murmurs in the courtroom ceased. It was pin-drop quiet.

He nodded toward the jury, "Who's the foreperson? Juror Number Five, could you hand the verdict forms to the bailiff, please?"

The bailiff boomed in a sonorous voice: "In the Superior Court of the State of California in and for the County of San Diego, people of the State of California, plaintiff, versus Sean Barclay Goff, defendant, we, the jury in the above entitled case, find the defendant guilty of the crime of murder, in violation of penal code section 187 (A) as charged in count one of the amended information, and fix the degree thereof as murder in the first degree. [His] victim: Joy Risker.

"We further find that in the commission of the above offense, the said defendant did personally use a deadly weapon, to wit: a knife, within the meaning of penal code section 12022 (B) (1). Dated July 27, 2006. Foreperson, Juror Number Five."

The judged asked, "Does either side wish to poll the jury?"

Greco shook his head, "No, your honor."

But Arena responded, "Yes, your honor."

The judge turned to the clerk. "Madame Clerk, would you please poll the jury?"

The clerk nodded and said, "Ladies and gentlemen of the jury, as I call your juror number, please answer yes or no to the following question: Was that and is that your verdict as read?"

Methodically, each juror responded with a yes.

The clerk then stated, "Twelve affirmative responses, your honor."

The judge nodded, "Thank you. Please record the verdict."

The clerk said, "So recorded."

The judge then questioned the prosecutor and defense attorney: "Counsel, do you waive the reading of the verdict as recorded?"

"Yes, your honor," Arena stated. Greco also said, "Yes."

The judge nodded. "Thank you. As to further items of business in this case, ladies and gentlemen of the jury, the final instructions on discharge of the jury is as follows. This is CalCrim Instruction 3950. You have now completed your jury service in this case. On behalf of the judges in the Superior Court, County of San Diego, State of California, please accept my thanks for your time and effort.

"Now that the case is over, you may choose whether or not to discuss the case and your deliberations with anyone. I remind you, under California law, you must wait at least ninety days before negotiating or agreeing to accept any payment for information about the case.

"Let me tell you some rules the law places in effect for your convenience and your protection. The lawyers in the case, the defendant, Mr. Goff, or their representatives may now talk to you about the case, including deliberation or your verdict. Those discussions must occur at a reasonable time and place with your consent.

"Please immediately report to the court any unreasonable contact made by the lawyers in this case, their representatives or by the defendant. A lawyer, representative or defendant who violates these rules violates a court order and may be subject to sanctions.

"I hereby order that the court record of personal juror identifying information, including names, addresses and telephone numbers be sealed until further order of this court. If, in the future, the court is asked to decide whether this information will be released, notice will be sent to any juror whose information is involved. You may oppose the release of this information and ask that any hearing subject to the release motion be closed to the public. The court will decide whether and under what conditions the information may be disclosed.

"At this time, the defendant is remanded to the custody of the sheriff of San Diego without bail pending sentencing." The judge went on, "Mr. Goff, sir, you have a right to be sentenced on a statutory date. For the convenience of court and counsel, do you agree to waive time so you can be sentenced on Friday, September 15, 9:00 A.M., this department?"

Sean looked away. "Yes."

The judge then announced, "Court accepts the time waiver. Thank you for that.

"Ladies and gentlemen of the jury, you have an opportunity to leave at this point in time. If you wish to talk to the attorneys, you may do so. That's entirely up to you. They will be out in the hallway. Also, you may talk to any representatives of the news media if you choose to do so. There is no obligation on your part to talk to anyone. It is frequently helpful for the attorneys to talk to jurors after a decision has been reached in a case. Many times, the attorneys like to have feedback as to their presentation of the case to the jury.

"Again, there is absolutely no obligation on your part to talk to any members of the news media or to talk to any of the attorneys or the defendant or the people's representatives. Any questions?"

The jurors sat still; not one raised a hand.

The judge nodded. "Thank you very much for your service. You are now discharged. We will report to the jury commissioner that you have completed your service in this department. And please be sure to take your personal property with you. Have a good day. Thank you."

The jury filed out of the room.

The judge turned to Arena. "Anything further on behalf of your client, Mr. Goff?"

Arena replied, "Just the official sentencing date. I believe we haven't done that yet."

The judge nodded, "Friday, September 15, 9:00."

"Thank you," Arena said.

"Mr. Greco, anything further?"

Greco shook his head, "No, your honor."

The judge addressed the courtroom, "Court is adjourned. Have a good day."

And so, on July 27, 2006, almost three years after he killed Joy Risker, Sean Goff was found guilty of murdering the young mother of two of his children, hacking up her body, dumping it in the Arizona desert and then lying about it for weeks.

No sooner was Sean convicted of the brutal murder and dismemberment of his junior wife than he went about the business of getting on with his life. First order: he regrew his goatee, peppered with gray, the one that he had shaved off for the trial. The absence of the goatee had significantly affected his appearance, making him seem heavier and pastier than he had ever looked.

A couple of months later, on September 15, 2006, three years minus four days after the last day Joy Risker ever viewed the cloudless San Diego sky, the last day she breathed the ocean air, the last day she got stuck in traffic on the 405, Sean received his sentence for depriving her of all those things.

But if Joy's loved ones thought Sean might finally cry real tears, might beg for mercy or lose control, they were wrong. Sean, even in defeat, still had control.

"It is said that confession is good for the soul," Sean said before the judge sentenced him. "The trial gave me an opportunity to confess a great many personal flaws and for this I am very appreciative."

Was he seriously using his sentencing to thank the court for letting him get his flaws out in the open? It seemed that was exactly what he was doing. Even in expressing contrition, Sean could not let the opportunity to promote his Christianity slip away from him. But he went even farther, claiming to be a doting father, even after he had been convicted of killing the mother of his children:

"I also express my sorrow...to my sons, who are without me," he said. "I make public apology and record of my deep and abiding love and affection that far surpasses that for my own life."

It was complete bullshit, of course. If his fatherly love truly surpassed his love for his own life, Sean would have found a way to make it work with the boys' mother instead of murdering her and depriving them of her. But he was on stage, and that meant he had one more opportunity to make himself into the hero of the story—one last attempt to pull martyrdom for himself out of the case of the woman he martyred.

"I mourn the loss of Joy for myself and our children," he continued, his speech falling on incredulous ears throughout the room. "I pray some day they understand my plight and my eternal love for them."

His plight? He wanted his children to understand *his plight*? The man who was about to find out how messy the pig sty he had landed himself in really was didn't see the need to apologize to his sons for killing their mother but instead wanted them to understand how hard *he* had it. And then, he had to take the opportunity to profess that, even as the judge was about to pronounce sentence on him for his horrific crime, a higher court had already absolved him:

"Sadly, I cannot apologize to Joy today," he said, the corners of his mouth bordering on a smile. "But I know in my heart that one day I will."

When I heard Sean speaking in such grandiose terms I realized his religious view of himself was completely out of touch with reality. Even if he believed that God had already forgiven him for murdering Joy, a room full of Joy's loved ones who were there to find some kind of closure, some kind of justice for a crime that made no sense was not the place to be grandstanding and proclaiming his innocence before God. A man, I thought, would suck it up and take his lumps from the people in the room who wanted nothing more than to express their hatred for him, their pain at his crime and their disbelief in his ability to calmly sit there while Joy was gone by his hand.

But Sean wouldn't even afford them that one small kindness, because he had too much to say about his own religion, the forgiveness of which he was sure—and unbelievably, how the entire experience had served to teach him a valuable lesson about his place in God's kingdom:

"I turned myself in because that's what God required of me," he said. Not, of course, because it felt like the authorities were getting too close. There was also no mention of the fact that his first wife had all but commanded him to turn himself in. No, it was because God, conveniently at the same time that the cops were about to start banging on Sean's door, decided it was time for Sean to stop lying and tell the police he had killed Joy—and then start stonewalling so Joy's remains wouldn't be found and mess up his planned defense. "Though I did not win my trial, through my obedience, I won a much greater victory, one with eternal implications."

Here, where he should be expressing his sorrow and apology, Sean again had found a way to portray himself as a righteous man, a misunderstood Christian who was fighting the good fight for Christ. It was his obedience, he contended, that had won the day, his faithful Christianity that had given him an eternal victory, forgiveness by God, even as the judge prepared to lower the boom of mankind's punishment. It was sickening to hear.

"My sufferings will continue to make me a better Christian," Sean continued, "and will continue to allow me to be an example to others of the saving grace of Jesus Christ and Jehovah our God. And I thank you for that opportunity."

It was a stunning and terrifying performance. Though he had said he was sorry, Sean expressed about as real a remorse as the tears he had cried on the stand. And he once again threw his religion, portrayed by him as holy and superior, into the faces of the people he had most wounded—those who loved and missed Joy. It was like a final stab wound, Sean refusing to relinquish control for one second of even Joy's memory. He would go to prison, but it was Joy who had put him through these *sufferings*, had thrust him into this *plight*.

Joy's father, Charles Risker, was outraged.

"Sean, you not only destroyed Joy's life," he said when he gave his statement. "You destroyed mine. You're a man who said he has his own kind of religion. What kind of religion was *that*?"

Risker, wearing a T-shirt with pictures of a smiling Joy plastered all over it, was working up to a fever pitch as he threw his vitriol at Sean, who was calmly sitting at a table, appearing to listen.

"Joy was my only child," he said. "She cannot be replaced. If you once loved her…why would you just desecrate her body in the way that you did? Barbaric! Monster!"

But the barbaric monster just sat there, emotionless, as the father of the woman he had brutally murdered let his emotions overflow.

"I hope you remember this," he said. "You deserve the death penalty. You deserve to die. I want them to give you the same consideration you gave Joy Risker, my daughter. I want…you deserve less than consideration. At the minimum, you should have life without parole."

And then a final parting shot.

"I hope you remember this for the rest of your life."

But Sean had long ago told me he had no respect for Charles Risker, who he felt had abandoned his daughter when she was just a baby. So he wasn't about to listen to the rantings of a man who claimed to love Joy while abandoning her. He was, after all, a man of God, and Charles Risker was just another deadbeat dad.

Then it was the judge's turn to speak, and he sentenced Sean to serve a term that shocked just about everyone who knew about the case: twenty-six years to life in prison. Not the death penalty, not life in prison. If Sean serves the minimum twenty-six years, he will be sixty-four years old when he gets out.

Chapter 21

THE AFTERMATH

The tragedy and glory of life is that it has this incessant way of moving on, of continuing, regardless of the pain and horror it left behind yesterday.

Joy's remains are long in the ground, mourned only by the friends she left behind. Her father, Charles Risker, died in 2011, still haunted by the loss of the daughter he had only just reconnected with after a long absence, following his nasty divorce from Joy's mother when she was little.

Joy's mother, thankfully, never lived to see her daughter murdered and sliced apart like a slab of meat. Joy had no siblings.

Sean's first wife divorced him before the trial and moved to the middle of America, where she has since remarried and continued to raise her son, who is almost an adult now, and keeps in contact with his father through letters to his prison cell in Chowchilla, California.

Joy's two children are being raised in the same area by one of Sean's brothers, who, thankfully, is Sean's polar opposite. Through many discussions with friends and relatives, it became clear that Joy's older son is aware of many of the details of the case, but the younger son is not.

The shock of my best friend murdering someone I knew and loved still simmers beneath the surface for me and, at the most inopportune times, it will pop back up in my consciousness. Invariably, the questions arise: *How could you not have known about him? What kind of cult were you in? Are you stupid? Are you crazy?* They're all questions I have asked myself.

Recalling those times for this book has been difficult and embarrassing. It's ugly to remember myself as the closedminded hypocrite I was during those times. It hurts me to remember being prejudiced against so many people: those of other religions, those of other lifestyles, those who wished to believe in no God at all—and that's exactly what Sean and his murder remind me of. I was wholeheartedly part of a worldview that was insular to the point of blindness. That period of my life reminds me of a child, plugging his ears, eyes slammed shut, running and screaming "La la la la la, I don't hear you" to everyone who disagreed with the things I believed at that time.

In 2003, partially because of Joy's murder and partially because it had been coming anyway, I started truly and thoroughly questioning everything that I believed. I had been pastoring a small church in my hometown since 2000—a job I had rejected several times until the congregation had finally prevailed upon me to take on the burden.

"Christianity's main problem is the same problem that infested its root: that most Christians are every bit as blind as the Pharisees of Jesus' day," I preached. "We suffer from the same smugness they did. We wrap ourselves in the same filthy cloak of false piety they did. We believe we're superior to everyone else in the area of religion simply because we believe in the right religion. Somehow—in our minds, anyway—we had the good grace to be born with the right stuff to believe the right way, bless God. But in our vanity, we ignore the fact that our corruption goes deeper than that of the Pharisees."

During that time, my congregation grew accustomed to hearing such sermons from me as I trudged one step at a time down the seldom-trodden road from fundamentalism to liberalism. While I was writing this book, I contacted dozens of people I used to know and my discussions with them were like cold splashes of water. Had I ever really been like that? Had I spoken that way? Had I used "Christianese" words and phrases peppered throughout every sentence?

Embarrassingly, I had. More damning, I had taken my natural smartass personality and applied it to religion and politics, leaving a wide path of destruction in my wake as I had moved blindly forward, not caring who I offended or hurt along the way.

Learning that my best friend—my spiritual mentor, the guy I had always respected as a good, giving, loving person, the man who had reached out to me and helped me along so many times—was a calculating, cold-blooded murderer was a shocking awakening to me.

As I had testified, all I really knew was that Sean had admitted killing Joy, and that later her body had been found in Arizona with the jaw removed. I was as shocked as everyone else when I learned the extent of the horrific things Sean had done. But I was more shocked than everyone else, because Sean had been more to me than he had to most other people.

In a life full of flippant comments and fights, I had made precious few true friends, and those I had made fell away from my circle as I had converted to the most judgmental and self-righteous religious person I knew. Only Sean stuck around. Even my family had become distant because of my offensive brand of religion.

As I began my journey out of that particular religious experience, it had seemed like Sean was coming along for the ride, relaxing his Midwestern morals on things such as drinking and listening to non-Christian music. But now, in jail, he was gone too, and I never expected him to be back. In that sense, Sean killed my best friend when he killed Joy. It wasn't that Joy was my best friend—she wasn't. I loved Joy, but it was a cursory kind of relationship. When she was gone, there wasn't a huge hole in my life, because we hadn't interacted that often.

But Sean left a big hole and that hole—like the proverbial black hole—has gravity. To this day, people act like they're joking when they look at me sideways and say things like, "Just what kind of guy must you be to have had a friend like that?"

I don't have an answer for them, even though I'm never sure if they're joking or really do want an answer. Surely, I think, it must be some kind of reflection on me as they suggest. Sean and I didn't just hang out. We were close. We laughed at the same things. We enjoyed the same things. For a long time, we were inseparable; when people saw one of us, they saw the other. What kind of person must I be to have been close to someone like Sean?

The answer is beyond my abilities of introspection. Could I ever be duped by a friend like that again? I'd love to think not. But who really knows? Who really knows what is going on in someone else's mind? In some ways, that fear affects me to this day in profound ways. Because of my business and the fact that I still play music and sing (mostly secular music these days), I have a lot of acquaintances. But I have very few actual friends. Could that be because I'm afraid of being duped again? I'm sure a psychologist would have a field day (and a fat bank account) trying to figure that out.

But for the most part, I have moved on. In the midst of the worst economy that America has seen since the Great Depression, I left the newspaper where I had worked for so many years and started an online competitor. My online newspaper quickly flourished and its readership overshadowed that of the local newspaper, which had been the only game in town since 1888.

In prison, Sean has thrown himself into a new kind of ministry—preaching the Gospel of Jesus Christ to the lost souls who have found themselves locked up with him.

I had written to Sean, letting him know I was writing this book—and even offering to let him read it before I submitted it for publication. Sean hadn't responded to me, but he had told his relatives, who told his in-laws, some of whom contacted me and expressed that I should just let the story die. But I had expected that he wouldn't respond.

Sean has reportedly disavowed polygamy, saying he made a mistake. But he has never admitted to murdering Joy Risker. He will readily admit he killed her, but when pressed, Sean still contends that it was all Joy's fault. Did Jesus teach him that lesson? It's anyone's guess.

Sean's confidence of God's direction in his life is foreign to me now, and it refreshes my wonder that I was ever involved in beliefs like that. I still believe in God. I still believe in a supernatural creator, but, like so many of the characters in the Bible, my understanding of faith is that it is defined by doubt, by skepticism.

Sean would certainly balk if he ever heard me preach, as I did in 2009, "Not one of us in this building is sure there is a God. Not one of us here is sure there is life after death. None of us knows any of those things, despite the preaching you hear in so many churches that you have to 'know that you know that you know,' for a simple reason: We don't know because none of us has ever been dead. We believe, but belief is the manifestation of hope, not assurance. I'm hopeful that there is a God. I'm hopeful that there is a life after this death and that in that life we are rewarded with paradise. But do I know that to be true? Absolutely not. And neither do you."

For Sean's beliefs, faith is the absence of doubt. For mine, faith is framed by the questions raised by doubt. When I'm wondering how it was that I could have been so close to someone who could do the things Sean did, I remind myself of that: those who claim to have such assurance are lying—to themselves, to others and to God. Anyone who doesn't admit the possibility of being wrong is a person who is capable of horrors unimaginable to those of us who are profoundly aware that some of what we believe is probably wrong.

Sean Goff's main failing wasn't rooted in the acts themselves; it was rooted far deeper, in his concept of faith that had been unshakeable since he had been six years old and allegedly had seen Jesus when he was eight. That faith told him that God spoke to people about the minutiae of their days, that he led them in the most intimate ways and that the ultimate example for our lives was to be found in the pages of a book that told the story of men who considered women their property, to be bought and sold.

The idea that the book itself was as infallible as the God who inspired it meant that the book, as the "Word of God," attained a sort of demigod status in the minds of those who were operating in the "blessed assurance" that its words were literally breathed out of the mouth of God. And Sean worshiped that book, though he would have denied that. That book led him to the logical conclusion that a man of God should have multiple wives. And that book led him to the logical conclusion that the ultimate solution for a woman who had turned her back on his version of the truth was to kill her to keep her from influencing his sons to follow the same infidel path as their mother.

I believe that book was indeed inspired by God, but that doesn't mean God dictated it to people. I believe it was inspired by God the same way the Mona Lisa was inspired by Leonardo da Vinci's model. And just as that iconic painting is not a photographic reproduction of its subject, the Bible is a good, if imperfect, representation of the God it aspires to describe. If Sean had believed that too, maybe Joy would still be alive, dancing her way across Europe, putting blush on celebrities, interpreting speeches for the deaf and raising her sons to be the life of the party, the magnets in every room they entered.

Sean, blind to that idea, is happily ministering to his fellow prisoners in prison at Chowchilla, blissfully oblivious to the irony of a man claiming to preach the truth while still lying about planning and executing the brutal murder of the mother of two of his sons. No doubt, his preaching is still electric, morally convicted, incisive and powerful. No doubt, his inmate congregants are convinced of and awed by his "anointing," just as so many were before he started accumulating wives. And no doubt, they flock to him for advice, spiritual and practical.

Sean hasn't changed. His surroundings have, his paper-thin mea culpa has and his audience has. Sean is still holding court from the pulpit, still fighting the good fight for Jesus, still being "led by the Holy Spirit." But today, there has been a significant change: he no longer has any women to lead or woo. The polygamist is now less than a monogamist. The patriarch of his biblical family now leads none of his family. He is simply a guy in jail who can really preach.

Trevor Whitken, now a music minister for a prominent Baptist church in San Diego, said this when I asked whether he thought Sean would be upset if Trevor gave me some quotes for this book:

"Well, he shouldn't have killed our friend."

Indeed.

ACKNOWLEDGMENTS

Abook like this is impossible to create without also creating a lot of indebtedness to those who support the author.

My writing this book was difficult for my wife, April, on multiple levels. Our baby turned a year old shortly after it was finished, and while I was writing it, he consumed every minute of her time while I was too busy to hold him and play with him. When we were able to get time together, this book, the case and Sean were all I could talk about, and she listened as I went over the details ad nauseum. I was absent from our marriage during that time, consumed instead with this—a subject that should have long before dissipated into the haze of my past. Then she celebrated with me the excitement and fears of the publishing process as the book again consumed our lives, becoming this new thing that demanded more and more of our time. And during the editing and rewrite process, she toughed it out again, sacrificing her personal time, her peace and relaxation, so I could babysit the monster this book had become.

Surely she had to be sick of hearing about the book and the case, but she carried on, encouraging and supporting me when a lesser woman would have hit me on the head and walked out.

April, I love you, and I owe you several months of "you" time and more of "us" time—a debt I look forward to paying.

My in-laws, Randy and Janice Woods, also gave me a lot of encouragement while reading the manuscript on a road trip, asking questions and giving suggestions that ended up helping me clarify parts of the book that had been difficult.

Special thanks also go out to Trevor Whitken, who went above and beyond the call of friendship in digging for materials I couldn't get to because I couldn't be where they were.

Dr. Laura Fulginiti at the Maricopa County, Arizona, Medical Examiner's Office was especially helpful in the creation of this book, taking a lot of time out of her incredibly busy schedule to explain small details and recount a story that had been by that time almost a decade old. I view her and Detective Bob Powers as the heroes of this story. Without their dedication and relentless efforts to figure out Joy's identity, Sean would likely have gotten away with murder.

Tara Walzel also went out of her way to unearth old photographs of Sean and Joy and to refresh my memory on incidents that I had long forgotten from when we both worked at Morris Cerullo's ministry. And I can't mention Tara without mentioning Ruth Kinser, without whom I wouldn't have been able to get in contact with so many of the people I eventually ended up talking to.

Rino Ortega deserves thanks for helping a stranger create a full and engaging memory of Joy.

The staff at the Carnegie Library in Wagoner, Oklahoma, exceeded my expectations to help me uncover information about Sean from before I knew him, when he was in high school.

My literary agent, Sharlene Martin, helped me wend the confusing and frustrating road of book publishing, and without her, you wouldn't be reading this right now.

Dr. Joan Dunphy and Caroline Russomanno at New Horizon Press also did amazing work in cleaning up the manuscript and making it more palatable.

Morris Cerullo communicated with me about a subject it would have been far more comfortable for him to stay silent about, and I thank him for it.

When he and I were young, Sean and his family helped me out more times than I can count when I was in need and no one else was stepping up—including my own relatives. I hate how our friendship ended up and I hate how Sean's life has ended up, snuffing out so much promise because of a cruel, selfish act that hurt so many people.

Lastly, I'd like to thank Joy for the light she brought into the lives of everyone around her. I hope that one day her children will be able to have a full picture of how truly special she was and how much she loved them. Her only mistake was falling for the manipulations of a much older, attractive yet scheming man.

Even in the midst of such great negatives, positives can develop, and her two wonderful sons are just that.